THE WORLD OF FOSTER CARE

The World of Foster Care

An international sourcebook on foster
family care systems

edited by
Matthew Colton
Margaret Williams

arena

Published by
Arena
Ashgate Publishing Limited
Gower House
Croft Road
Aldershot
Hants GU11 3HR
England

Ashgate Publishing Company
Old Post Road
Brookfield
Vermont 05036
USA

British Library Cataloguing in Publication Data
The world of foster care
　　1. Child care services　　2. Child care services –
　　Cross-cultural studies
　　I. Colton, M. J., 1955–　　II. Williams, Margaret, 1943–
　　362.7'3

　　ISBN 1 85742 339 9

Library of Congress Cataloging-in-Publication Data
The world of foster care : an international sourcebook on foster
　　family care systems / edited by Matthew Colton, Margaret Williams.
　　　　p.　cm.
　　includes index.
　　ISBN 1-85742-339-9
　　　1. Foster home care–Cross-cultural studies.　2. Child welfare–
　　Cross-cultural studies.　3. Child care services–Cross-cultural
　　studies.　I. Colton, M. J. 1955–　.　II. Williams, Margaret. 1943–
　　HV875.W67　1997
　　362.73'3–dc21
97-19599
CIP

Typeset in Palatino by Raven Typesetters, Chester and printed and bound in Great Britain by Hartnolls Ltd, Bodmin.

Contents

About the authors

Argentina

Oscar Francisco Toto holds the following degrees: Social Worker, La Plata (Provincia Buenos Aires), 1965; Doctor in Social Work, Universidad del Museo Social Argentino (UMSA) Buenos Aires, 1972.

He worked as a social worker for the Tribunal de Menores Poder Judicial, Provincia de Buenos Aires, from 1965 to 1995, and also gained considerable teaching experience between 1987 and 1995. He was Principal Professor, Universidad Nacional de Buenos Aires from 1984 to 1987, and was appointed through examination as Professor, Universidad de Mar del Plata. Currently, he is Vice-Dean, Facultad Ciencias Sociales de la Universidad de Buenos Aires, a term of office that runs until 1998.

Martha Susana Kliun holds a degree as a psychologist from Universidad Nacional de La Plata. From 1975 to 1978, she worked at Caritas (a foster family care service), La Plata, and since 1978 she has been employed as a psychologist, Tribuna de Menores Provincia de Buenos Aires.

Susana Ines Sozzani de Montalvo has a degree in Psychology, Universidad Nacional de La Plata, and a post graduate degree as a specialist in the legal aspects of psychology. From 1960 to 1970 she worked as an Educational Consultant, Dirección Gral de Menores, Ministerio de Acción Social de la Provincia de Buenos Aires. Since 1978 she has been employed as a Psychologist, Tribunal de Menores, Poder Judicial Provincia Buenos Aires.

Australia

Susan Pitman works with a large welfare agency called Oz Child. At the beginning of her career, after a period working at Monash University as a laboratory assistant to a zoology lecturer researching the reproductive cycle of echidnas, she succumbed to the call of adventure and went to Papua New Guinea. As her previous employment experience was singularly useless in the then-colonial environment, she ended up as an Accounts Clerk with the Public Works Department at Goroka, in the Highland District. Exposure to the cultural diversity of Papua New Guinea awakened a desire to become an anthropologist, so she returned to Monash University and completed a BA with a double major in Anthropology and Sociology.

She conducted fieldwork on an island in the Coral Sea to the south-east of Papua, and finished her MA thesis three weeks before producing her first daughter. After eleven years' farming and child rearing, she returned to the workforce, carrying out contract evaluations in the family support service field. Nearly two years later, she exchanged the uncertainties of contract work for a full-time position as a Research Officer with Oz Child, and has continued undertaking practice research with this agency for the past ten years. The agency itself runs a range of family support services, including four foster–care programmes and a number of educational support programmes. It also has a Research and Policy Unit and a subscription information service specializing in child and family welfare.

Botswana

Lengwe-Katembula Mwansa, formerly a Lecturer and a Co-ordinator of the Social Work Division at the University of Zambia, is currently a Senior Lecturer in the Department of Social Work, University of Botswana. He holds a BSW with Merit from the University of Zambia, an MSW from McGill University in Canada, and a PhD in Social Welfare from Brandeis University, Waltham, MA, USA.

His research interests include social policy, public health, child welfare, and youth and social development. He has published several works in these fields.

Pempelani Mufune is an Associate Professor, Department of Sociology, University of Namibia. He obtained his BA (Sociology and Psychology) with Distinction from the University of Zambia, and his MA and PhD (Sociology) from Michigan State University.

His primary research interests are in the evolution of African class structures, and the impact of work on individual social psychological functioning. He has consulted widely for a number of national and international agencies, such as the Irish Institute and the Commonwealth Youth Programme Africa Centre. He has published extensively in various journals, including *International Sociology, Africa Today* and *Economic Quarterly*.

Kwaku Osei-Hwedie is a Professor and Head of the Department of Social Work, University of Botswana, Gabarone. He received his BA, *Summa Cum Laude*, in Sociology; his PhD in Social Welfare from Brandeis University, Waltham, MA, USA, and a Postgraduate Diploma in International Law from the University of Zambia, Lusaka. He has previously been a Senior Lecturer and Head of the Department of Social Development Studies at the University of Zambia, Lusaka.

Dr Osei-Hwedie's academic and professional interests are in the areas of youth and social development, social service provision, social policy, social welfare theory and the indigenization of social work education and practice in African societies. He has co-edited and authored some sixteen books and several articles on socio-economic development in Africa.

Canada

Judy Krysik, PhD, is an Assistant Professor at the Faculty of Social Work, University of Calgary. She is a former child welfare worker in the province of Alberta, and is currently piloting a family reunification programme for children in government guardianship who reside in long-term care. Her research interests include cross-national comparisons of family policy, child welfare design and programme evaluation.

Finland

Kari Salavuo, Dr Soc. Sc., is a Professor of Social Policy at the University of Turku, Finland. He has worked at the university for over thirty years, and has published many books and articles on various issues in social policy, for example: income distribution in Finland, poverty, social assistance clients, and a comparative analysis of welfare states. His current special research interest lies in the social networks and care of the elderly, and he is the Finnish director of a research project on the care of the elderly in Japan and Finland.

Dr Salavuo has worked for many years on the International Council on Social Welfare. He is a widower with two sons, interested in reading, tennis and cross-country skiing.

France

Michel Corbillon began his career as a professional social worker, which included periods as a community worker and residential care worker. He then completed a sociological thesis on intellectual deficiency. In 1984, he founded a research group on social reproduction and innovation (GERIS, Groupe de recherche sur la reproduction et l'innovation sociale). He has participated in several research projects undertaken by the group, including a nationwide study of child welfare services in France. In 1989 at UNESCO, he co-ordinated a conference on French and international research on children placed away from home ('L'enfant placé, actualité de la recherche française et internationale').

Dr Corbillon is now Lecturer in Educational Sciences, University of Paris X-Nanterre. He is a member of the Executive Committee of the European Scientific Association on Residential and Foster Care for Children and Adolescents (EUSARF). He has published many articles and books on children in care and child welfare services.

Germany

Jörg Maywald was born in 1955 in Karlsruhe, southern Germany, the son of war refugees from eastern Germany. He studied sociology and psychology in Berlin and Amsterdam. He took five children consecutively into short-term foster care as part of a neighbourhood scheme for disadvantaged families.

Jörg Maywald set up and worked in the Berlin Child Protection Centre (1975–86). He carried out research in Paris, and worked with psychotic youths at the Ecole Expérimentale de Bonneuil (1986–87). He also worked as a teacher. After German reunification, he led a Federal Youth Ministry project from 1991 to 1994, entitled The Promotion of Foster Family Care in the New German States (*Forderung des Pflegekinderwesens in den neuen Bundesländern*). Since 1995, he has been the Director of the German League for Children in the Family and in Society (Deutsche Liga für das Kind in Familie und Gesellschaft).

Jörg Maywald is married and has three children.

Peter Widemann was born in Berlin in 1937. During the war, he was evacuated, and as a child and youth, spent several years in homes and in foster care.

He completed an apprenticeship as a confectioner, worked in children's homes and spent one year (1959–60) in California as a home help and educator. After studying social work, he worked in youth welfare offices, and while working, also studied part-time at the College for Administration (Verwaltungsakademie) in Frankfurt/Main.

Since 1969, he has worked in the Youth Department of the Berlin State Government, where he is responsible for the supervision of homes, for the planning and co-ordination of foster care, and most recently, for all residential and non-residential care. Peter Widemann also has an MA in Educational Science from the Free University, Berlin.

He has had several papers published on residential care topics, and is a member of youth welfare commissions. He has also worked as a teacher.

Hong Kong

Christopher Bagley is Professor of Social Work at the University of Calgary, and was a Visiting Lecturer at City University, Hong Kong, from 1991 to 1994. He and his wife are former foster parents, and currently have two adopted, mixed-race children.

Grace Po-Chee Ko is Lecturer in Social Work at City University, Hong Kong. She is an adoptive parent, and is active in Mother's Choice, an adoption and fostering agency in Hong Kong, and in Happy Parents' Association, an agency for the support of adoptive parents. Her doctoral research is on adoption by Chinese couples.

Charles O'Brian is Senior Lecturer in Social Work, City University, Hong Kong. He is of mixed Pakistani and Irish descent, and has a focus on multi-cultural issues in social work. His current research includes a study of transracial adoption by European parents in Hong Kong.

Hungary

Maria Herczog holds a BA in Economics from the University of Budapest, an MA in Sociology conferred in 1989, and a PhD (1994) on the structural and professional dilemmas of the Hungarian child welfare and protection system. She is presently Head of the Child Youth Protection Unit for Training and Methodology, and is conducting research at the Hungarian Institute of Criminology. As a lecturer, she teaches social work courses, including evaluation and international child welfare practices.

Dr Herczog edits the *Family, Child and Youth* bi-monthly journal, and has written and edited numerous articles and book chapters on child welfare, child protection and foster care. In an attempt to make family and child welfare problems more visible to the general public, she takes part regularly in radio and television programmes as a member of various panels of experts. In addition, she is a Member of the Executive Committee of the International Federation of Social Workers, and is the co-founder and former president of the Hungarian Association of Social Workers.

India

R.R. Singh is currently a Professor in the Department of Social Work, University of Delhi, and has been the President of the Association of Schools of Social Work in India since November 1993. He has travelled widely in connection with seminars, workshops and conferences throughout the United States, Austria, the Netherlands, Thailand, Japan and New Zealand.

He was formerly a Member of the Research Advisory Committee, Ministry of Welfare, Government of India (1989–91), is currently a Member of the Editorial Committee, *Encyclopaedia of Social Work in India* (2nd series in Hindi), and a member of the advisory committee on research and courses in many departments and schools of social work. He has directed several seminars, training programmes and workshops, and has presented papers in the following areas: human rights, social work and welfare, ageing, youth development, social policy, family welfare, and fieldwork.

Dr Singh directed the Research Project on the Social Care of Children in Delhi (1982–87), and is a former consultant for the Project on Family Welfare Services for the Urban Poor in Cochin City – A World Bank-assisted project of the Popular Environment Management Services, Kerala. He is a Member of the Mental Health Authority, Government of Delhi, a Member of the Advisory Committee for *Contemporary Social Work*, and a Member of the Rehabilitation Committee, Institute of Human Behaviour and Allied Sciences, Delhi. Dr Singh is currently working on a project concerning voluntary action and social development; he is also involved with a study of rural/urban trends in community welfare, and with the dynamics of community leadership, particularly with respect to the Chipko/ Anti-Alcohol Movement in Uttarakhand.

Ireland

Robbie Gilligan is Senior Lecturer in Social Work and Co-ordinator of the Advanced Diploma in Child Protection and Welfare in the Department of Social Studies, Trinity College, University of Dublin. He is the author of a range of publications on child welfare, including *Irish Child Care Services* (Institute of Public Administration, Dublin, 1991). He was the Director of Studies for the Council of Europe Study Group which produced the report *Protection of Youth against Physical and Moral danger* (Council of Europe, 1990). He has a wide range of experience in child welfare services, as a social worker, foster parent, researcher, consultant and board member.

Israel

Zmira Laufer was first introduced to foster care in her own home, when her parents took it upon themselves to become foster parents to a young girl – a survivor of the horrors of the Holocaust – who remained with the Laufer family until she married.

Dr Laufer's next contact with foster care occurred when she became a youth movement counsellor and maintained close ties with those children living in foster homes in the group under her care who needed the additional support of an older sister beyond ordinary activities. Little explanation is needed as to why she thereafter chose to become a social worker and specialize in children's welfare.

Her career began at the Child Guidance Clinic in the Hadassah Hospital in Jerusalem, for the Ministries of Health and Labour and Welfare, where she was promoted to the senior position of Counsellor and Co-ordinator of Social Work. The next stage in her career involved developing and administering services for children's welfare for both offices. The years 1975–79, when she established and held the position of Head of the Preschool Unit of the Ministry of Labour and Welfare, were especially relevant to her work in the area of foster care. The unit was in charge of locating children who had been 'forgotten' in foster or residential care, introducing and implementing the concept of 'permanency planning' for these children, and for preschool children in general who needed to be placed out of the home. Within this framework, the use of foster families for preschool children was increased, as opposed to transfer to residential care, which had been the accepted solution up to that point. Recruitment efforts were made, and a training programme was developed. The data collected by the unit greatly assisted the political activities which led to the changes introduced in the Adoption Law for Neglected Children or Children Whose Parents are Found to be Unsuitable.

Since 1979, Dr Laufer has been a faculty member at the School of Social Work, University of Haifa, where she established a Continuing Education Department, and was its Director for nine years. In 1986, she received her PhD from the Hebrew University of Jerusalem. Today, she heads the Undergraduate Social Work Programme (BA) and teaches courses in research, staff development, social work in residential care, crisis inter-vention and task-centred treatment.

Her current areas of research and writing are child placement and the organizational behaviour of social workers.

Italy

Tiziano Vecchiato has, since 1989, been scientific director of the Emanuela Zancan Foundation, a centre for studies, research and training in the area of social policy. The foundation was established thirty years ago, and works in co-operation with central, regional and local governments, universities and other research centres.

During the last few years, he has also co-ordinated projects and research studies on services for children and families. His recent publications include *Etica e servizio sociale* (co-editor, Via e Pensiero, 1995) and *La valutazione dei servizi sociali e sanitari* (Fondazione E. Zancan, 1995).

Japan

Sadao Atsumi is currently President of the Japan Medical Food Association.

He was born in Tokyo in 1921, and graduated from the Faculty of Law, Tokyo Imperial University, in 1943. He was an official of the Nagasaki Prefectural Government in 1945, and in 1951 took up a position concerned with the foster care service in the Protection Section of the Department of Child and Family, Health and Welfare Ministry. He finally became the Director of the Department of Child and Family in the Health and Welfare Ministry.

In 1956, he became Adviser to the Foster Parent Association of Japan, and was President of the Association in 1968. He has been a registered foster parent himself under the Tokyo Prefectural Government, beginning in 1966.

Netherlands

Tjalling Zandberg is Associate Professor at the University of Groningen, and has been active in the Department for the Education of Exceptional Children since 1988. Previously, he worked for several years as the director of a centre for visually handicapped children and adults in Surinam, South America, and as senior staff member in a residential treatment centre for adolescent boys and girls.

He is a specialist in foster care and residential treatment, focusing on the integration of research and practice in these areas. During the last few years, his research projects have been concerned with: the development, implementation and effects of foster day care; the development of treatment plans in a government residential institution for delinquent boys, and the effects of community-based treatment in group homes.

Philippines

Maria Paz U. de Guzman is a *Magna Cum Laude* graduate in Psychology from the University of Santo Tomas. She received training in Child and Adolescent Psychology in the United States as a Junior Fellow in Clinical Psychology at the Department of Institutions and Agencies, New Jersey, USA. She attained her MA in Psychology at the New School for Social Research in New York City. After practising psychology and teaching for twenty years in various universities in Manila (fifteen years of which were at the UP Department of Psychiatry, College of Medicine), in 1987 she cofounded the Parenting Foundation of the Philippines Inc., whose main programme is foster care for abandoned and neglected children. She is currently a Trustee and Regional Secretary for Asia of the International Foster Care Organization (IFCO). In May 1995, she was one of the IFCO delegates who participated with the

Special Working Group that drafted the international guidelines for foster care. The workshop was sponsored by the Swedish International Development Authority and hosted by the Department of Public Welfare, Kingdom of Thailand.

Pazie, as she is fondly called by family and friends, was appointed by the President of the Republic of the Philippines to the newly-created Intercountry Adoption Board (ICAB) as specified by Republic Act 8043, in August 1995. She is one of the seven-member Central Authority defining policies and setting guidelines to oversee all adoption of Filipino children by foreign families.

She has four children, the youngest of whom is adopted. She and her husband constitute a licensed foster family. They have fostered a number of children, all of whom have been permanently placed in loving, adoptive homes.

She is a Charter Member of the Zonta Club of Manila II Inc., Zonta International, a worldwide socio-civic club of women professionals/entrepreneurs known for their support of women's welfare in various forms.

Poland

Zofia Waleria Stelmaszuk is an Assistant Professor at the University of Warsaw, Faculty of Pedagogics, Department of Social Pedagogy. She holds two Masters degrees (in Child Psychology and Social Pedagogy), a PhD in Child and Family Studies, and she teaches and conducts research in the child welfare field.

Currently, she is working on a family reunification project sponsored by the National Committee on Scientific Research in Poland. Her special interest is in modern social work theory and empowerment-based practice. She has recently become involved in re-establishing social work education at the university level in Poland.

She is involved in foster care advocacy, and collaborates with other activists across Poland. After the recent political changes, she also became involved in international collaboration. She recently spent a semester at Columbia University School of Social Work in New York as a Kosciuszko Foundation Fellow, and has been invited to join The West–East Dialogue on Social Know-How Transfer, the Austrian project whose main focus is foster care. She joined IFCO after the Berlin Conference, where she was one of the keynote speakers, and has recently agreed to act as the IFCONET person.

Wanda Klominek established and organized the Adoption and Fostering Centre in Cracow in 1963, under the auspices of the TPD (Towarzystwo Przyjaciol Dzieci) Children's Friends Centre. She worked there for the next thirty years.

Until 1989, she was engaged in finding adoptive and foster families for a total of about 25,000 children. She is the author of the book *Adoption and What After. . .* (Nasza Ksiegarnia, 1976) and of numerous articles on the subject of adoption published in Poland and abroad. Since 1993, she has been the Chairperson of the Cracow Foster Parents Association.

United Kingdom

Clive Sellick is a Lecturer in the School of Social Work at the University of East Anglia, Norwich. His special interest is foster care, and he is the author of two related books: *Supporting Short-term Foster Carers* Avebury, (1992), and, with John Triseliotis and Robin Short, *Foster Care: Theory and Practice* B.T. Batsford, (1995). He has recently directed his university's work in Romania, assisting in the re-establishment of social work training and practice in conjunction with Unicef, and is the Programme Director of the University of East Anglia's Masters degree in International Child Welfare. Formerly a social worker, manager and guardian ad litem throughout his twenty years in social work, Clive Sellick also served as a magistrate for five years on the former Inner London Juvenile Panel.

June Thoburn is a Professor of Social Work at the University of East Anglia, Norwich. She has written widely on child and family social work, child protection and child placement, and her book *Child Placement: Principles and Practice* (Arena, 1994) is a widely-used text. Before joining the staff at the University of East Anglia in 1980, she worked in child and family social work in the UK and in Canada.

United States of America

Eileen Mayers Pasztor, DSW, is the International Projects Programme Director and Western Office Director for the Child Welfare League of America. Dr Pasztor has over twenty-five years of experience in the field of child welfare. She is experienced as a foster care and adoption caseworker, supervisor and programme administrator in public child welfare, as a social work educator, trainer and consultant working both nationally and internationally, and as a foster parent and adoptive parent.

Dr Pasztor's primary work has been developing policies, programmes and practices for the recruitment, selection, preparation and retention of foster parents and adoptive parents for children with special needs. Her work also involves supporting the role of foster parents as partners in permanency planning.

At the Child Welfare League of America, Dr Pasztor was Staff Director for the National Commission on Family Foster Care and for the North American

Kinship Care Policy and Practice Committee. She served on the committee revising the Child Welfare League of America (CWLA) Standards for Excellence for Family Foster Care Services, and served as the CWLA's liaison to the American Academy of Pediatrics Committee on Child Care, Foster Care and Adoption.

Dr Pasztor is principal developer of several CWLA publications: *The Ultimate Challenge – Foster Parenting in the 1990s* (1992); *HOMEWORKS* (1993) (at-home training resources for foster parents and adoptive parents); and *Foster Parent Retention and Recruitment: State of the Art in Policy and Practice* (1995). She also helped develop *Foster PRIDE/Adopt PRIDE* (1996), a new competency-based curriculum for prospective foster parents and adoptive parents, and for foster parent in-service training.

Dr Pasztor has been interviewed on local and national radio and TV shows. She has presented over 500 workshops and keynote addresses on kinship and on family foster care and adoption services for local, state, national and international programmes and conferences.

Kathy Barbell is Director of Foster Care for the Child Welfare League of America in Washington, DC. Ms Barbell is a social worker with an MSW degree from the University of South Carolina. She has twenty-seven years of experience in child welfare, including casework, supervision and administration of programmes at the local and state levels in New York, South Carolina and Connecticut. She is responsible for developing and implementing the CWLA's family foster care initiative, focusing on practice and policy. She provides consultation and technical assistance to public and voluntary child welfare agencies across the country on family foster care issues.

Venezuela

Elsa Levy is a Venezuelan citizen and a psychologist. She graduated as a family therapist and community worker, and worked as a Family Therapist for ten years in the Children's Diagnostic Centre. Later, she was a volunteer in the Government Centre for Child Protection, advocating for the placement of children in small family-type homes rather than in larger institutions.

In 1992, she founded a Home called Los Chiquiticos 1 ('The Little Ones 1'), together with FUNDANA (Fundación Amigos del Niño Abandonado). Los Chiquiticos 1 shelters about ten children aged 7 or under who are abandoned or in danger, providing them with a warm and loving home as well as the basic necessities of life. A second home with the same function was opened in 1995.

Iliana Kizer is a lawyer who graduated from the Santa Maria University in Caracas, specializing in the area of families and children. She is presently legal adviser to FUNDANA, and has a special interest in the placement of children who are over the age of 6, or have special needs, or are part of a sibling group. Usually, once these children have been declared abandoned, they live in large institutions which do not even provide the basic necessities of life.

Iliana Kizer has been authorized by the INAM – the institution designated by the Venezuelan government for the protection of minors under the guardianship of the state – to make all the necessary arrangements for placing children who are over the age of 6 or who are physically or mentally disadvantaged. She has been successful in this, and has placed internationally children with Down's syndrome, Beckwich-Weideman syndrome, deafness, chronic terminal renal deficiency, heart conditions, and mental disadvantage, among others.

After observing children's progress through reports, photographs and films, and working on the principle that every child is entitled to belong to a family, Iliana Kizer believes that there is a parent somewhere waiting for every abandoned child, and it is our responsibility to find these parents and bring them together with the children who need them. She would like to share her feeling that adoption is no longer just the satisfaction of a personal need (the filling of an emptiness), but has become instead a social mission.

Zimbabwe

Rodreck Mupedziswa holds an MSc (Social Planning) from the London School of Economics and Political Science (University of London), and is currently a PhD candidate (part-time) with the University of Zimbabwe. In addition, he has attended a number of short courses at such institutions as the University of Reading and Brighton Polytechnic in the United Kingdom. He is a member of the International Association of Schools of Social Work (IASSW), International Refugees Advisory Panel (IRAP) and the Southern African Universities Social Sciences Conference (SAUSSC).

Rodreck Mupedziswa is the Deputy Principal of the School of Social Work, an affiliate of the University of Zimbabwe. He is author of the book *Uprooted: Refugees and Social Work in Africa* (1993), and has co-edited the book *Social Policy and Administration in Zimbabwe* (1995), both published by the School of Social Work. Two manuscripts for books, 'Social Work in Africa: Critical Issues in the Struggle for Relevance' and 'AIDS and Social Work in Africa' are currently being considered for publication.

In addition, Rodreck Mupedziswa has published several chapters in books, as well as several papers in reputable journals such as *International Social Work* and the *Journal of Social Development in Africa*. His primary research interests lie in the field of African social welfare policy, socio-economic development and employment issues. He has consulted with a number of international organizations, including the Scandinavian Institute of African Affairs, the World Institute for Development Economics Research (UN) and the Refugee Studies Programme (Oxford University). He has travelled extensively, and has presented papers at numerous international workshops and conferences.

Leontina Kanyowa was born in Mbala, Zambia. She trained as a social worker at the University of Zambia, where she attained a Diploma and Bachelor of Social Work degree. Her first job as a social worker was with the Zambia Association for Children with Learning Disabilities.

In 1986, Leontina Kanyowa moved to Harare, Zimbabwe, where she worked for the Norwegian Agency for Development Cooperation (NORAD) and the University of Zimbabwe, before joining the School of Social Work. Leontina obtained her MSW from the University of Zimbabwe in 1994, and is currently lecturing in the Certificate and Diploma in Social Work programmes. She also supervises BSW (Honours) dissertations. Leontina Kanyowa's areas of interest are maternal health, children, and issues pertaining to AIDS/HIV.

Preface

As its title suggests, *The World of Foster Care* is an international reference book which describes the role and structure of foster care systems in different countries of the world. Each chapter addresses the foster care system in a particular country and is written by an expert or experts from that country.

The book has been endorsed by the International Foster Care Organization (IFCO) in order to provide, in one volume, an easily accessible, compact and fairly comprehensive description of foster care as it operates in different countries. People attending IFCO conferences have asked for this information, but until now, it has not been available. The book is designed for students at the undergraduate and graduate levels, teachers, scholars, policymakers, and providers in the fields of child care, social work, administration and public policy.

In order to make comparisons easier, many of the contributing authors have followed a standard outline, organizing their material under the following headings:

- Jurisdiction (background of the country)
- History and origins
- Administration and organization
- Who is placed in foster care?
- Care providers
- Financial support
- Major problems
- Major trends
- Role of national foster care association
- Research

Following this outline has been a challenge for some authors, since not all sections are relevant to the foster care system in their countries; indeed, some have decided that their material would best be presented in a different way. Nevertheless, a number of commonalities and interesting disparities have emerged, which are discussed in the concluding chapter.

With respect to the language difficulties which are always very much to the forefront in a book of this type, readers should note that some chapters have been extensively edited and may therefore contain errors due to the editor's lack of understanding of what was intended. In addition, the necessary retyping of references to books written in languages other than English (on machines intended for English only) may have entailed some sacrifice of accents. We apologize to any author whose work may have been distorted in this way.

Our contacts in some countries, while extremely willing to be helpful, were able to provide us with only minimal information: not enough to constitute a chapter. For example, the Secretary General of the Indonesian National Council on Social Welfare forwarded our request to a number of directorates and foundations, and received a response from the Indonesian Child Welfare Foundation. The information contained in this response is summarized below, followed by a summary for Brazil.

We hope that readers will enjoy this brief insight into the operations of foster care in different countries. Following this first edition, it is expected that future editions will include additional countries, and will allow the diversities between the countries to be addressed more fully.

Foster care services in Indonesia

Under the Constitution of Indonesia, the government is responsible for the care of children in difficult circumstances: for example, abandoned, neglected and orphaned children. A number of programmes have been established to aid these children, one of which is the Foster Parents Programme, launched by the government in 1994, and involving not only government agencies but also non-government organizations and the private sector.

The underlying aim of the programme is to contribute to the success of the Compulsory Education Programme. Those who are eligible to be provided with a good education under the Foster Parents Programme are children from poor families, handicapped children, children who live in remote areas, and students between the ages of 7 and 12. Carers fostering these children are eligible for a grant to a maximum value of 60,000 rupiah, which is dependent upon the foster carers' income, and may be given to cover such items as clothes, food, and educational fees and materials.

Other provisions for children in difficult circumstances include orphanages, sponsorship for the child in his or her own home, and foster family care, where the child lives with another family. Foster family care is not officially promoted by the government, but is an integral part of the traditional Indonesian culture. For example, a rich family may offer the child of a poor family an opportunity to go to school, and after schooling is completed, the child then has an obligation to help with domestic work in the rich family's home.

Foster care services in Brazil

Our contact person in Brazil was one of several who wrote to say that they could not provide the information requested because there were no foster care programmes in their country. However, Rosana Karam, writing from Porto Alegre, was able to enlighten us on a number of points.

Brazil – the fifth largest country in the world, with an area of 8,511,996 square kilometres – has been experiencing severe socio-economic problems since the 1980s; wealth is unequally distributed, and a high proportion of the population lives in poverty. Indeed, according to data from the Brazilian Institute of Geography and Statistics, 53.5 per cent of Brazilian children and adolescents belong to families whose monthly income is lower than half the Brazilian minimum salary (equivalent to $US50).

Brazil does not have a cultural or legal tradition of foster family care, but a foster family care programme was established in Porto Alegre by Fundaçao Estadual do Bem Estar do Meñor (FEBEM – State Foundation for the Protection of Minors), which tried for a number of years to assist partially or totally abandoned children. Unfortunately, the programme failed owing to a number of factors: lack of financial resources, the low socio-economic status of candidate foster families, lack of training for candidates, and labour claims against the state.

At present, FEBEM is still working to assist abandoned children as well as delinquent children, with or without physical or mental difficulties, through other programmes and specialized facilities organized according to national and local social policy.

Acknowledgements

A book of this type cannot be produced without becoming indebted to a great many people. The editors would like to thank the International Foster Care Organization (IFCO) for its initial sponsorship, and particularly John Meston, who provided contacts and encouragement in equal measure. Dr Joe Hudson of the University of Calgary deserves a special word of thanks, since it was he who carried out much of the groundwork required before contact could be made with prospective authors.

In addition to the contributing authors, to whom our debt is obvious, there are people in various countries who assisted us by giving advice, making contact with others on our behalf, passing on our letters, providing telephone numbers and addresses, and so on. Book chapters did not always result from these efforts, but whatever the final outcome, we would like to express our gratitude to these colleagues who devoted so much of their time on our behalf.

We would like to thank:

- in Victoria, Australia, Sherrie Coote, Director of Kildonan Child and Family Services, incorporating Whittlesea Family Services, and also Sandra de Wolf of the Amalgamation of Berry Street and Sutherland Child Youth and Family Services;
- in Bolivia, Celia Ferrucino from La Paz;
- in Brazil, Dr Seno Cornely, International Council on Social Welfare, Porto Alegre;
- in Egypt, Dr Saad Nagi of the Social Research Centre, American University in Cairo;
- in Ghana, Professor J.M. Assimeng, Head of the Department of Sociology, University of Ghana, Legon;
- in Budapest, Hungary, Ms Zsuzsa Szeman of the Institute of Sociology, Hungarian Academy of Sciences, and Ms Kati Levai, Head of the

Department of Sociology, University of Debrecen;

- in Lebanon, Dr Julinda Abu Nasi, Director of the Insitute for Women's Studies in the Arab World, Lebanese American University, Beirut;
- in Macedonia, Dr Divina Lakinska, Faculty of Philosophy, University of St Ciril and Metodi, Skopje;
- in New Zealand, Dr Rajen Prasad, Social Policy and Social Work Department, Massey University;
- in Russia, Dr Arkadi Nekrassov, Principal Adviser, President of the Association of Social Workers, Ministry of Foreign Affairs, Moscow;
- in Singapore, Ms Chee Lee Chin, Assistant Director, and Mrs Indra Chelliah, Deputy Director of the Family and Women's Welfare Section, Ministry of Community Development;
- in South Africa, Mrs Margot Davids, Manager of the Foster Care Department, Johannesburg Child Welfare Society;
- in Thailand, Mr Sakol Boonkhum, Director of the Child and Youth Welfare Division, Department of Public Welfare, Bangkok, and also Mr Somporn Thepsithar, Vice President of the National Council on Social Welfare of Thailand;
- in Uganda, Professor Patrick Mazaale, Department of Social Work, Makerere University, Kampala;
- in Venezuela, Irene de Peralta, from Caracas.

Special thanks are due to Professor Rajeshwar Prasad, Senior Fellow at the G.B. Pant Social Science Institute in Jhusi, Allahabad, India, whose long experience and distinguished scholarship have been invaluable in providing us with much-needed assistance and advice.

Above all, we would like to express our heartfelt thanks to Ms Susan Roberts, Department of Social Policy and Applied Social Studies, University of Wales at Swansea, for her unflagging efforts and patience in helping us to put the manuscript together.

1 Argentina

*Oscar Francisco Toto, Martha Susana Kliun and
Susana Ines Sozzani de Montalvo*

Jurisdiction

Location

The Argentine Republic is situated at the southern extreme of South America,
covering a surface of 2,780,792 square kilometres; its population amounts to
32.6 million, according to the latest census in 1991. In the last inter-census
period, 1980–91, the annual average population growth amounted to 1.5 per
cent, comprising 1.4 per cent growth within the country and 0.1 per cent
growth through migration.

The province of Buenos Aires is the largest and most densely populated in
the whole country. It covers 307,571 square kilometres, an area larger than
countries such as Italy, and even larger than a whole group of European
nations, such as Austria, the Netherlands, Belgium, Denmark and the former
East Germany put together. The population of the province amounts to 10.9
million inhabitants, according to the 1980 census. Population density in the
province as a whole is 35.2 inhabitants per square kilometre, while in Greater
Buenos Aires, where 7 million people live, the density is 1,859.6 inhabitants
per square kilometre.

Demography

Together with Uruguay and Cuba, Argentina may be characterized
historically as one of the precursors of demographic transition in Latin
America, since demographic data have shown it to be a country of moderate
population growth over the last few decades. Along with Uruguay, Cuba,
Chile and Puerto Rico, it is one of the nations that have reached the post-
transitional period, with low growth at present and predicted for the near
future.

An outstanding characteristic of the age distribution of the population is the increasing tendency towards demographic ageing: a decrease in fertility has led to a reduction in the proportion of people younger than 15 and an increase in the proportion aged 60 or older. The latter group represented 13 per cent of the population in 1991, and it is expected that it will rise to 16 per cent by the year 2025. The lower life expectancy of men means that women are predominant within the older age group. These data should be taken into account when analysing the demands on social services, as well as when considering aspects of human development related to emotional support for this sector.

With respect to reproduction, the overall fertility rate – the average number of children per woman at the end of the female reproductive period – amounted to 2.8 in 1991. However, there is a wide contrast when analysing the different regions and social and economic groups within the country. If present trends continue, the rate will drop to 2.2 children per woman by 2025.

There are also important variations when considering child mortality, which amounted to 23 deaths for every 1,000 children born alive in the entire country in 1993. In the Federal District, the mortality rate is 15 per 1,000 children, whereas it is 34 per 1,000 in the province of Chaco in the north-west of Argentina. Life expectancy at birth for the period 1990–95 is estimated at 74.8 for females and 68.1 for males, an average of 71.35 years for both sexes combined.

Migration

International migration, which played an outstanding role in the formation of Argentine society, has undergone a change in composition dating from the mid-twentieth century. In the past, migrants came mainly from Europe, but now they are coming from countries adjacent to Argentina. Recent data show a decrease in the net migration balance between 1980 and 1991 compared to the previous decade: the proportion of foreigners in the population has fallen from 6.8 per cent in 1980 to 5 per cent in 1991. These data demonstrate the low incidence of international migration in Argentine population growth.

With respect to internal migration, in the last two decades, there has been a decrease in the migration flow between the provinces and the Metropolitan Area of Buenos Aires. This change in the scale of migration is indicative of improved conditions over the country as a whole, since people migrate in order to find jobs, secure an education or generally to raise their economic status.

History and origins

Until the institution of the Civil Code in 1871, foster care was governed by Spanish legislation included in the laws of Castile. However, Velez Sarsfield, the author of the Civil Code, discarded the Spanish laws – possibly motivated by their lack of use, and also by the inadequacies of the Napoleonic Code, which limited recipients of foster care to adults, and did not meet the main goal of foster care: the protection of helpless children.

Many years elapsed before initiatives appeared which addressed children's issues. Not until 1933 was a bill on foster care presented to parliament by Senator Ramón Castillo. That bill was not passed, and neither were bills pertaining to a child code presented by Jorge Coll in 1938 and by Senator Alfredo Palacios in 1943.

Finally, foster care was introduced in 1948 under Law 13.252. Various bills were presented to improve and modify this law, but none were passed. Eventually, Law 19.134, passed in 1971, replaced the previous legislation, and divided foster care into the two institutions now in existence: full foster care and simple foster care.

General provisions of the legislation now in force

Law 19.134, in force at present, declares in Article 1 that: 'Fostering of non-emancipated minors shall take place by *judicial decision* on the initiation of the foster carer.' Current knowledge and beliefs and the conclusions of specialized congresses have emphasized the fact that foster care provides most benefit to the child when the foster care relationship is established in the child's earliest years. It should be stressed that the necessary *judicial decision* is an unavoidable prerequisite to foster care, according to the legislation now in force.

Article 2 of the law provides that: 'Nobody can be fostered by more than one person except in the case of a couple.' This provision is complemented by Article 5: 'Adoptive or foster parents may not be younger than 35 except in the case of couples who have been married for more than 5 years or couples married for less than 5 years who are not able to procreate.' Grandparents intending to foster a grandchild are also allowed to foster or adopt.

These provisions mean that any person older than 35, whether single, widowed, divorced or married, is able to foster. This minimum age does not apply to couples who have been married for more than five years and have no children. In order to foster, a married person must obtain the consent of their spouse.

Under the current legislation, it should be noted that under Article 6, a carer must have had custody of the child for a period of one year prior to fostering. A bill which has already been passed by one of the houses of parliament would reduce this period to six months. However, even under the present law, there is no obstacle to initiating the necessary judicial proceedings before the custody period has expired.

An important provision of the legislation allows fostering even when the foster carer already has children. In such cases, the right to foster may be granted as an *exception*.

The law pertaining to foster care is divided into five chapters and includes 35 articles. The general provisions are contained in Chapter I (Articles 1–13). Chapter II (Articles 14–19) covers full foster care, which places the fostered child in the new family with full rights, even those related to succession. Chapter III (Articles 20–29) covers simple foster care, whose main characteristic is that ties with the natural family are preserved. Chapter IV (Articles 30 and 31) govern placement breakdown and the documenting of placements, and finally, Chapter V (Articles 32–36) covers inter-country fostering.

Inter-country fostering

When Argentina approved the United Nations Convention on the Rights of the Child (through Law 23.849, 1990) it expressed some concern about paragraphs b, c, d and e of Article 21. Article 2 of Law 23.849 provides that: '[these paragraphs] will not apply within the area under jurisdiction because their application requires reliance on strict legal procedures to avoid the traffic and sale of children coming into foster care, which may not be in place'.

The rules agreed by the convention regarding foster care appear to contradict not only the principle which underlies all its other regulations – the welfare of the child, translated into juridical standards as *the best interests of the child* – but also the articles that grant the child the right to his or her nationality and the right not to be taken out of the country or kept abroad illegally (Articles 7 and 11).

Argentina's decision to object to Article 21 of the Convention on the Rights of the Child implies that:

- fostering by inhabitants of other countries does not constitute another way of taking care of the child, because *the domicile of choice is required to be in Argentina;*
- Argentina will not pass laws on inter-country fostering equivalent to the laws in force regarding fostering inside the country;
- no legislation will be passed which would allow unlawful financial profits;
- there will be no promotion of fostering through bilateral or multilateral agreements.

Such a position reflects a complete rejection of the trafficking in children, which nowadays, together with trafficking in weapons, drugs and wild animals, constitutes one of the most prevalent international illegal activities. From the standpoint of laws about minors, it is evident that the minor is degraded as a person so long as he or she is seen as an object, available for appropriation and sale.

Administration and organization

In Argentina, foster care is an institution that belongs exclusively to the judicial field. In the provinces, where legislation has provided Youth Courts, the whole process takes place within that field. In the province of Buenos Aires, at the Youth Tribunals, the process is as follows:

1 the child becomes endangered, helpless or abandoned;
2 measures are taken to ensure the protection and guardianship of the child;
3 the biological parents are sought; if they are found and identified, they are observed in order to evaluate their capacity to fulfil their parental role by looking after, protecting and loving the child;
4 a decision is made regarding the legal situation of the child, either by a declaration of abandonment or/and the disenfranchisement of *patria potestas*;
5 all candidates who wish to foster the child are included in a roll held at the Youth Court in the appropriate jurisdiction;
6 all candidates are interviewed by a Youth Court judge;
7 interviews are held to determine whether the candidates are psychologically fit to foster;
8 social-environmental studies on the candidates are carried out;
9 the minor is placed in the custody of the selected couple, with the intent that they should later be permitted to foster;
10 during the one-year custody period, home visits occur, guidance is provided to the family if necessary, and the situation is periodically reviewed;
11 after the custody period has elapsed and the correct procedures have been completed, the couple is permitted to foster.

Foster care organizations may be associated with state-run bodies, or they may be private institutions, working together with the judicial authorities. Organizations associated with the state may fall under the auspices of health care (hospitals) or the area of social action, which is the responsibility of the Undersecretariat for Children and Families.

The tasks that foster care organizations undertake are: investigation of risk situations, identification of children at risk, and referral to the appropriate protective body, and the provision of support to the guardians or future foster carers of the child, sometimes through meetings and activities in which the guardians may participate but are not obliged to do so. During the custody year, the judicial authorities require that the guardians are supervised, with referral to psychological services if necessary.

Private organizations limit their activities to the overall evaluation of the future foster carers. This evaluation includes medical records, psychological assessments and social-environmental studies. The evaluation results are sent to the judicial department, where they are reviewed by the appropriate judge.

The origin of these private organizations may be traced back over twenty years to Catholic family movements. At present, the number of private organizations is insignificant, and the majority work in those jurisdictions where there are no Youth Courts, or in places where courts cannot count on the services of specialized technical–professional staff.

Who is placed in foster care?

In Argentina, foster care is considered appropriate for any child or young person who has been abandoned, either because of the absence of relatives or the breaking of family ties. Data show that potential carers prefer to foster healthy, young children less than 12 months old. Physically or mentally handicapped children are not fostered to any significant extent, and there is no special programme devoted to such children in the province of Buenos Aires.

Major problems

A major difficulty associated with foster care in Argentina lies in the fact that the number of people who wish to foster far exceeds the number of children whose situation is such that they can be placed in the custody of potential foster carers with a view to being fostered later on.

This situation partly results from a legal requirement that the *patria potestas* should already have been relinquished before a child is eligible to be put in the custody of a potential foster carer. Biological parents possessing the *patria potestas* have the right to at least one contact per year with the child, who comes under the authority of the Youth Court judge. Hence, in some cases, the process which must be gone through before the child is eligible for custody takes a long time, and the child, who is growing up throughout this period, no longer falls within the preferred age range of 0–12 months by the time the process is completed.

In the case of older children, from 4 to 11 years old, difficulties occur in the integration of the child into the guardian's or foster carer's family. These difficulties arise because guardians of older children may not have been evaluated with respect to their wish to foster a child, and they may reject a child who does not live up to their ideals or expectations. In addition, some older children do not wish to be fostered, perhaps because they have already established ties with their biological parents, and the longer these ties continue, the harder they are to break. Some children become frustrated with the whole lengthy process of becoming eligible to be fostered, and reject everything to do with it as a result.

Role of national foster care association

There is no national foster care association, but a number of private organizations concerned with foster care services are located in the Federal District of Buenos Aires.

Contact: Equipo San José, Concepción Arenal 3540 (CP 1427), Buenos Aires, Argentina *Telephone*: (+54) 771-4615 *Fax*: (+54) 771-7390. ANIDAR, Remedios de Escalada de San Martín, 1886 PB Dpto A (CP 1416), Buenos Aires, Argentina *Telephone*: (+54) 581-0061 *Fax*: (+54) 581-9198. Consejo Nacional del Menor, Departamento de Adopción, Presidente Peron 700, Piso 4 (CP 1038), Buenos Aires, Argentina *Telephone*: (+54) 326-0414/3023/3551/5822.

Research

The following studies are recommended:

Chavanneau de Gore, S. (1993) *Mujeres que Entregan a sus Hijos*, Buenos Aires: CENEP.
Minyersky, N. (1992) *Adopción, Mito o Realidad*, Facultad de Derecho y Ciencias Sociales de la Universidad de Buenos Aires.

Bibliography

Dantonio, D. (1994) *Derecho de Menores*, Editorial Astrea, Buenos Aires.
Giberti, E. (1987) *La Adopción*, Buenos Aires: Editorial Sudamericana.
Giberti, E. and Chavanneau de Gore, S. (1992) *Adopción y Silencios*, Buenos Aires, Editorial Sudamericana.
Zannoni, E. (1972) *La Adopción y su Nuevo Régimen Legal*, Buenos Aires: Editorial Astrea.

2 Australia

Susan Pitman

Jurisdiction

Australia is a large continent dominated by an arid centre but with a range of climates, stretching from tropical in the north to cool, temperate in the south. The population is almost 18 million, with around 29 per cent under 19 years of age. While the overall population density for Australia is 2.3 per square kilometre, the reality is that over 80 per cent of the population is concentrated in the higher-rainfall areas along the eastern, south-eastern and south-western coastal areas. The likelihood that Australian children will live in an urban setting is high in that 71 per cent of the population lives in cities with populations of over 100,000 (Boss et al., 1995).

Migration to Australia has contributed significantly to population growth. In earlier times, migrants came largely from the United Kingdom and Ireland. Post-war migration shifted the focus to Europe, but in recent times, migrants have tended to come from non-European countries, particularly those in Asia. As a result of this process, the cultural heritage of the population in contemporary Australia is one of considerable cultural diversity, the value of which is recognized by a strong governmental commitment to a policy of multi-culturalism, and community support for it.

Australia's indigenous population consists of around 250,000 people of Aboriginal descent and around 25,000 Torres Strait Islanders, with the latter living mainly in Queensland and in the Torres Strait (Boss et al., 1995). Aboriginal people reside throughout the country, living a range of lifestyles from the predominantly traditional in the north of Australia to urban in the major cities. While some Aboriginal people have achieved success and status in mainstream society, Aboriginal people as a whole are over-represented on all indicators of social disadvantage, despite governmental recognition of the need for special consideration, along with considerable, if sometimes misguided, expenditure of funds. Historically, the Aboriginal experience had

9

much in common with that of other indigenous peoples colonized by Europeans, with disease and deliberate destruction being responsible for a dramatic decline in the population after contact. A consistent element in the 'management' of the Aboriginal population which continued until 1969 was the removal of Aboriginal children from their families, and their placement in institutions and with white foster families as a means of enforcing a policy of assimilation into the dominant, white culture.

Politically, Australia is a federation of six states (New South Wales, Victoria, South Australia, Tasmania, Western Australia and Queensland) and two territories (Northern Territory and the Australian Capital Territory). The system of government is a democratic one, derived largely from the Westminster model; Queen Elizabeth II of the UK is also the Queen of Australia. However, there is growing support for Australia to become a republic by the year 2000. While the main revenue-raising powers are held by the federal government, the administration of community welfare services, such as foster care, is mainly the responsibility of the states and territories.

History and origins

In the first half of the nineteenth century, children who were orphaned, abandoned or who lived in socially unacceptable conditions were cared for in large orphanages or asylums, which were run with a mixture of governmental and charitable-voluntary support. Around the middle of the nineteenth century, social reformers imported the idea of foster care from the UK and began promoting it as a way of circumventing the harmful effects of institutional care on children. Foster care had the additional attraction for the authorities of being a cheaper alternative. South Australia was the first state to officially experiment with foster care, or 'boarding out' as it was known, in 1872, and by 1890, the idea had spread to New South Wales, Victoria and Tasmania. Official enthusiasm for foster care subsequently waned to some extent, partly in response to concerns about abuses arising from inadequate reimbursement to foster parents and poor supervision of foster homes, and partly because institutional care was easier to control, and offered operational advantages.

However, the socio-economic conditions prevailing between the latter part of the nineteenth century until the First World War ensured that foster care continued to provide an alternative to institutional care. Foster children were valued for their work potential, especially in rural areas, and the regular payments associated with foster care provided an additional source of income for many families. Both foster care and institutional care during this period operated, to a large extent, independently of the family. Children who came into care were unlikely to return home, and contact between the parents and foster parents was rare. Selection and supervision of foster parents by volunteers proved to have limitations, and inspection by departmental officials became the norm by the 1920s.

During the 1920s and 1930s, some departments began to recruit professional foster parents, but this activity coincided with a gradual decline in the popularity of foster care as a result of continuing administrative difficulties and changes in the general social-economic conditions.

In the 1960s, there was a retreat from institutional care, largely in response to Bowlby's (1971, 1973, 1980) seminal work on maternal deprivation, with the result that the more family-centred foster care experienced a revival of interest. The underlying assumptions guiding the development of foster care at this time were that when difficulties being experienced by the parents were likely to be temporary, the child would benefit from family life, and be able to contribute to it, and that foster care should be one of a range of services available to families experiencing a crisis.

The promotion and use of foster care as a family support service continued until the late 1980s, when an increase in the number of substantiated child abuse cases coincided with a policy shift towards de-institutionalization and a greater linking of government funding to designated outcomes. As a result, the scope for foster care agencies to engage in preventive family support work was limited by their need to place children in care for protective reasons.

Administration and organization

Foster care, or 'home-based care', as it is increasingly known, is the most commonly used form of out-of-home care throughout Australia, accounting for around 80 per cent of placements nationally. This reflects a widely-held practice belief that when a child is unable to remain at home for whatever reason and cannot be placed within his or her kinship network, the next best option is a home-based programme such as foster care. However, within the broad definition of foster care, a range of placement types are available to respond to the different needs of children and families. In Victoria, for example, the Health and Community Services Department recognizes six types of foster care for planning and reimbursement purposes:

- Emergency – short-term placements arranged at short notice to provide time for the resolution of difficulties that prevent children remaining with their families;
- Respite – short-term placements, often arranged on a regular basis, to support parents and strengthen their capacity to meet the care, protection, nurturance and developmental needs of their children;

- Reception – placement to provide safe custody for children removed for their own protection from their home by the court or protective interveners;
- Short-term/transitional – planned placements for children unable to reside with their families while processes are organized to support the return home, or as a transitional period prior to independent living;
- Transitional to permanent care – planned placements for pre-adoptive children or children who are to be placed permanently;
- Permanent/long-term – permanent placements or planned extended placements where other types of permanent placement are unavailable or unsuitable.

The daily average number of placements for each type of foster care in Victoria for 1993/94 is shown in Table 2.1.

Table 2.1   Average number of placements per day in Victoria, 1993/94

Type of intervention	No.
Emergency	121
Respite	80
Reception	154
Short-term/transitional	272
Transitional to permanent care	145
Permanent/long-term	543

Source: Health and Community Services (1994a).

In addition to conventional foster care, specific programmes have been developed to enhance the placement potential and success of hard-to-place children, such as those with disabilities, adolescents and those with behavioural disorders. The programmes developed in Victoria which are listed below are broadly representative of those in other states.

Kinship care

The first placement option sought for children within the protective system who need to be removed from their home is within their own kinship network. Assessment of potential carers from within the kinship network is not as rigorous as for foster parents, and approval is given to care for a particular child. However, carers are entitled to foster care reimbursements and other support available to foster parents. Supervision is usually provided from within the protective system, rather than through a foster care agency.

Shared family care

This programme is targeted to meet the needs of children with developmental delay and intellectual disability. It incorporates the funding of disability resource worker positions, targeted recruitment of carers, additional support to carers, high payments to agencies for placements made under the programme, and in some instances, higher reimbursement to foster parents caring for children with disabilities. The caseload ratio is 1:6, compared to 1:12 in programmatic foster care.

Adolescent community placement

This separately-funded programme recognizes the increased difficulties of finding home-based placements for adolescents (aged 12–17 years) through providing additional reimbursements to carers and to the patron body. This home-based care programme is mainly provided by non-foster care agencies.

Specialized home-based care

This new programme was introduced to assist children and young people in residential services to gain access to home-based care. The children who are placed within the programme may have behavioural difficulties, be part of a large sibling group, or have such needs that they have been precluded from home-based care in the past. Specialized home-based care placements receive increased case management support, increased caregiver payments and establishment costs to meet the additional cost of caring for these children, based on an assessment of need.

Table 2.2 shows the number of children in the different types of home-based care in Victoria on census day, 30 June 1994.

The majority of agencies providing foster care programmes are non-governmental organizations (NGOs), which contract with the relevant state or territory government department to arrange and support foster care placements. In Victoria, for example, 94 per cent of foster care placements are delivered by NGOs. In New South Wales, the Northern Territory and Western Australia, however, the situation is reversed, with their respective community services departments being the major providers of foster care programmes. In Western Australia, for example, only 14 per cent of children are placed through NGOs, while in New South Wales, the figure is around 30 per cent. However, there is a move in each of these states to shift service

Table 2.2   Numbers of children in different types of care, Victoria, 30 June 1994

Type of care	No.
Foster care	1,193
Adolescent community placement	173
Shared family care	77
Kinship care	566

Note: Specialized home-based care was not operational at this time.
Source: Health and Community Services (1994b).

provision into the non-governmental sector. In New South Wales, transition to 100 per cent NGO service provision is intended to be completed by 1999.

Who is placed in foster care?

The main sector of the population for whom foster care is utilized is children and young people who have been removed from parental care because of concerns about their safety. Referrals in these situations come from the government protective services, and they involve children for whom some statutory intervention has applied. Notifications of child abuse and neglect across Australia increased by 39 per cent in the four years from 1988/89 to 1992/93, occurring at the rate of 19.4 per 1,000 in 1992/93. In 1992/93, 87 per cent of the 6,156 children under a Care and Protection Order who were in foster care were under a Guardianship Order, which made them wards of the state or territory, while the remainder were under non-guardianship orders, the definition of which can vary across states and territories. Over half (55 per cent) of the children under Care and Protection Orders in foster care were aged between 8 and 15 years. The peak age for children in foster care was 13 years, while numbers declined rapidly from 15 years of age onwards. The number of children under Care and Protection Orders in foster care in 1992/93 for the various states and territories is shown in Table 2.3.

Apart from children under a statutory order, there is also a further target group of children from families where the level of family functioning is such that the use of respite or short-term foster care is deemed beneficial for both child and family. In many of these family situations, there are serious concerns about the child's wellbeing, and foster care is actively used to prevent the occurrence of abuse. Foster care is also used to support families unable to utilize their own networks for emergency or respite care. Referrals for cases in these last two groups come from the community services

Table 2.3   Children under Care and Protection Orders in foster care,
1992/93

State/territory	No.
New South Wales	1,785
Queensland	1,638
South Australia	966
Australian Capital Territory	77
Victoria	1,068
Western Australia	345
Tasmania	229
Northern Territory	48

Source: Zabar and Angus (1995).

department, hospitals, community-based family support agencies and self-referrals.

The fourth main group of children utilizing foster care is those with special needs. In some cases, the need is for respite foster care; in others, where the family is unable to continue caring for a child with a disability, it is for long-term care.

Data on children in home-based care are not collected or reported in a consistent manner across the states and territories. In some annual reports, total numbers of children and/or placements are given; in others, the average daily number is given. It is therefore not possible to give an Australia-wide picture of the total number of children placed in home-based care in any one year.

Having recognized the tragic consequences of the assimilationist policy of forced removal of Aboriginal children, governments are now committed to the child placement principle, which recognizes Aboriginal children's right to out-of-home care in their own cultural community. Recruitment of indigenous foster parents is generally and preferably the responsibility of Aboriginal child welfare organizations. There is also recognition by government funding bodies of the need to exercise flexibility in carer selection and assessment criteria in order to give due consideration to the cultural context.

Care providers

Foster parents in Australia are recruited from all walks of life. They may be married, single or living in a *de facto* relationship, and may or may not have children of their own. However, potential carers are carefully screened, and are given both initial and ongoing training to assist them in their role. Recruitment, screening and training of carers is largely the responsibility of the organization providing the foster care, be it governmental or non-governmental. However, in some states and territories, such as Queensland and South Australia, greater standardization occurs through the use of guidelines, standards and training manuals set out by the relevant government department. In others, such as Victoria, agencies exercise more autonomy over the process, but duty-of-care requirements and a nominal licensing system ensure appropriate standards are met. A National Foster Care Week to support recruitment is held annually through the co-ordinated efforts of the major child welfare bodies in each state and territory.

Victoria is unique, in that the recruitment of carers is co-ordinated by a non-governmental umbrella organization, the Children's Welfare Association of Victoria, through a project known as Homesharers. Initiatives include community service announcements on television and radio, Foster Care Week, training and recruitment videos, publications, and general support to agencies conducting their own local recruitment campaigns. The project has found that an average of 245 people per month enquire about becoming foster parents, and between 5 and 10 per cent actually foster children. Across all the foster care agencies in Victoria, there are approximately 1,780 active carers.

Financial support

The rate of reimbursement to foster parents varies across states and territories, but in each case, it is intended to cover the costs incurred in caring for a child. However, the reality is that most foster parents are out of pocket to some extent. Payments increase with the age of the child. They may also include a disability loading, when relevant, and negotiated payments to respond to a child's special problems, needs and/or special events. A further variable in relation to payments can be the type of out-of-home placement involved.

In Victoria, standard reimbursements range from $A55 ($US41) per week for young children to $A107 ($US79) per week for older adolescents. Carers of young people placed under the Adolescent Community Placement programme receive a higher payment of $A120 ($US89) per week in recognition of the difficulties associated with these placements. Young people aged 16–17 years are also eligible for a Commonwealth Austudy benefit if they are at school, and unemployment benefits if they are not. The recommended amount of this benefit to be paid as board to their foster parent is $A60 ($US44). In contrast to Victoria, there is a flat rate of $A76 ($US56) per child in the Northern Territory, with provision for payments above the standard rate in cases of special need.

In New South Wales, current payments range from $A64 ($US48) for 0–4-year-olds to $A99 ($US73) for those aged 16 and over. However, there is a current proposal for restructuring the payments to carers in New South Wales whereby the base costs will be increased to range from $A69 ($US51) to $A155 ($US114), with a loading of between 50 and 80 per cent for up to 26 weeks for different types of care other than long-term. Money will also be made available to meet the special needs of children, to be paid to the service provider, who may, at times, be the carer.

Major problems

A range of problems are being experienced in the foster care field, some of which are common across the states and territories and some of which are particular to the state or territory involved, such as those relating to the operation of the particular legislative framework within which foster care operates.

Changes in community work patterns have meant that the assumption that women will be at home full-time, on which the volunteer system of foster care was based, no longer applies in the majority of families. This has caused difficulties both in the recruitment of adequate numbers of carers in general and in recruiting for particular types of foster care involving longer-term and/or more open-ended commitment on the part of the carer.

A policy direction of least intrusive intervention combined with an emphasis on supporting families to maintain children at home, while widely supported, has had a number of consequences for foster care. First children who require out-of-home placement are now more likely to be older, more behaviourally disturbed and/or emotionally damaged; second, at least in Victoria, a reluctance on the part of magistrates to issue Care and Protection Orders as a first response to cases brought before the court because of protective concerns has meant that children removed from the home situation can be left for unacceptably long periods in reception foster care without having their legal status resolved and an appropriate case plan implemented.

A greater emphasis on output-based funding has led to concerns that quality practice may be an inevitable casualty. An associated funding issue is that the trend towards narrowing the focus of the target group to clients of the particular government department funding the service has meant that using foster care in a preventive fashion, as one of a range of integrated family support services, is becoming increasingly difficult.

There are a range of issues concerning the funding of carers. The degree of difficulty associated with many of the children in out-of-home care, and the skill required to manage them, combined with problems in attracting sufficient carers, has raised the possibility of introducing models of foster care based on the use of professional carers. Apart from raising issues about competency standards, training and registration of carers, there is a debate about how such models may be introduced to avoid inequities occurring with foster parents already caring for children on a voluntary basis. There is some evidence that 'professional' levels of payments are being introduced in an *ad hoc* fashion through the development of specialized foster care services for hard-to-place children which have higher carer payments, and also through retention of a residential care placement level of funding for children and young people transferred into home-based care.

A final problem area for foster care is the conflict which can sometimes be experienced between the best interests of the child and the rights of the parent(s). As foster care has shifted from an essentially child-centred service to that of a family-centred one, the priority given to the child's best interests has sometimes been compromised. An example in Victoria was the introduction of a court-based review of guardianship extension through the Children and Young Persons Act, which allowed for the option of a Permanent Care Order. However, the outcome in many cases was to undermine the security of long-term placements for both child and foster parent, as magistrates were forced by the Act to review the option of returning the child to the natural parent, even when the child had been in the placement for a number of years.

Major trends

A major nationwide trend in the provision of foster care is the greater recognition given to the role of the family in a placement over the past ten years. For example, recruitment of potential foster parents now includes assessment of their capacity to engage and support the family; access facilitated by the foster parents can be an important element in a case plan; length of stay in foster care tends to be shorter, and reunification is the goal for the majority of children, even when protective concerns have prompted the placement. In Western Australia, for example, 60 per cent of children separated from their families for protective reasons were reunited with them within 12 months.

There has also been a trend towards the development of specialized models of home-based care to meet the needs of specific, hard-to-place client groups, such as behaviourally disturbed adolescents and severely disabled children. Most of these models recognize that a greater level of resources is needed to support such placements, and that the support provided needs to be tailored to meet the individual needs of both child and carer. Underpinning this trend is the ongoing policy of moving children and young people out of group care into home-based care.

The need to recognize and accommodate the demands of contemporary lifestyles within a volunteer-based foster care programme has led to the development of innovative ways of supporting foster parents, for example, through accessing community-based child care, after-school care, holiday programmes and respite services.

Role of national foster care association

There is no national, incorporated foster care association, despite attempts over the years to establish one. However, each state and territory has its own foster care association, which acts primarily as an advocacy and lobby group, and these associations do meet annually at the Annual Forum of Foster Care. Apart from the state bodies, there are also local carer associations in each state and territory which play a more active support role. In Victoria, for instance, the Foster Care Association of Victoria Inc. is a state-wide, incorporated association with representatives from most foster care programmes. In addition, most foster care programmes have their own foster parents interest group, which provides ongoing training, social events and mutual support.

Contact: Ms Janice Hughes, Foster Care Association of Victoria Inc., 37 Main Road, St Andrews 3761, Victoria, Australia *Telephone*: (+61) 3-9710-1391 *Mobile*: 019-41-7137.

Research

Little research has been conducted into foster care in Australia. The main research interest appears to be issues related to the impact of long-term foster care, and to a lesser extent, issues related to the recruitment of foster parents. Some examples of recent research, drawn largely from Victoria:

Cowling, C. 'Permanent Care of Children with a Psychiatrically Disturbed Parent', Melbourne University, unpublished research. (A study which looks at the impact of the foster family.)

Evans, S. and Tierney, L. (1995) 'Making foster care possible: A study of 307 foster families in Victoria', *Children Australia*, Vol. 20, No. 2. (A study of why families offer to help others through fostering.)

Gardiner, H. 'Concept of Family: Perceptions of People in Foster Care', Swinburne University of Technology, Melbourne, unpublished research. (A study which compares the perceptions of children in long-term foster care and adults who had been in foster care, with those of matched control groups from intact families.)

Harvey, I. (1988) 'Processes and Outcomes of Fostering Long Term', Macquarie University, New South Wales, PhD thesis. (Psychology aspects of non-government foster care.)

Lawrence, R. (1994) 'Recruiting carers for children in substitute care: The challenge of programme revision', *Australian Social Work*, Vol. 47, No. 1. (An evaluation of different means of recruiting trialed in a non-government agency.)

O'Neill, C. 'Supporting Permanent Placement', Melbourne University, research in progress. (A long-term study of the support needs of birth parents, foster parents and children in long-term placements.)

Further information on foster care in Australia can be found in:

Goddard, C. (1993) *Responding to Children: Child Welfare Practice*, Melbourne: Longman Cheshire.

Murphy, H., Howe, C. and Kearsey, D. (1991) *Publicity and Recruitment: The North East Foster Care Experience*, Melbourne: Capital Press.

Bibliography

Boss, P., Edwards, S. and Pitman, S. (eds) (1995) *Profile of Young Australians: Facts, Figures and Issues*, Melbourne: Churchill Livingstone.

Bowlby, J. (1971) *Separation and Loss, Vol. 1: Attachment*, Harmondsworth: Penguin.

Bowlby, J. (1973) *Separation and Loss, Vol. 2: Separation, Anxiety and Anger*, Harmondsworth: Penguin.

Bowlby, J. (1980) *Separation and Loss, Vol. 3: Sadness and Depression*, Harmondsworth: Penguin.

Health and Community Services (1994a) *Health and Community Services Annual Report 1993–94*, Melbourne: Health and Community Services.

Health and Community Services (1994b) *Placement and Support Client Census*, Melbourne: Health and Community Services.

Zabar, P. and Angus, G. (1995) *Children under Care and Protection Orders, Australia 1992–93*, Australian Institute of Health and Welfare, ACT.

3   Botswana

Pempelani Mufune, Lengwe-Katembula Mwansa and Kwaku Osei-Hwedie

Jurisdiction

Botswana is a landlocked country, bounded by South Africa, Namibia, Zambia and Zimbabwe. It is relatively large, with an area of 582,000 square kilometres, and is about the size of Kenya, France or the state of Texas, USA. It is at the centre of the Southern African Plateau, at an altitude of 1,000 metres above sea level.

Botswana has an arid and semi-arid climate, with an annual rainfall ranging from over 610mm in the extreme north-east to less than 250mm in the extreme south-west. The rainfall is highly erratic and unevenly distributed. About 90 per cent of the rain falls in the summer months, between April and November. Temperatures are high and vary between 22°C and 33°C from July to January. Consequently, evaporation rates are also high, ranging from 6mm to 12mm daily (Central Statistics Office, 1986). Partly because of this, there is very little surface water, and rivers flow only after intensive rain, except in the extreme north-west. The Okavango and the Chobe drainage systems are the only major permanent surface water. It should be noted that over 66 per cent of the country is covered by either the Kalahari sand or the Kalahari desert (Republic of Botswana, 1973; 1976; 1985; 1991). Most of the country has scrub and savannah vegetation, and only 5 per cent of it has both adequate rainfall and suitable soils to provide potential for agriculture. However, even over this small area, the unreliability of rainfall, combined with high evapo-transpiration rates, lead to a high risk of crop failure. The climate also results in grasses of poor quality and productivity, particularly in the desert area.

In 1991, according to the last census (Central Statistics Office, 1991), Botswana's population was 1.327 million, having increased from 550,000 in 1966. The average annual rate of increase was 3.7 per cent between 1966 and

21

1981, and between 1981 and 1991 the rate declined slightly to 3.5 per cent. These figures indicate that the population has almost trebled in a period of 25 years. Based on present trends, the population is expected to reach 1.6 million by 1996, and 1.8 million by 2001. Part of the reason for this is the high fertility rate, which stood at 5.3 in 1991, having declined from 7.1 in 1981 (Duncan et al., 1994).

Most of the population is below 15 years of age, pointing to a high dependency ratio. In general, infant mortality is declining (from 112 per 1,000 in 1965 to 39 per 1,000 in 1989), and life expectancy is increasing (Central Statistics Office, 1991).

According to the *Household Incomes and Expenditure Survey: 1985/86*, the average household size in 1985 was 4.0 persons in urban areas and 5.3 persons in rural areas (Central Statistics Office, 1988). Forty per cent of households were headed by women in urban areas, and nearly 18 per cent in rural areas. Duncan et al. (1994) provide a similar picture of high percentages of female-headed households, but differ with respect to the percentages in urban and rural areas respectively. According to these authors, 45 per cent of all households were female-headed in 1981, rising to 47 per cent in 1991: in rural areas, 52 per cent of households were headed by females, while in urban areas the figure was 34 per cent.

Another important demographic factor is migration from rural to urban areas. Duncan et al. (1994) again point out that Botswana's population has moved from villages to the most prosperous urban areas along the railway lines, and from small villages to larger villages. Thus, whereas in 1964, 4 per cent of the population lived in urban areas, by 1991, 24 per cent were in towns and 20 per cent were in the big villages that have relatively more urban characteristics.

Botswana obtained its political independence from the UK in 1966. At that time, it was among the world's 20 poorest countries in per capita terms. Thus, there were no domestic resources to finance the state's capital spending, no source of finance for recurrent annual expenditures, and the country was extremely dependent upon expatriate labour (Colclough et al., 1988). At the time of independence, the country's main source of income was cattle raising, subsistence agriculture and money sent home by workers who had migrated to South Africa (Hoppers, 1986).

From the outset, Botswana was part of the South Africa-dominated customs union. Through the provisions of this union, South Africa-based firms were allowed unhampered access to the Botswana market. However, these firms did not create enough employment opportunities in Botswana, with the result that many Tswanas sought work elsewhere. At this time, the number of Tswanas employed in South Africa was greater than the official number employed within Botswana itself. By 1968, the number of people employed in Botswana's formal work sector was barely 25,000 – 7 per cent of the country's total labour force (Hoppers, 1986).

What has been remarkable about Botswana has been its dramatic rate of economic growth. This growth began not long after independence, and was sustained long after it. Botswana's economic growth rate was higher than any other country in the world from 1966 to 1986. From 1968 to 1978, GDP trebled in real terms (Hoppers, 1986). In 1987, GDP was about 2.5 billion pulas ($US960 million), and this represented an eightfold increase over the previous decade (Republic of Botswana, 1985). All sectors have experienced tremendous growth. However, the importance of agriculture has decreased because of drought and the tremendous increase in mining. In general, the generation of employment has lagged behind population growth, as shown in Table 3.1.

Table 3.1   The growth of population and formal employment, 1964-86

	1964	*1971*	*1981*	*1986*
Population	503,000	574,000	941,000	1,128,000
Formal employment	20,000	37,000	97,000	129,000
Annual average growth in employment as % of population	4.0	6.4	10.4	11.4

Source: Colcough et al. (1988), p.4.

With the availability of various revenues, Botswana was able to improve on the provision of social services. According to Harvey (1992), there were significant improvements in the provision of health and education, government services and the building of infrastructure. In health, for example, whereas there were 3.6 doctors per 100,000 of the population in 1965, there were 14.5 doctors per 100,000 in 1984. Similarly, whereas there were 5.6 nurses per 100,000 in 1965, there were 142.8 nurses per 100,000 in 1984. In terms of education, the percentage of children enrolled in primary school increased sharply from 65 per cent in 1965 to 96 per cent in 1988. The figures for secondary school enrolment rose from 3 per cent in 1965 to 33 per cent in 1988.

Botswana's growth has not been without its problems. Despite the country's expanded opportunities, it has neither developed the capacity nor attracted enough investment to create the estimated 12,000 new jobs it needs per year to accommodate its school leavers or make a dent in its unemployment rate, estimated at 25 per cent (Republic of Botswana, 1985).

The over-stimulation of mining and other industries at the expense of agriculture has contributed to rural–urban migration, resulting in soaring numbers of unemployed and creating the phenomenon of street children, who add to the pressures on urban social services.

A significant proportion of children and young people do not attend school, and much of this is due to poverty (Republic of Botswana, 1985). The limited financial and human resources available to the education sector only emphasize the need to prioritize investment in education and training (Colclough et al., 1988). So far, the country has continued to depend heavily on expatriate labour. In addition, dependency on South Africa and the customs union has not been reduced.

According to National Development Plan 7, government revenues have been greatly strengthened by the inflow of aid funds. Botswana was among those countries receiving the highest per capita levels of foreign aid in the world between 1970 and 1990 (Duncan et al., 1994).

Organization of social services in Botswana

In general, public social services in Botswana are organized and provided through government agencies. A few non-governmental organizations (NGOs) are also involved in the provision of social services.

Government services

Public social services are provided by two government ministries: the Ministry of Local Government, Lands and Housing (see Figure 3.1), and the Ministry of Labour and Home Affairs.

Ministry of Local Government, Lands and Housing (MLGLH) As Figure 3.1 shows, the MLGLH contains the Social Welfare and Community Development Unit (S&CD), which is the major unit concerned with social services provision. The MLGLH also includes the Remote Area Dwellers Unit, which is mandated to deal with ethnic and marginal communities. In addition, the MLGLH houses the Food Resources Department (FRD), which takes responsibility for organizing food relief and supplementary feeding programmes, especially during times of drought.

The Ministry of Labour and Home Affairs (MLHA) This ministry deals with women's affairs, youth and sports, and is also concerned with social welfare. The Social Welfare Unit of the MLHA formulates social welfare policies, supervises and implements laws and regulations concerning social welfare, and renders support to voluntary organizations involved in social welfare provision. The Women's Affairs Unit is charged

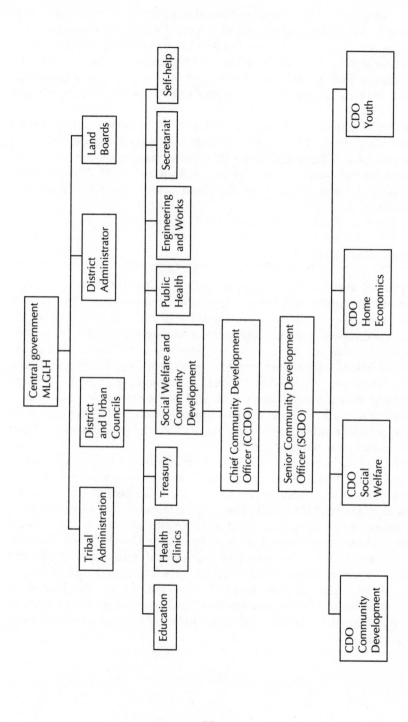

Figure 3.1 The structure of social service provision in Botswana

with the integration of women in national development. Specifically, it is supposed to co-ordinate women's activities, disseminate information to relevant women's groups and ensure that gender issues are incorporated into the development programmes of government and non-governmental organizations. The Youth and Sports Unit is charged with formulation of policy relating to public and private initiatives towards youth and sports.

It is important to note that the MLHA is mainly responsible for policy formulation, while the MLGLH is mainly concerned with service provision. The S&CD in the MLGLH is responsible for social welfare provision relevant to foster care for children and youth. The organization of this department will be discussed under 'Administration and organization'.

History and origins

The history of formal foster family care in Botswana is intertwined with the process of community development during the colonial era. The first step was the creation of a Welfare Unit in the Department of Education of the colonial government. Initially, foster care was barely considered – welfare was concerned with education, poverty, Scouting and Guiding, and aid to soldiers who were returning from the Second World War. In 1952, the Social Welfare Department reported that social problems experienced by Africans in Botswana were most effectively dealt with at the level of the tribe and its customs. Thus, social welfare schemes officially provided at the time were meant to augment rather than replace those schemes operating within tribal social structures (Hedenquist, 1992).

In 1964, the Department of Welfare was transferred from the Ministry of Education to the MLGLH. However, social services were placed within the Ministry of Labour and Social Services. In the latter part of the 1960s, the welfare department of the MLGLH became the Department of Social Welfare and Community Development. This department (the S&CD) was divided into six sectors: Audio-Visual Aids, Community Development, General, Home Economics, Social Welfare, and Youth and Women. Only in 1970 did the S&CD voice concern about children. In a community development handbook (Republic of Botswana, 1970) issued under the banner of Ipelegeng (self-help), the department listed child welfare programmes as an area of major importance in its activities. Implicitly, this also included foster care for children.

Administration and organization

Government services

The MLGLH is the central national-level organization for the co-ordination of community development and social welfare services in Botswana.

The MLGLH has statutory responsibility for administering local government institutions. The minister is ultimately responsible for the efficient operation of the local authorities. He approves council budgets and bylaws. A major part of councils' recurrent budget income is received as grants from central government, and these are disbursed through the MLGLH. Development budget grants for local authorities are also funded through the MLGLH (Hedenquist, 1992, p.68).

Below MLGLH in the organizational structure come District and Urban Councils (see Figure 3.1). At this level, central government activities are co-ordinated by the Commissioner, who works in conjunction with the District Council Secretary. Below the District and Urban Councils are the Departments of Education, Health Clinics, Treasury, Public Health, Engineering and Works, Secretariat, Self-help and Social Welfare and Community Development. The most important department in the provision of social services (including foster care) is the S&CD.

According to the National Development Plan 7, 1991–97, the objectives of the S&CD include: assisting local communities in co-ordinating efforts to provide for health, welfare and recreation; assisting family groups and their members in adjusting to their circumstances; helping young people channel their energy into useful activities, and helping them integrate into their communities; assisting individuals, groups and communities in promoting their psychological wellbeing and realizing their potential, and co-operating with NGOs in the provision of social welfare services (Government of Botswana, 1991). Specifically, the S&CD is charged with organizing and monitoring community programmes, such as those concerned with destitution, juvenile delinquency, paupers' burials, bursaries, the disabled, needy children, day care centres, school casework, family counselling, marital disputes and divorces, probation work, and aid to the unemployed. The S&CD is also responsible for working with Village Development Committees (VDCs) and voluntary organizations. In addition, it is charged with responsibilities pertaining to youth and home economics.

The officers charged with facilitating the above-mentioned activities are the Chief Community Development Officer and his subordinate, the Senior Community Development Officer. They are assisted by Community Development Officers in charge of community development, social welfare, home economics and youth. Foster care is the responsibility of the Community Development Officer in charge of social welfare (Hedenquist, 1992).

Non-governmental organizations

There are several NGOs involved in the provision of social services.

SOS Children's Village

The SOS Children's Village Association of Botswana was founded in 1985 through the initiative of Lady Ruth Khama (the country's first First Lady) with the help of SOS Children's Village, UK. In 1987, the SOS Children's Village in Tlokweng was fully commissioned to care for Botswana's abandoned, abused and orphaned children.

The purpose of the village is to help children in need of care who have lost their parents or have been abandoned for other reasons. Homes are provided for children in small, family-type groups. Usually, 10 to 12 children live in each house under the care of a foster mother and an assistant as a family unit. Care is taken not to separate siblings. The SOS Village is run by a director, whose job is to advise the various foster mothers and to ensure that proper care is provided to the children. Services provided to the children include education, health and recreational facilities. Wherever possible, children in the SOS Village remain in contact with their extended families.

SOS educational facilities also cater for children from the larger community, and SOS children attend neighbourhood schools. This is part of the integration process of SOS children into mainstream life. SOS also provides a youth centre for children over 18 years of age. The idea is to care for the children until they are able to look after themselves. SOS receives an annual grant from the government. Currently, the annual subvention that SOS receives from the Department of Culture and Social Welfare has been doubled to 100,000 pulas (about $US38,500). SOS receives 80 per cent of its funds from foreign donors (SOS, 1995a).

Child to Child Foundation

This is a non-political and non-profit voluntary organization. It is mostly concerned with poor and disadvantaged children in rural areas, and its primary focus is on early learning and health education. The foundation began in 1979 with the financial support of the American Women's International Association. Over the years, it has become involved with over 51 schools in Botswana and with over 50,408 schoolchildren at both pre-school and primary school levels. This involvement has often led to the identification of children in need of foster care or adoption. Where necessary, the foundation has reported cases to the relevant authorities for action. In 1995, the government provided a grant of 65,000 pulas (approximately $US28,000) to this organization.

Childline

Childline is another facility that provides services to children and their families. It mainly operates as a phone-in helpline for distressed children and their families. Its objectives include: providing an emergency service for all children in danger or distress; helping parents who are experiencing difficulties with their children; providing opportunities to members of the public to report suspected cases of child abuse, and acting as a referral source for professionals such as social workers, nurses and doctors who need guidance in dealing with problem cases.

It is important to emphasize that Childline processes cases and refers them to appropriate institutions, mainly the S&CD, SOS, the police and the courts.

Since its inception, Childline has been funded from voluntary sources. However, in 1995, the government provided a first annual grant of 36,000 pulas (approximately $US14,000).

Policy framework

The policy framework for foster care in Botswana is based on the Children's Act (1981), the Adoption of Children Act (1952), the Affiliation Proceedings Act (1970), and the Deserted Wives and Children's Protection Act (1978).

The Children's Act

This was passed in 1981 with the intention of preventing the deprived and delinquent children of today from becoming the deprived, inadequate, unstable and criminal citizens of tomorrow (Dow and Mogwe, 1992). The Act defines a child as anybody under the age of 14. It is aimed at protecting children who: are in need of care, defined as those who have been abandoned or are without visible means of support; have no parent or guardian, or have an unfit parent or guardian; are engaged in any form of street trading, unless deputed by parents to help in the distribution of merchandise with respect to a family concern; are in the custody of a person who has been convicted of neglect, ill-treatment or corruption of children; or are frequenting the company of an immoral or violent person or are otherwise living in circumstances calculated to cause or conduce seduction, corruption or prostitution.

The Act provides for a Commissioner of Child Welfare, who must either be a magistrate, a district commissioner or a chief. The commissioner is mandated to protect infants from abuse and to preside over a Children's Court in respect of children in need of care. Citizens are required by law to report to the social welfare officer or police officer in their district any child in need of care. These officials have the authority to remove the child from the circumstances to a place of safety, and ultimately, to bring the child to the Children's Court of the district. The social welfare officer is required to furnish the court with a report on the child's general conduct, home environment, school records, medical history, and to provide any other relevant information pertaining to the child.

Section 19 of the Act sets out the powers of the Children's Court with respect to children in need of care. After holding an inquiry in which the child is declared to be in need of care, the Children's Court is empowered to return the child to the custody of the parents or guardians, or the person in whose custody the child was before the commencement of the court proceedings. The court is also empowered to place the child in the custody of a suitable foster parent, send the child to a children's home, or send the child to a school of industries.

When a child is placed in the custody of a parent or guardian, a foster parent or a custodian, that child may be placed under the supervision of a social welfare officer. The social welfare officer is required to provide a progress report on the child to the commissioner of the district.

In general, a parent, guardian or any person having custody of a child who neglects, ill-treats or exploits that child is guilty of an offence.

The Adoption of Children Act

This Act came into force on 12 December 1952 and has undergone several amendments, the latest in 1966. It addresses matters relating to both the entry and exit of children from care. It specifies the qualifications for adopting children and for the appointment of guardians for the purposes of adoption. It also defines the role of the courts in the adoption process, and sets out the adoption process in general.

According to the Act, married couples are allowed to adopt jointly, or divorced or separated spouses are allowed to adopt alone. However, the Act also makes the proviso that: 'no person under the age of 25 years shall adopt any child either alone or jointly with his or her spouse' (s. 3, para. 2). In addition, no person is permitted to adopt a child aged 16 years or older unless he or she is at least 25 years older than the child. There is an exception to both provisions which states that a husband and wife may jointly adopt any child born to either of them, even though one or both are under the age of 25, or the child is aged 16 or over.

A qualification related to this states: 'a person shall not adopt otherwise jointly with his/her spouse, a child less than 25 years younger than the said person, unless the child is of the same sex as that person or that person is a widower, widow, unmarried or divorced and is a natural parent of the child' (s. 3, para. 2).

Most of these provisions are aimed at avoiding any possible sexual relationship between the adoptive parent and an adopted child of the opposite sex. Nevertheless, some cases are still being reported of sexual abuse by adoptive fathers towards adopted daughters and by adoptive mothers towards adopted sons. It should be noted in this context that most of the people in Botswana who have opted for legal adoption did not receive a full explanation of the Act, and probably did not understand clearly what it meant. They therefore should not be blamed if their relationship with an adopted child is not the kind of relationship specified in the Act.

There are several steps in the adoption process. An order must be obtained from the court of the district in which the child resides. This court will continue with the adoption process only if it is completely satisfied that the child is eligible to be adopted and the parents are qualified to receive the child. The proposed adoption is primarily intended to serve the interests and promote the welfare of the child.

The prospective adoptive parents should never have been guilty or under suspicion of neglecting a child. They must have a demonstrated capacity to look after the child, in that they must be of good reputation, fit to be entrusted with the custody of a child, and they must possess adequate means to maintain and educate the child.

An adopted child is given the surname of the adoptive parent, and is deemed by law to be the legitimate child of that parent. The court allows the natural parent or guardian to visit the adopted child during a two-year period after the adoption. The Adoption Order may be rescinded within six months if the applicant is the child's natural parent and did not consent to the adoption, or if the adoption was entered into on the basis of fraud or misrepresentation. An Adoption Order, a rescission of an Adoption Order, and a refusal of an application for the rescission of an Adoption Order are all subject to appeal to the High Court. The appeal may be brought by a parent, guardian or adoptive parent.

An adopted child may not be removed from Botswana within 12 months after adoption without a written explanation to the minister. A child of 10 years or older has to give consent to his or her adoption. The adopted child retains the right to choose whom to marry or not to marry, on the understanding that the only eligible marriage partners are those who would have been eligible had the adoption never taken place. However, the same section of the Act goes on to stipulate that the adoptive parent may not enter into legal marriage with an adopted child who is less than 21 years of age.

The Affiliation Proceedings Act

This is 'an Act to provide for the determination of the paternity of an illegitimate child, and is concerned with the making of orders for the maintenance of such children, together with other matters connected therewith or incidental thereto' (Preamble).

Once the natural father has been identified, the court issues a Maintenance Order and specifies the amount to be paid. This amount is usually 40 pulas (about $US15), which is grossly inadequate, and various interest groups are fighting to raise it. Moreover, very few women ever collect it. The Maintenance Order continues to be in effect until the child is 13 years old, and may be extended by the court to age 16.

The Deserted Wives and Children's Protection Act

This Act provides for the maintenance of married women and their children. It broadly defines a married woman to include one married either by law or custom. A child is defined as a person under 16 years of age or between 16 and 21 years, provided that he or she is not earning a living. Dow and Mogwe (1992, p.27) indicate:

> A child may have recourse to this Act in cases where s/he has been deserted by the father, where the father has neglected to provide the child with food and other necessities of life, where the child has left or been removed from the home because of the father's act of cruelty or the father is an habitual drunkard.

A child may exercise his or her right to complain. In that case, the father is ordered to appear before the court to explain his neglect of the child. The court determines how much the father must pay in maintenance, taking into account his means, the number of children in his family, his wife's capacity and other relevant aspects of the situation.

Who is placed in foster care?

Foster care

Formal foster care in Botswana consists of placing children in need of care into a formal institution. At present, all children formally deemed to be in need of foster care are placed in the SOS Village, Tlokweng. This may explain why there were no foster care cases in Botswana until the late 1980s, as the SOS Village had not yet been opened.

The concept of children in need of care, including foster care, is widely understood within the Tswana culture. It is traditional for grandparents, uncles and other members of the extended family to take children into their care if, in their judgement, the children are not receiving proper treatment. It is also traditional for natural parents to give away children to other people, be they relatives or not, who for some reason might be in need of children (Schapera, 1984).

In the rural districts of Central, Gantsi, Kgalagadi and the South East, there are significant numbers of children in need of care. In the Central District, there were five cases in 1991, with four ongoing and one closed. In Gantsi, there were nine cases still pending in 1991. In 1992, Kgalagadi had a high number of cases (18) of children in need of care. Only two of these had been resolved by the end of 1993. South East District had eight cases, with seven resolved and one pending in 1992/93 (Gantsi District Council, 1995; Kgalagadi District Council, 1993; South East District Council, 1993).

On average, the figures for children in need of care in urban areas are higher than those in rural areas. Gaborone reported 22 such cases in 1994/95; Francistown had seven cases in 1992/93, four of which were disposed of; Jwaneng had three cases in 1992/93, while Lobatse had only two cases in 1994/95, which were successfully dealt with (Gaborone City Council, 1995; Francistown Council, 1993; Lobatse Town Council, 1995).

Adoption

Cases of adoption are relatively recent in Botswana. The procedure for adoption is as laid down in the Adoption of Children Act (1952). The scale of adoption in the country is not known, as the information available is patchy and thus only reflects certain years and districts. The data presented here refer to selected districts and years for which data are available, so allowances must be made for this.

From the data, the little adoption that takes place occurs mostly in urban areas, especially in Francistown, Lobatse, Gaborone and Jwaneng (a mining centre). Thus, in Francistown, the second biggest town in Botswana, there were five cases of adoption, of which four were dealt with in the 1991/92 period. In 1992/93, the number of cases increased to 15, of which 10 were dealt with, while five were ongoing. These are the only available figures for Francistown. The 1990/91 annual report of the Francistown Social and Community Development Unit (Francistown Council, 1993) indicates that there had not been cases of adoption in Francistown before 1991.

Reported cases of adoption in Jwaneng cover the 1992/93 period (Jwaneng Town Council, 1993). There were six cases of adoption, and by the end of 1993, they were all pending. According to the Jwaneng Social and Community Development Office, these cases were influenced by benefits associated with adoption. Beginning in the 1990s, the mining company, the main employer, decided that married people and those with children should be entitled to certain types of housing, educational benefits and medical aid schemes. Realizing that they were missing opportunities to gain access to such benefits, many workers started to adopt the children of their partners. This has raised the rate of adoption in the town.

Gaborone, the capital city, records the highest number of adoption cases (Gaborone City Council, 1995). According to the Gaborone City Council Progress Report for 1994/95, 18 cases of adoption were being processed. However, it is not clear how far these cases have progressed. Lobatse (a meat processing town) had 11 cases of adoption in 1993/94, with four new cases opened in 1994/95.

Most rural areas do not report cases of adoption, because whatever adoption occurs in those areas is not based on the Adoption of Children Act, but is based instead on customary law. For example, informal adoption occurs frequently where herd-boys, maids or relatives employed by the Botswanans stay for long periods, or even permanently, with their employers.

With regard to formal adoption, S&CD officers in Kgalagadi in the 1989/90 annual report indicated that there were cultural taboos which militated against the formal adoption of children (Kgalagadi District Council, 1993). People in the area feel that formal adoption may exacerbate the disintegration of the extended family system which is already occurring. Given the history of oppression and subordination of the Basarwa, who are the main inhabitants of this area, the adoption of children by outsiders, especially foreigners, is seen as totally unacceptable.

The only rural area showing a high adoption rate is the South East District, where there were 11 cases in 1992/93 (Duncan et al., 1994). All of these occurred in the big villages of Ramotswa, Tlokweng, Otse and Mogobane, which, in essence, are outlying areas of Gaborone. Legal adoption, as defined by the Adoption of Children Act, is basically known and understood by only a few people among the more educated town dwellers. This may explain why there are more cases of adoption in urban areas.

Care providers

Foster care, understood broadly as 'the relocation or transfer of children from biological or natal homes to other homes where they are raised and cared for by foster parents' (Isiugo-Abanihe, 1985, p.53), is widely practised in Botswana. In many cases, mothers working in urban areas in Botswana tend to 'post' their children to their parents in rural areas, so that the children can be cared for by their grandparents. This is done because the mothers cannot afford to pay for child care services in the urban areas where they are living.

'Posting' is very widespread, especially among single, female parents, and is seen as an informal system of foster care.

According to Isiugo-Abanihe (1985, p.56), discussing foster care in Africa:

> fostering here is rooted in kinship structures and traditions, children are sent out not only in the event of family crisis or when one or both natural parents cannot, for some reason, manage to bring them up. Rather, the sending out of children is practised by both stable and unstable families, married and single mothers, healthy and handicapped parents, rural and urban homes, and wealthy and poor parents.

In view of this, fostering in a traditional context is motivated by kinship relationships, since children are thought of as belonging not only to the natural parents but also to the extended family. Such traditional fostering may occur in many different circumstances: in a crisis, such as divorce, separation, death, sickness or teenage pregnancy; because of economic pressures, when, for example, low-income parents who cannot afford domestic help post their children to live with grandparents, or when children are sent from rural to urban areas to stay with relatives and help with household chores; and finally, when children are sent to live with relatives in places where they can have access to educational facilities (Isiugo-Abanihe, 1985).

Figures from the 1991 Population and Housing Census (Central Statistics Office, 1991) support the view that fostering is widespread in Botswana, and provide indications of why people are motivated to foster their children. Table 3.2 shows the number of women whose children are being fostered, according to marital status, educational status and area of residence.

Major problems

According to the Children's Act (1981), anyone who sees a child in need of care must report the case to a social welfare officer in the Social Welfare and Community Development Unit of the local council. In practice, however, people report to the police, Childline and other agencies. Once reported, a social welfare officer or any responsible citizen is supposed to take up the matter with the Magistrate's Court, so that an order can be made declaring that the child is in need of care. Once the order has been obtained, proceedings for foster care are then put into place.

The first difficulty here has to do with lack of knowledge. Most people do not know that they have to apply to the Magistrate's Court for a Child Neglect Order. This delays progress. The second problem relates to the court orders themselves. The annual meeting of Chief Community Development

Table 3.2   Number of women fostering children according to marital status, age, educational status and area of residence

Category	Children at home	Children elsewhere	Total
Marital Status			
Never married	96,747 (65.2%)	51,520 (34.8%)	148,267
Married	85,759 (78.8%)	23,095 (21.2%)	108,854
Living together	44,819 (66.7%)	22,411 (33.3%)	67,230
Separated	3,533 (59.5%)	2,400 (40.5%)	5,933
Widowed	2,621 (53.0%)	2,321 (47.0%)	4,942
Age			
12–14	122 (80.7%)	29 (19.3%)	151
15–19	11,112 (82.1%)	2,418 (17.9%)	13,530
20–24	45,789 (68.8%)	20,786 (31.2%)	66,575
25–29	78,911 (68.1%)	36,828 (31.9%)	115,739
30–34	100,848 (70.6%)	41,864 (29.4%)	142,712
Educational status			
No education	64,376 (70.7%)	26,676 (29.3%)	91,052
Primary Education	83,964 (24.0%)	263,304 (76.0%)	347,268
Junior secondary	30,753 (59.5%)	20,897 (40.5%)	51,650
Senior secondary	7,524 (68.4%)	3,461 (31.6%)	10,985
Above senior secondary	4,338 (72.0%)	1,682 (28.0%)	6,020
Area of residence			
Rural	120,562 (75.4%)	39,187 (24.6%)	159,749
Urban	116,126 (64.9%)	62,738 (35.1%)	178,864

Source: Central Statistics Office (1991).

Officers held in Mahalapye on 28–30 April 1993 expressed concern over the orders provided by the High Court. They contended that the orders did not contain enough information to enable them to carry out thorough investigations. In particular, the court orders do not cite full names and house numbers, nor the relevant information on relatives, headmen, place of work, addresses and phone numbers to make it possible for social workers to track down the culprits. In another meeting of Chief Community Development Officers held in Jwaneng on 14 June 1993, it was indicated that there is a need for facilities to cater for children in need of protection. These facilities should be run by councils, since SOS does not have the capacity to receive all such children. Such facilities would also cater for children in need of care and protection while they were waiting for a court order.

Procedures for data collection and reporting are inadequate. This leads to lack of information on a yearly basis. First, there appears to be a duplication between the Ministry of Home Affairs and the Ministry of Local Government. It is not clear as to whether S&CD officers based in the Ministry of Local Government are supposed to provide information to the Ministry of Home Affairs. It seems that the Ministry of Home Affairs cannot compel the Social Welfare Officer in the Ministry of Local Government to provide the necessary statistics.

The Children's Act, the main policy framework for dealing with children in need of care and protection, has major gaps. Primarily, the institutional framework necessary for implementing the Act has not been created. Homes, schools and institutions for the reception of children in need of care and protection provided for under the Act do not yet exist.

As Table 3.2 shows, it appears that the majority of women having their children fostered fall into the 20–34 age group. This is the age group entering the labour force and perhaps struggling to get settled.

With regard to marital status, Table 3.2 shows that the separated and widowed lead in terms of fostering their children. Thus, 40.5 per cent of the separated foster their children out, while 47 per cent of the widowed do so. This may be due to crises and instability in the household. Married people are the least likely to foster their children out, which may indicate the importance of stability and integration within the family.

In terms of education, those with no education (70.7 per cent) and those with senior secondary school education or above are least likely to foster their children out. This may be because those with higher education are more settled in jobs which enable them to look after their children without financial difficulty. Conversely, those with primary and junior secondary school education are most likely to foster their children out. These people are more likely to have lower-status jobs, and hence are likely to post their children, since they cannot hire domestic help to take care of the children.

Finally, it seems that urban dwellers are more likely to foster their children out than rural dwellers, probably for economic reasons. When people send their children from urban to rural areas, they are likely to send money from time to time to help with the children's upkeep. However, the average frequency of sending funds and the amounts involved are not known.

Major trends

There is much activity in the traditional systems of foster care, but there is little research to ascertain the scope, type of care, finances involved, impact of fostering on the children and their families, and related activities or issues.

Partly because of the informal system of fostering, the formal system, based on the Children's Act and the Adoption of Children Act, is not well developed. Most of the children in need of care are provided for within the confines of the extended family system, but this is breaking down due to industrialization, urbanization and modernization. Increasingly, children in need of care are not being helped by the extended family system. This has necessitated the increasing use of formal structures such as the S&CD. The establishment of SOS must be seen in this light.

Despite the emergence of a formal system of foster care, there is only one institution providing direct care to needy children; there are no families formally fostering children, and there is no significant research on foster care in the country. The increasing number of needy children is forcing the government and other organizations to increase their interest in the issue of foster care. The call by chief community development officers for council-run homes should be seen as an important effort to deal with the situation. Similarly, there are plans afoot to establish a second SOS Village in Francistown.

It is hoped that the Child Welfare Association, which co-ordinates the activities of all organizations involved in child welfare activities, will help to stimulate more child fostering and adoption activities.

Bibliography

Colclough, C., Cumming, C. and Sekgoma, G. (1988) *Investment Options in Post Secondary Education*, Gaborone: Ministry of Education, Government of Botswana.

Central Statistics Office (1986) *Country Profile*, Gaborone: Government Printers.

Central Statistics Office (1988) *Household Income and Expenditure Survey: 1985/86*, Gaborone: Government Printer.

Central Statistics Office (1991) *Population and Housing Census*, Gaborone: Government Printers.

Dow, U. and Mogwe, A. (1992) *The Convention on the Rights of the Child and the Legal Status of Children*, Gaborone: UNICEF.

Duncan, T., Jefferis, K. and Molutsi, P. (1994) *Social Development in Botswana: A Retrospective Analysis*, Gaborone: Government of Botswana and UNICEF.

Francistown Council (1993) *Annual Report 1992/93*, Social and Community Development Unit.

Gaborone City Council (1995) *Annual Report 1994/95*, Social and Community Development Unit.

Gantsi District Council (1995) *Annual Report 1994/95*, Social and Community Development Unit.

Harvey, C. (1992) 'Botswana: Is the economic miracle over?', *Journal of African Economics*, Vol. 1, No. 3, November, pp.335–68.

Hendenquist, J. (1992) *Introduction to Social and Community Development Work in Botswana*, Gaborone: Ministry of Local Government, Lands and Housing.

Hoppers, W. (1986) *After Training What? Youth Training and Self-Employment in Botswana and Zambia*, London: Commonwealth Secretariat.

Isiugo-Abanihe, U.C. (1985) 'Child fosterage in West Africa', *Population and Development Review*, Vol. 2, No. 1, March, pp.53–72.

Jwaneng Town Council (1993) *Annual Report 1992/93*, Social and Community Development Unit.

Kgalagadi District Council (1993) *Annual Report 1992/93*, Social and Community Development Unit.

Lobatse Town Council (1995) *Annual Report 1994/95*, Social and Community Development Unit.

Republic of Botswana (1970) *Community Development Handbook*, Gaborone: Ministry of Local Government and Lands.

Republic of Botswana (1973) (1976) (1985) (1991) *National Development Plans*, Gaborone: Government Printers.

Schapera, I. (1984) *The Tswana*, London: Routledge and Kegan Paul.

SOS Children's Village Botswana (1995a) News Flash, Gaborone, June.

SOS Children's Village Brochure (1995b) Gaborone.

South East District Council (1993) *Annual Report 1992/93*, Social and Community Development Unit.

4 Canada

Judy Krysik

Jurisdiction

Canada is a federal state organized into ten provinces and two territories. The British North America Act of 1867 united the provinces of Quebec, Ontario, Nova Scotia, and New Brunswick into the Dominion of Canada. Sharing its borders with the continental USA and Alaska, Canada has the third highest land mass of any country in the world. Perhaps best known for its climate, Canada varies from temperate in the south to sub-arctic in the north, accounting at least partially for the fact that 80 per cent of the population lives within 100 miles of the continental US border.

Demography

The age distribution pyramid for Canada reflects the effects of the baby boom generation. Of the approximately 27 million inhabitants, 14.1 per cent are aged under 10, and 14.6 per cent are aged between 10 and 19. The bulk of the population, 35.1 per cent, is aged between 20 and 39. The average life expectancy, 81 years for females and 74 for males, is a testimony to the relatively good standard of living enjoyed by Canadians.

Cultural diversity

Canada is often described as a cultural mosaic, a place where culturally diverse groups are encouraged to maintain their ethnic ties (Thomlison and Foote, 1987). In its early years, however, Canada was immersed in a struggle between the British and the French, a circumstance which has afforded Quebec greater measures of sovereignty, and which remains unresolved as Quebec deals with the possibility of separation. British and

41

French represent the largest ethnic groups in Canada. Recent estimates indicate that 33.6 per cent of Canada's population have British backgrounds and 24.4 per cent French (White, 1994). In 1986, 3 per cent (about 750,000) of the population reported at least some American Indian origin (Ponting, 1994). Finally, approximately 16 per cent of the total population are immigrants, a proportion that has held constant over the last four decades. However, changes have occurred in the numbers of immigrants coming from different parts of the world, a factor which makes Canada's population increasingly diverse. Asian-born immigrants comprise the largest group of newcomers arriving between 1978 and 1986, and there have also been substantial increases from other non-European areas (White, 1994).

The national economy

The 1992 United Nations Human Development Report ranked Canada as the world's best country for its residents, based on national income, life expectancy and educational attainment. The Canadian economy relies to a large extent on its natural resources, a factor that has created great regional economic disparities. Agriculture constitutes 4 per cent, industry 36 per cent and services 60 per cent. The majority of the population, 77 per cent, is urban-based.

The structure of child welfare service delivery

Health, education and welfare matters – formerly in the domain of the local parish or municipality – were assigned to the provinces under the British North American Act (1867). Funding for these services is shared between federal and provincial governments, and each province has developed legislation that sets out guidelines for service delivery. With regard to child welfare services, generally there has been an attempt to achieve uniformity across the country. In the provinces of British Columbia, Alberta, Saskatchewan, New Brunswick, Prince Edward Island, Newfoundland, and in the Yukon and North West Territories, child welfare services are delivered directly by government departments or by government contract. In Ontario and Nova Scotia, child welfare services are delivered through local, community-based and board-run agencies, such as the Children's Aid Society. Manitoba possesses a mixture of government and children's aid societies, and Quebec fulfils its child welfare mandate through semi-public agencies known as Centres de Services Sociaux.

History and origins

The earliest type of communal care facility for children was the orphans' asylum. First developed in Montreal around 1822, the asylums were operated by the local parish or municipality. In the mid-nineteenth century, the orphans' asylums expanded to eastern and central Canada, and thereafter to western Canada. Initially, the orphans' asylums were general facilities, housing children, the aged, and women. In 1891, J.J. Kelso, father of the Humane Society in Toronto, helped found the Children's Aid Society (CAS). The CAS is credited with developing specialized institutional facilities for children, based on the rationale that segregation was necessary for proper socialization (Bullen, 1990). As the nineteenth-century institutions became overwhelmed with children, indenturement was employed as the solution. Institutions maintained children in their earliest years until they could be indentured at age 12, or sometimes earlier if there was demand. Females could be indentured until age 18 or marriage, and males until age 21.

The shift from institutional care to foster care was based on the argument that institutional life for children, even when segregated from adults, contributed to an early and lasting dependency on public charity. In 1893, the Ontario government passed the first Children's Protection Act, which formed the legislative basis for foster care. Foster care has since become, and remains, the most important resource for out-of-home care in Canada. Placement in foster care usually requires a change in legal status, whereby the biological or adoptive parent's rights to the guardianship of a child are legally terminated on a temporary or permanent basis. This termination can be initiated either voluntarily by the guardian(s) or mandated by the court. Once the guardianship of a child is permanently transferred to the state, the child becomes eligible for adoption.

Institutions, having their function usurped by foster care, moved from providing residential services to all children requiring out-of-home care to providing pre-foster care placement and treatment for the handicapped and emotionally and behaviourally disturbed. Thus the introduction of foster care did not replace institutional care, but broadened the continuum of out-of-home services for children.

Child protective legislation also created the authority to monitor foster homes, with the intention of enforcing the shift from child indenturement to child socialization within a family context. Given the fact that the majority of foster parents came from a class that needed extra income, an economic motive was present at times in the decision to foster. The status of foster children often proved to be no different to that of indentured servants. Not until the introduction of compulsory education did the focus on nurture succeed the notion of economic usefulness.

However, foster care was not the panacea originally hoped for. As early as the 1920s, there were reports of shortages of foster care placements, of children being moved about from one home to another (foster care drift), and of screening and supervision processes that could not prevent child maltreatment. These problems persist as major challenges in the provision of foster care services today.

The philosophical context of foster care

Over time, acknowledgement of the problems inherent in foster care has prompted certain shifts in philosophy. Two major paradigm shifts have occurred. One is a move towards permanency planning. The second is a shift from amelioration of the child's past towards family preservation. Both of these shifts have demanded legislative change.

Permanency planning attempts to deal with foster care drift. It recognizes that children who have been in care for longer than 18–24 months have a significantly reduced chance of returning home or of being adopted. By creating a comprehensive plan of action that sets out contracted goals and responsibilities and involves natural and foster parents, children, and agency personnel, the likelihood of foster care drift is greatly reduced, and family contact is more likely to occur.

The second shift, towards family preservation, views the child's relationship with his or her natural or adoptive family as important regardless of whether that family is able to provide residential care for the child. Under family preservation philosophy, foster care has come to be considered more of an interim resource, as opposed to a long-term solution. Foster parents are now instrumental in facilitating the child's transition back to the biological family, maintaining the child's ties with the biological family when returning home is not an option, and connecting the child with his or her cultural, social and religious heritage.

Administration and organization

Foster care services are administered by both government and private agencies. Provincial governments provide public foster care, and contract with private agencies to provide additional foster care resources. The development of specialist foster care in the private sector initially created conflict between public and private foster care providers, because specialist foster care providers received more training and support, and generally, better pay. In addition, conflict was created between residential and treatment foster care agencies because funds were diverted from residentially-based centres to treatment foster care. In Alberta, the tension has been resolved to a certain extent through the sharing of professional development opportunities between public and private agency providers. The government has maintained control over setting foster care standards, but has also worked with specialist foster care agency associations to standardize the two systems (Jaeger and Stavert, 1995).

While the administration of foster care has been carried out primarily by the public sector, there is a growing trend towards more private, non-profit involvement. In the Calgary Region of the Province of Alberta, a one-year pilot project saw the takeover of the public system by a community-based council. This trial model of governance was developed on the initiative of the local Foster Parents Association. It involved foster parents and interested individuals in the overall responsibility for foster care services for a one-year period beginning 1 September 1995. The newly-created council was responsible for foster parent recruitment, home assessments and approval, matching and placement, training, management and support of children placed in the programme, monitoring and evaluation, and financial operations excluding rate setting. Currently, the Calgary Region has approximately 255 public foster homes serving 400 children at any one time. The government also contracts with 12 private agencies to provide an additional 170 foster care spaces.

Who is placed in foster care?

The shift to child welfare services supporting families with in-home services was expected to produce fewer children with permanent guardianship status, a decreased demand for foster care, and shorter stays in out-of-home care. In 1981, Levitt reported that there were 79,440 children in out-of-home care in Canada. In 1995, the Child Welfare League of Canada reported that 50,000 children were in out-of-home care, 40,000–45,000 of whom were in foster care. While there are fewer children in out-of-home care today than in previous years, the children who receive foster care services are more likely to be older and have more severe problems and special needs.

One of the most striking characteristics among the foster care population is the over-representation of North American Indian children. North American Indian children, including status, non-status and Metis, make up approximately 3.5 per cent of the total child population, and an estimated 20 per cent of children in out-of-home care (Peters and Fong, 1995). In Alberta, 47 per cent of children in out-of-home care in March 1994 were of North American Indian descent (Whitford et al., 1995). These children also tend to be younger, and are more likely to be in government guardianship (Rosenbluth, 1995). During 1986 and 1990, there was an overall decrease in the time that children spent in foster care. In 1990, non-North American

Indian children were in out-of-home care for six months less than they had been in 1986, whereas there was no difference for North American Indian children (Rosenbluth, 1995).

Care providers

The change in the foster care population has required a change in foster care providers. Fostering has changed from a voluntary service that provided temporary care for most children to a system of taking in older children with multiple individual and family problems. As a consequence, the demands on foster parents have increased. Whereas foster parents were once mother and father substitutes, they are now required to be surrogate therapists. Traditional foster care services are no longer sufficient to meet the needs of most consumers, and what has in the past been described as 'specialist' or 'treatment' foster care has become the norm.

Specialist foster care retains the emphasis on the normative family and community-based experience of traditional foster care, combined with a more formal treatment approach which is based on goal setting, treatment planning and skilled intervention (Gabor and Kammerer, 1983). The Alberta Parent Counsellor Programme, for instance, began in 1974 as a demonstration project with the purpose of developing and testing specialized, treatment-oriented foster care for children with emotional and behavioural problems. The programme has since been operated as part of the foster care programme in Alberta. Under this programme, the foster parent is a parent counsellor, and is viewed as central in the helping system. Parent counsellors assume responsibility for providing services to both children and their biological families, while the social worker's role is that of a resource (Gabor and Kammerer, 1983). There are also foster care providers who specialize in caring for and treating children with alcohol and drug addiction, criminal or delinquent behaviour, AIDS, and physical and mental disabilities (Nutter et al., 1995).

With the introduction of specialist foster care, a new type of foster parent has emerged. Many foster homes are Caucasian and middle-class. This contrasts sharply with the population needing care – children from one-parent, low-income, non-Caucasian families. Thomlison and Foote's (1987) study of treatment foster care parents in Alberta revealed that these providers were generally young and highly educated. The mean age was 36 years for mothers and 39 for fathers. Forty-eight per cent of mothers and 69 per cent of fathers had completed university education. No mothers had less than high school education, and 93 per cent were two-parent families.

The change in foster parent roles, combined with more women entering the paid labour market, has further reduced the pool of potential foster parents, and has also led to an overburdening of available foster parents. Steinhauer (1984) reported that 1 in 4 Ontario foster homes closed each year, and between 1966 and 1978, the total number of homes decreased by 40 per cent. In addition, some homes remain vacant because of the lack of an appropriate match. Recruitment and retention of foster families are major issues in foster care administration across Canada.

In recent years, there has been an emphasis on extended family members as foster parents. This practice, referred to as 'kinship care', is currently acknowledged as an underdeveloped resource. Kinship care has developed at a time when family preservation efforts have grown increasingly popular and are recognized as more humane and cost-effective.

Financial support

The acute shortage of foster homes in Canada is in part attributed to the poor financial incentives. Tax-free payments to foster parents vary from province to province, but are relatively low compared to the actual costs of raising a child. Generally, the parent is paid for basic maintenance of the child, based on a daily rate that is intended to cover day-to-day costs such as food, clothing and personal needs, transportation and babysitting. The amount can depend on the child's age, the parents' experience and expertise, and can be adjusted depending on the level of difficulty of the child. Clothing allowances are available to meet a child's needs when the child enters foster care. All treatment, such as medical, dental, optical and counselling, is covered, as well as all educational fees and supplies. Occasional costs, such as vacation money and camp fees, and recreational or cultural costs, may also be covered.

Specialist foster care programmes in Canada generally pay caregivers at rates above those provided in public foster care. Some homes serving children with special needs or in emergency situations are paid a retainer fee, based on the available number of placements.

For more specific information on current foster care rates payable in all provinces and territories, contact: Shelley Holroyd, Social Programme Information and Analysis Directorate, Strategic Policy Group, Human Resources Development Canada *Telephone*: (+1) 819 997-9458. *Fax*: (+1) 819 994-0203.

Major problems

Although foster care is the resource most commonly utilized for out-of-home care, several concerns persist. Seven areas of major concern are discussed below.

A lack of culturally appropriate foster families

Foster care services are often not culturally appropriate. Rosenbluth's (1995) publication on foster care in Saskatchewan compared the placements of North American Indian and non-North American Indian children. He found that placements in the same cultural background occurred in 90 per cent of cases for 234 non-North American Indian children, compared to only 9.4 per cent of cases for 483 North American Indian children.

Punishment of low-income families

The foster care system often treats families in need of adequate housing, income and health care support as unable or unwilling to provide for their children. It is ironic that children in care are often better off economically than those who remain with their families of origin. This creates tension for parents who are unable to provide the same level of care the child received while in foster care, and a disincentive for children to reunite with their families.

Maintaining sibling ties

There is recognition of the importance of maintaining sibling ties for children in foster care. The devastating effects of separation from siblings have been noted from the early records of children sent from England to Canada in the nineteenth and early twentieth centuries (Ward, 1984). A number of reasons are given for separating brothers and sisters in foster care, but these are all administrative. Such reasons include home recruitment, home size, family income, or wide differences in the ages of the children involved.

Poor health care and social development

Children in foster care are at greater risk of health problems and inadequate social development. Moffatt et al. (1985) assessed the health of 900 children in foster care in the province of Quebec through a review of medical charts. Evidence of complete immunization was present in only 48 per cent of the 900 cases and the prevalence of short stature was four times the expected rate. Overall, the agency was aware of only 40 of the 77 problems uncovered during the medical examination, including the fact that 14 children were not able to pass an auditory screening test. Of the 23 adolescents in the study, 10 were smokers, and 4 had sexual behaviour judged to place them at risk of venereal disease. Of 25 who were of school age, almost 50 per cent had failed at least one grade, and 35 per cent had scores below the second percentile of normal on the school progress scale of the Child Behaviour Checklist.

A lack of biological family involvement

The importance of biological family involvement has been emphasized over the past decade. Research findings support the fact that greater contact between parents and children increases the likelihood of return home (Levitt, 1981). In the absence of a comprehensive plan involving biological and foster parents, children and agency personnel, the likelihood of foster care drift greatly increases. On an administrative level, Richardson et al. (1995) found that those agencies with written policies addressing biological family involvement were more likely to be successful in increasing family involvement.

Poor preparation for leaving care

The age for termination of foster care varies among the provinces and territories from 16 to 19 years. However, many young people are not prepared for the transition. Some provinces have legislative measures in place to extend care until the age of 21 if the young person is handicapped or attending school or university. The interpretation of this policy option is restricted by tight budgets and is not well communicated or encouraged (Meston, 1988). Each province has a programme to prepare young people for independent living. Programmes for independent living range from non-residential support programmes to apartment/shared living programmes and supported boarding programmes. Most young people do not have the financial or social support to go on to post-secondary education, such as college or university. One of the greatest needs voiced by young people in out-of-home care is for someone to take an active interest in their lives, not as a job, but as a matter of interest and concern: a concern that should extend past the age of majority (Peters and Fong, 1995).

Inadequate screening, training and licensing of foster family carers

Although the trend is towards making foster parents para-professionals, screening varies, as does training and licensing. Edmonton, Alberta, has one of the longest training programmes for foster parent applicants in Canada: 40 hours. In some instances, however, people have been accepted as foster parents without the completion of a home assessment, and licensing has been virtually a 'rubber-stamping' process.

Major trends

As noted above, under family preservation philosophy, foster care has come to be considered more of an interim resource than a long-term solution.

Foster parents are now expected to be instrumental in maintaining children's ties with their biological families and with their cultural, social and religious heritage. There is also a growing trend towards making specialist or treatment foster care the norm, and viewing foster parents as equal members of a professional treatment team.

In recent years, there has also been an emphasis on extended family members as foster parents. This practice taps what is currently acknowledged as an underdeveloped resource.

A major priority for the second half of this decade will be the recruitment of a more culturally diverse group of foster parents. This will facilitate a greater number of culturally appropriate foster care matches. But retention and support of foster parents can only follow increased recruitment rates. Relief, in the form of respite services and support and training for foster parents, is essential in order to retain and increase foster care resources.

Role of national foster care association

The Canadian Foster Family Association (CFFA) was established in 1978, and was incorporated as a national, non-profit, charitable organization in 1987. Membership includes the 12 provincial/territorial foster family associations, as well as individual, association, and corporate donors. The mandate of the CFFA is to promote quality foster care services in Canada, and to act as a collective voice to address issues of concern. Association activities include publication of a quarterly newsletter, recognition of long-term foster parent service, an annual educational symposium, and special educational projects. A code of ethics for foster families was developed and approved in 1994, as well as a set of national foster care guidelines. The CFFA also participates in the International Foster Care Organization. Each province has a provincial foster parent organization and local associations. The provincial organizations are responsible for setting standards and providing support and advocacy services to foster parents.

Contact: The Canadian Foster Family Association, No. 608, 251 Bank Street, Ottawa, Ontario K2P 1X3 Canada *Telephone*: (+1) 613-237-2032 *Fax*: (+1) 613-237-0362.

Research

Foster care providers, child welfare practitioners and academics in Canada are actively involved in foster care research. Areas of current research interest include safeguarding against abuse in foster family care, family reunification, developing North American Indian ties, leaving foster care, and biological family involvement. For further reading, the following resources are suggested:

Hepworth, P. (1980) *Foster Care and Adoption in Canada*, Ottawa: Canadian Council on Social Development.

Hudson, J. and Galaway, B. (eds) (1995) *Canadian Child Welfare: Research and Policy Implications*. Toronto: Thompson Educational Publishing.

Mackenzie, B. (ed.) (1994) *Current Perspectives on Foster Family Care for Children and Youth*, Toronto: Wall & Emerson.

Raychaba, B. (1993) *Pain ... Lots of Pain*, Ottawa: National Youth in Care Network.

Bibliography

Bullen, J. (1990) 'J. J. Kelso and the "new" child -savers: The genesis of the Children's Aid Movement in Ontario', *Ontario History*, Vol. 82, pp.107–28.

Gabor, P. and Kammerer, K. (1983) 'A meeting point: Developing treatment oriented foster care', *Child Care*, Vol. 1, pp.87–97.

Jaeger, D. and Stavert, D. (1995) 'Private and public partnerships: The Alberta experience', *Focus*, Vol. 4, pp.5–6.

Levitt, K.L. (1981) 'A Canadian approach to permanent planning', *Child Welfare*, Vol. 60, pp.109–12.

Meston, J. (1988) 'Preparing young people in Canada for emancipation from child welfare care', *Child Welfare*, Vol. 67, pp.625–34.

Moffatt, M.E.K., Peddie, M., Stulginskas, J., Pless, I.B. and Steinmetz, N. (1985) 'Health care delivery to foster children: A study', *Health and Social Work*, Vol. 10, No. 1, pp.5–14.

Nutter, R.W., Hudson, J., Galaway, B. and Hill, M. (1995) 'Specialist foster care programme standards in relation to cost, client characteristics, and outcomes', in Hudson, J. and Galaway, B. (eds), *Child Welfare in Canada: Research and Policy Implications*, Toronto: Thompson Educational Publishing, pp.201–18.

Peters, S. and Fong, S. (1995) 'Reforming Social Security as if Children Matter: The Voices of Child Welfare Participants', unpublished manuscript.

Ponting, J.R. (1994) 'Public opinion on Aboriginal peoples issues in Canada', in McKie, C. and Thompson, K. (eds) *Canadian Social Trends*, Vol. 35, No. 1, pp.19–27.

Richardson, G., Galaway, B., Hudson, J., Nutter, R. and Hill, M. (1995) 'Birth parent participation in treatment foster care program in North America and the United Kingdom', in Hudson, J. and Galaway, B. (eds) *Child Welfare in Canada: Research and Policy Implications*, Toronto: Thompson Educational Publishing, pp.219–32.

Rosenbluth, D. (1995) 'Moving in and out of foster care', in Hudson, J. and Galaway, B. (eds) *Child Welfare in Canada: Research and Policy Implications*, Toronto: Thompson Educational Publishing, pp.233–51.

Steinhauer, P.D. (1984) 'The management of children admitted to child welfare services in Ontario: A review and discussion of current problems and practices', *Canadian Journal of Psychiatry*, Vol. 29, pp.473–83.

Thomlison, R.J. and Foote, C.E. (1987) 'Child welfare in Canada', *Child and Adolescent Social Work*, Vol. 4, pp.123–43.

Ward, M. (1984) 'Sibling ties in foster care and adoption planning', *Child Welfare*, Vol. 63, pp.321–32.

White, P.M. (1994) 'Ethnic origins of the Canadian population', in McKie, C. and Thompson, K. (eds) *Canadian Social Trends*, Vol. 35, No. 1, pp.3–6.

Whitford, D., Manyfingers, B. and Tom, T. (1995) 'Reshaping Child Welfare: Improving Services for Aboriginal People', unpublished manuscript.

5 Finland

Kari Salavuo

Jurisdiction

Compared with other European countries, Finland is small in terms of population, but in terms of area, it is of medium size. The population is 5 million, giving an average density of only 17 people per square kilometre. The demographic pyramid resembles that of most other industrial countries, with middle-aged groups predominating. Nineteen per cent of the population are under 14 years of age, and 14 per cent are over 65 years of age. During the next few decades, the proportion of elderly people is projected to rise very rapidly. Along with the current reduction in the younger age cohorts, this will lead to a radical change in the age distribution of the country. The need for social services is related to the population structure. The ageing of the population will tend to increase the demand for welfare and health services, possibly at the expense of children's welfare services (*Statistical Yearbook of Finland*, 1994).

Culturally, Finland is very homogeneous. There are only very small minorities of Lapps (4,000), refugees (11,000) and foreigners (46,000). Ninety-three per cent of the population speak Finnish, and 6 per cent speak Swedish. Lutheranism has been the dominant religion in Finland since the seventeenth century, and 88 per cent of Finns belong to the Evangelical-Lutheran Church, while 1 per cent belong to the Orthodox Church. Because of its history and geographical position, Finland has been influenced by both East and West (*Statistical Yearbook of Finland*, 1994).

Finland is one of the rich, Western industrial states. In terms of its GNP, it ranks among the 15 most affluent nations of the world. The economic recession in the 1990s has reduced the Finnish GNP by about 15 per cent. In 1995, the GNP increased by 3.8 per cent. At the end of 1993, the GNP was about $US84 billion and the GNP per capita was $US14,700 (adjusted for purchasing power parity). Average monthly earnings were $US2,270 for men and $US1,845 for women at the end of 1994 (*Statistical Yearbook of Finland, 1994*).

In order to compare the level of wellbeing in the various parts of the world, the United Nations Development Programme (UNDP) has developed a Human Development Index. This measure is based on indicators of national income, life expectancy and educational attainment, and ranks countries according to their scores. On this scale, Finland is very close to the top: life expectancy is 75 years, and 52 per cent of the population have completed post-primary education, while 14 per cent have a university degree or its equivalent.

Organization of social services

Finland's welfare and health services are of a high standard, and all Finns are guaranteed a livelihood. This has been achieved at an outlay that is slightly below the European average: in 1990, welfare expenditure accounted for 27 per cent of GNP. As a result of the economic recession, total welfare expenditure rose in 1993 to 38 per cent of GNP, despite certain reductions in the volume of welfare and health services.

The Finnish model of social welfare is in transition. It is generally feared that children, especially those in need of child welfare services, may be ignored, and the risk of deprivation may even grow in the future.

One characteristic of the Finnish welfare state is that the public sector has the main responsibility for organizing social services. It is regarded as essential that people enjoy the same services and opportunities regardless of their economic situation, social class or place of residence. Almost all social and health services are publicly financed and provided. Municipalities are responsible for welfare implementation. According to the Social Welfare Act (1982), each Social Welfare Board is required to organize social services for the people in its area. Municipal boards can organize social and health services, either alone or jointly with other municipalities. They can also purchase services from the state, other municipalities, inter-municipal establishments, or private organizations, firms or individuals. State subsidies cover part of municipal welfare expenditure, depending on the municipality's living expenses category, and the rest is covered by its own tax revenues. There are fees for some social and health services, and these are adjusted according to the client's means.

Child welfare services are also the responsibility of the local authorities. Child welfare practice has traditionally been divided into three categories in Finland: general services, prevention, and care. General services include health care, education, cultural activities, and improvement of the overall environment. These services are provided universally to all children and families. General services also include various forms of financial support and social security. Preventive services in 'open' care include family guidance and counselling, lay helpers and hobby activities. Care comprises provision of foster care or residential care, and after care. In practice, distinguishing between these categories is difficult; the borders between prevention and care are especially blurred.

History and origins

The basis for the Finnish child welfare system was created in the late nineteenth century, when urbanization and industrialization spread, and long working hours in mills and factories left many children without care. In order to save children from an unsettled life in private homes, and from begging and being auctioned, the so-called 'ladies' societies' began to establish children's homes in different parts of the country in the 1850s. The years of the Great Famine in the 1860s drove thousands of families to begging, and created a large number of orphans (over 26,000). The obvious needs of these orphans accelerated the founding of children's homes, and the period 1850–80 can be regarded as the first period of their large-scale development. The first local authority children's home was established by the city of Helsinki in 1881. As was normal in those days, the children's homes functioned as annexes or departments of the poorhouses.

The second period over which a large number of children's homes was established, came after the Civil War (January–April 1918). This again left a great many orphans, since many parents had died in the war or were in prison camps or in exile. It was then felt that the authorities had a role to play in placing these children in good homes. At first, it was planned to place the orphans in foster homes in the countryside, but the mothers of children who had lost their fathers opposed this, and a new state subsidy system was created to care for these children in their own homes or in children's homes. In 1919 alone, about 2,500 children were placed in children's homes, 1,700 were placed in foster family care, and 6,000 were assisted in their own homes. By the end of that year, there were 183 children's homes, of which 61 were maintained by voluntary organizations (Utrianen, 1989; Kemppainen, 1991).

The first state reformatory school began its work in 1981. The reformatories were under the auspices of the Prison Department, and were clearly punitive institutions. Educational programmes were gradually introduced between 1910 and 1920 for the rapidly increasing number of children in the reformatories.

The 1920s saw not only the expansion of public services in these spheres, but also the birth of the two largest private child welfare associations, which continue to function to this day: the Mannerheim League for Child Welfare, which seeks to improve the health of Finnish children through child health clinics, and the Finnish Child Welfare Association, which began to work in adoption and foster care services.

Child welfare regulations had been included in general legislation for a long time. After thirty years of preparation, the first Child Welfare Act became law in 1936. While it did not add much to services, it did state the conditions under which a child should be taken into care, and authorized the intervention of the social welfare board if parents were not willing to accept the measures taken.

The Second World War had dramatic consequences for Finnish children, and approximately 50,000 of them were orphaned. Some of the wartime child welfare problems were solved in part by the establishment of reception homes and a high-calibre network of residential institutions, which became the pillars of child welfare development.

By the end of 1946, Finland had 104 local authority children's homes and 103 homes maintained by voluntary organizations, together housing 7,416 children – about 40 per cent of all children in care. In addition, more than 600 children under the age of 17 were placed in old people's homes. In the 1940s, institutions, as a rule, were old and large. From the middle of the 1950s until the 1980s, there was a decrease in the number of children taken into care, and the number of residential institutions also fell. The number of children taken into care was at its lowest level in the 1970s, when there were great hopes for open-care measures.

Legislative basis of foster care

Child welfare legislation in Finland has been under reform from the middle of the 1970s onwards. In the past two decades, both Finnish society and the status of the child have changed a great deal, so the old legislation proved insufficient to meet new needs. Six Acts concerning child welfare were passed during the 1970s and 1980s, and a new Family Carer Act came into force in April 1992.

The reforms have comprised an overhaul of the entire network of social service organizations, and provide more flexible and effective safeguards for the child's health and happiness. The Acts pay special attention to improving the conditions in which the child grows up. They cover schools, health services, building, housing, the family and culture, and consider that all these areas must be co-ordinated to take the priorities of child welfare into account.

The fundamental principles underlying these reforms are the best interests of the child and a preventive approach. The child's own wishes and views are given more weight than in former times. The new child welfare legislation also lays greater emphasis on the children's families – on their natural environment and resources – and it obliges child welfare workers to co-operate with families.

The Child Welfare Act (1984) identified supporting families in bringing up their children as the most important principle of child welfare, thus directing the authorities of the Social Welfare Office to a concern for the whole family. In family-oriented and individual child welfare, the aim is to secure the best interests of children primarily by open-care measures – through interventions which do not involve residential care or fostering. This means helping parents or other custodians understand the child's physical, psychological and social needs.

Amendments to the Child Welfare Act in 1990 emphasized preventive, non-stigmatizing and supportive measures and services. One of the central objectives of the reform was to shift the emphasis of child welfare from extrafamilial care to measures that encourage and support the maintenance of children in their own homes.

As a result, all the work methods of welfare services were adapted towards strengthening child rearing by custodians. Maternity and child health clinics were expanded, family training was diversified, and co-operation with families was intensified. In the day care service, various forms of co-operation to encourage and support parental participation were developed. Home help services have also been developed to support child rearing by parents.

Administration and organization

The three major Acts governing foster care are the Social Welfare Act (1982), the Child Welfare Act (1984) and the Family Carer Act (1992). According to the Social Welfare Act, child welfare is the responsibility of the local authorities: the municipalities. On the local authority level, the Social Welfare Board is the organ responsible for general principles and directives, as well as for day-to-day decisions in child care. Accordingly, the Child Welfare Board makes decisions on whether or not the child shall be taken into care and on the provision of substitute care. The Provincial Administrative Court must confirm the Care Order if a child is taken into care against the will of his or her parents. It also functions as the Court of Appeal.

At the end of the 1980s, a new form of extrafamilial care was developed which lay somewhere between traditional residential care and foster care. This new form of care is called 'family homes', and it means that private families care for children professionally as private providers of services. They number approximately 40, and provide about 200 places. Earlier, family homes were considered to be on a par with residential homes, so that the regulations regarding residential care were applied to them, for example with respect to staffing levels. The permission of the County Administrative Board was required in order to establish a family home. Today, all types of care in private homes are defined as family care or foster care.

According to amendments to the Social Welfare Act which came into force in 1992, 'foster care' means arranging the care, upbringing or other round-the-clock tending of a person outside his or her own home in a private home. The aim of foster care is to give the person cared for an opportunity to obtain family-like care and close human relationships, and to promote his or her basic security and social development. Foster care is provided for a person when appropriate arrangements cannot be made to tend, care for or bring that person up in his or her own home, even with the help of other social and health services, and when that person is not considered to be in need of institutional care.

According to the Family Carer Act, a 'family carer' is a person who, on the basis of an agreement made with a municipality or federation of municipalities, is responsible for providing care, and provides family care in his or her own home. A person can be accepted and considered suitable as a family carer on the basis of his or her education, experience or personal qualities.

Foster care is the responsibility of the municipalities. The majority of foster family care clients are Child Welfare cases. They could also be old people or developmentally disabled. Child Welfare arranges foster care in municipalities on a commission agreement basis. In 1993, 15 per cent of municipalities purchased foster care from private family homes. The number of children and young people in Child Welfare foster homes has increased in the past decade. However, as shown in Table 5.1, the proportion of foster homes has fallen in relation to the number of child placements.

Table 5.1   Proportion of child placements in foster homes

	No. of children	No. of family homes	Ratio of children/homes
1985	4,557	3,489	1.3
1989	4,576	3,074	1.5
1993	5,556	3,306	1.7

Source: Antikainen and Kivinen (1995).

As Table 5.2 shows, only a relatively small number of foster family care placements are arranged through private agencies, although the municipality can purchase foster care from these. The proportion of private agencies has increased in the last two years.

Table 5.2   Increase in the number of placements
by private versus public agencies, 1990–93

	Public agencies		Private agencies		Total
	No.	*%*	*No.*	*%*	
1990	6,683	97.6	115	2.4	4,796
1993	5,302	95.4	225	4.6	5,556

Source: Antikainen and Kivinen (1995).

Who is placed in foster care?

The need for child welfare intervention is clearly greater in urban areas. The most common reasons for admission to care are the parents' or custodians' abuse of intoxicants, neglect of the children's care, and psychological problems. Together, these account for nearly half the principal reasons for admission to care. About 16 per cent of developmentally disabled children have been placed in foster family care. Over half of the children who have been placed in foster family care are under 12 years of age. During the 1990s, the number of new placements into care has decreased, but the total number of children in care has increased by about 1,000, as Table 5.3 shows.

Table 5.3   Admissions to care, 1991–93

	Total no. of admissions	*No. of new admissions during each year*	*New compulsory admissions*
1991	8,724	2,470	9.4%
1992	9,414	2,539	8.9%
1993	9,688	2,312	8.5%

The data in Table 5.3 indicate longer placement periods, particularly in open-care placements. The growth in the number of placements has been accompanied by an increase in placements other than into institutional or family care. Especially in the 1990s, new forms of after care and other suitable arrangements have been developed: examples include supported independent living arrangements, and schemes whereby the family of a placed child lives in the same residential unit as the child.

Care providers

Since the 1970s, one essential feature in the development of child welfare has been a relative increase in open care and a reduction in substitute care (see Table 5.4). Foster care, as opposed to residential care, has been the more widely used form of substitute care since 1976. Over half of the children who have been taken into care have been placed in foster family care. The number of placements in independent supported homes has increased, mostly catering for young people as part of the after care service. Recent years have seen the development of a group of professional foster care units, lying somewhere between institutional and foster family care, and placement in these units has also increased.

**Table 5.4   Numbers and proportions of children in
different types of care, 1991–93**

	Foster care		Residential care		Other		Total no.
	No.	%	No.	%	No.	%	
1991	4,342	50	3,669	42	709	8	8,720
1992	4,698	50	3,732	40	984	10	9,414
1993	4,917	51	3,555	37	1,216	12	9,688

Source: Kivinen and Majamaki (1995).

Financial support

The foster care population consists mainly of children. Sixty per cent of foster care placements are made because of child welfare concerns. The number of private foster homes has decreased during the past few years, and the new Family Carer Act (1992) aimed to increase the number of persons willing to work as foster parents. The new Act gives caregivers the right to a fee, compensation for expenses, a pension based on the fee, and 12 weekdays' leave per year.

A person considered to be a family carer under the terms of the Family Carer Act shall be paid a remuneration of at least $US253 per person being cared for per month, to a maximum of $US760, provided that the family carer undertakes foster care on a full-time basis. When the carer does not take care of the person on a full-time basis, the maximum is $US380. The level of remuneration varies between municipalities and usually lies between $US382 and $US765 per month. With respect to child welfare, carers are paid between $US368 and $US551, but carers who look after people with mental disabilities are paid nearly $US714 per month. It seems that foster care in child welfare services is viewed as less exacting and time-consuming, because remuneration is generally lower here than in other sectors.

The Family Carer Act is a very remarkable law, because it determines the legal employment status of the family carer and provides social security to him or her. This reform has improved the status of family carers, but in practice, many problems still remain.

Major problems

According to the Family Carer Act (1992), the family carer shall be given an opportunity for free time. Family carers tend to be devoted to their work: more than half of them had not had any free time during 1993. The provision of free time seems to be the most difficult point to implement, compared to all the other provisions in the contracts.

The municipality is responsible for providing adequate training, job supervision and educational advancement for the carer. Almost all municipalities organize training for family carers, but at present, only 17 per cent of family carers looking after children have received training, and job-related guidance has been quite sporadic as well. The right of family carers to receive education, training and guidance varies across municipalities and according to the area of activities. Currently, 16 per cent of carers work without guidance. A central role in the education of family carers is played by organizations, especially the Finnish Federation of Foster Care Associations (Perhehoitoliitto) and the Finnish Child Welfare Association (Pelastakaa Lapset ry), from whom the municipalities purchase training services.

One problem in carrying out family care is the lack of time available for training family carers. Another problem is lack of communication. Levels of co-operation between the family and the social worker are often good, but working together has nevertheless presented difficulties in many areas. Some authorities prefer to make decisions on behalf of others, and often tend to treat foster parents as if they were clients, not partners in the caring process.

The implementation of foster care requires ongoing recruitment of new foster homes and carers. In child welfare, there is a permanent lack of both carers and foster homes, especially in the cities. Despite a conscious effort to maintain a close relationship between placed children and their biological parents, this relationship still presents a problem in foster family care. It is interesting to note the results of a recent study, which showed that children placed in foster care considered cohabiting as the main factor in the development of a child–parent relationship. Consequently, foster children felt that it was easier, on a psychological level at least, to regard substitute parents rather than biological parents as their real parents.

As a rule, foster care has been long-term, and the families have undertaken to act as caregivers for children for many years. Typically, more than half of the children have been admitted to care after a short period of open-care assistance. Most of these admissions are expected to be long-term, and in such cases, residential establishments function as 'waiting rooms' for foster care. Seventy per cent of children placed in residential care for the first time will be placed again, usually in foster homes. Forty-two per cent of the children placed in foster homes have been moved, in most cases to a new foster family.

Major trends

The legal reforms regarding foster family care had many aims. The first purpose was to strengthen and develop extramural care, and to ensure that care was similar to normal family life. In order to achieve this goal, no family can provide care for more than four children. However, when at least two persons are responsible for care, one of whom has education sufficient for the task and adequate experience in care and educational work, the maximum number of children may be seven. The second purpose of the reforms was to improve the status and legal rights of family carers.

The nature of foster care as a social service has changed. Crisis or emergency services linked with child welfare are new activities. Similarly, professionalized foster home care has increased in the 1990s, and has offered new, alternative services for children and young people. Foster care not only offers more advantages than, for example, residential care: it is also cheaper. Even if more resources are provided for the education and supervision of foster carers in the future, thus increasing the cost, it is still possible that financial considerations will persuade municipal authorities to make more use of foster care than has previously been the case.

Foster care in Finland has a special character, in that private and public bodies come together, and the resources of both professionals and volunteers are combined to serve the unique needs of individual families and all the different children coming into care. Implementing and supporting the foster care service requires special knowledge and appropriate attitudes on the part of authorities, as well as a commitment to devote time and careful attention to the development of foster care. Any emphasis on foster care as a service should not be based on short-sighted political-ideological pressures, but on ethical considerations about the best way to serve children and young people.

Child welfare in transition

In recent years in Finland, greater emphasis has been placed on preventive work and on extramural support measures. In spite of this, there are situations where protection of the child's welfare and the appropriate organization of care requires that the child be cared for in an out-of-family placement. Foster and residential care, as two of the forms of out-of-family placement, are also part of the wider spectrum of child welfare services of the future. The estimated number and proportion of places in residential care following developments in child welfare have shown a continual decrease. The institutions are smaller, the number of people working in educational or supervisory roles has risen, and the services provided by the institutions have been diversified. In addition, somewhere between traditional residential care and foster family care, a new kind of small unit has come into being. These trends will continue.

The content and extent of extrafamilial care will depend to a large extent on decisions made outside child welfare, and indeed outside the whole area of social welfare. During the past few years, child welfare, together with the entire Finnish social security system, has been undergoing great changes. The deep economic recession afflicting the country has posed serious challenges to the welfare services. While families increasingly need support from social welfare agencies – due to the rapid growth of unemployment and economic difficulties – the unfavourable economic situation of the country has led to the tightening of the public purse strings, and consequently, to fewer opportunities for the state and local authorities to provide, let alone increase, services. The increase in the need for living allowances has taken social work resources away from child welfare.

At the same time, the administration and financing of social welfare and health care have been thoroughly reformed. The new state subsidy system, which came into force in 1993, considerably increases the independent decisionmaking powers of the local authorities, with the objectives of improving the efficiency and effectiveness of their activities, as well as of securing the provision of basic services in the municipalities.

The increased economic independence of municipalities has gradually led to changes in the methods of service provision. In child welfare, this can be seen, for example, in fiscal competition between public and private care units, as well as between institutional care and family care. While earlier, the task of the social worker was to concentrate in finding a place which best satisfied a child's individual needs, now the social worker has to compare the costs of these units and consider what the payment covers. Social workers are expected to estimate the price–quality relationship of foster care and foster family homes, and to follow up to see that their estimates were correct. The task becomes more difficult as the variety of these units increases, and social workers have less and less freedom to study alternatives with respect to the best interests of the child. The most favourable scenario is that a variety of alternatives makes it possible to select the best placement for the child; the worst is that concentrating on the cost of the service biases the decision towards the most suitable solution for the municipality.

It is likely that lack of money and overcompetitive attitudes between the private and public foster care sectors will increase regional differences in the level of services, and will threaten the further development of child welfare measures.

Role of national foster care association

In Finland, in the field of child welfare and youth work, there are about 18 federations. All of them act to safeguard the rights of children, and families with children. The activities of these organizations may be categorized as: expert functions, lobbying, the maintenance of welfare and health services, various organizational activities, and international co-operation.

The Finnish Federation of Foster Care Associations co-ordinates 26 organizations which support fostering, both in homes and institutions, promote the training and recreational activities of their members, and maintain co-operation between families, the communities concerned and the relevant authorities. The federation is a member of the IFCO, and supports the care of children, young people and the disabled through contact with relevant voluntary organizations and authorities: it arranges training and recreational activities, supports research into fostering, and maintains international contacts.

Contact: Leea Markkanen, The Finnish Federation of Foster Care Associations, Yrjönkatu 8 B 16, Jyväskylä, Finland 40100 *Telephone*: (+358) 41-616-699 *Fax*: (+358) 41-611-646.

Research

There have been relatively few studies on foster care in Finland, and most of these have concentrated on foster care in child welfare, examining foster care from the viewpoints of the foster child, his or her biological parents, the social worker and the foster family. The most recent studies are follow-ups of the foster care law reform. This type of research has mostly been undertaken in the University of Jyväskylä and in the National Research and Development Centre for Welfare and Health (STAKES). Three of the most recent books and articles are:

Laurila, A. (1993) *Foster Home: Experiments and Ideas,* Jyväskylä: Gummerus.
Kivinen, T. and Majamaki, P. (1995) *Ajankohtaiset muutossuunnat lastensuojelussa,* Dialogi 1/1995, Helsinki: STAKES.
Antikainen, E. and Kivinen, T. (1995) *Perhehoitoa koskevan lakiuudistuksen seuranta,* Helsinki: STAKES.

Bibliography

Antikainen, E. and Kivinen, T. (1995) *Perhehoitoa koskevan lakiuudustuksen seurantaa,* Aiheita 8/1995, Helsinki: STAKES.
Children in Residential Care in Finland (1992) Helsinki: The Central Union for Child Welfare/The Consultative Committee on Residential Care.
Jaakkola, J. et al. (1994) *Areliaisuus, yhteisöapu, sosiaaliturva: Suomalaisten sosiaalisen turvan historia,* Helsinki: Sosiaaliturvan keskusliitto.
Kemppainen, M. (1991) 'Residential child and youth care in Finland', in Gottesman, M. (ed.) *Residential Child Care: An International Reader,* London: Whiting & Birch.
Kemppainen, M. (1994) 'Finland: Trends in Finnish child welfare', in Gottesman, M. (ed.) *Recent Changes and New Trends in Extrafamilial Child Care: An International Perspective,* London: Whiting & Birch.
Kivinen, T. (1992) *Lastensuojelun moninaisuus. Pitkittäisselvitys lasten asiakkuudesta,* Sosiaali-ja terveyshallitus, Raportteja 59/1992, Helsinki: Vapkustannus.
Kivinen, T. (1993) *Lastensuojelun perhehoidon pohjoismainen kirjo,* Aiheita 52/1993, Helsinki: STAKES.
Kivinen, T. and Majamaki, P. (1995) *Ajankohtaiset muutossuunnat lastensuojelussa,* Dialogi 1/1995, Helsinki: STAKES.
Laurila, A. (1993) *Lainaksi annettu lapsi. Sijaiskoti kokemuksia ja ajatuksia.* Jyväskylä: Kirjapaja.
Palonen, A. (1992) *Huostaanotto ja perhesijoitus lastensuojelullisina toimenpiteina. Turun yliopiston oikeustieteellisen tiedekunnan julkaisuja,* Turku: Yksityisoikeuden sarja B:24.
Social Welfare and Health Care Organizations in Finland (1994) The Association of Voluntary Health, Social and Welfare Organizations and The International Council on Social Welfare and The Finnish Federation for Social Welfare. Forssa.
Statistical Yearbook of Finland (1994).
Utriainen, S. (1989) 'Child welfare services in Finland', *Child Welfare,* Vol. 68, No. 2 / March–April.
Valkonen, L. (1995) *Kuka on minun vanhempani? Perhehoitonuorten vanhempisuhteet,* Tutkimuksia 52/1995, Saarijärvi: STAKES.

6 France

Michel Corbillon

Jurisdiction

Situated on the Atlantic Coast of Europe, France has a surface area of about 549,000 square kilometres and a population of about 58,000,000 (Covet, 1994). Contrasting changes are occurring at both ends of the age distribution curve: the proportion of people under 20 years old (currently 26 per cent of the population) is diminishing, while the proportion of those over 65 (currently 15 per cent of the population) is increasing. As is the case in the other European countries, the present demographic situation is characterized by a low fertility rate (though recent trends point to a stabilization of the birth rate), a slight decrease in the mortality rate and a tendency for couples to be slightly older than in the past when they have children (Lévy, 1995). The present unemployment rate is 12.6 per cent, according to data published by the International Labour Organization (Bezat, 1995).

In 1983, a number of areas – especially child protection – which had been the exclusive responsibility of the state were transferred to local government departments under a move towards decentralization. These departments (*départements*) reflect divisions which stem from the French Revolution. Metropolitan France includes 95 departments, the nature and population of which vary widely. In relation to children, the central government retains only legislative and statutory power and the authority to assume control, mainly with respect to legislative matters. The local General Council (Conseil Général) is now in charge of the organization of child welfare services and facilities, staff management, financing, and the fixing of the fee scale for services. (The Conseil Général is an elected assembly which manages departmental affairs.) Between 1984 and 1986, laws and decrees defined this transfer of responsibility. Several principles were asserted or reaffirmed:

- priority is given to keeping the child in his or her natural family, with help provided by social services;
- importance is placed on maintaining the full responsibility of families who find it temporarily necessary to entrust their children to other agencies, especially through the provision of better information concerning their rights and duties, and by closer involvement of the families in decisions taken concerning their children;
- there is an obligation to reassess the situation of each child at least once a year.

The placement system for children is included in the broader field of social services. The placement of children and teenagers is entrusted to several institutions in France: the Child Care Office (Aide Sociale à l'Enfance, roughly equivalent to the British Children's Bureau), the Judiciary Protection of Minors (Protection Judiciaire de la Jeunesse), maladjusted children's services, and infant and juvenile psychiatric services. The term 'maladjusted children' refers to 'children who have a physical, mental or behavioural handicap and who are unable to adapt to normal life in their family, at school or in social or occupational spheres without an educational effort which usually includes medical, psychological, pedagogical, educational and social measures' (Thévenet, 1989, p.160).

Two ministries in particular are in charge of the monitoring of services: the Ministry of Social Affairs and the Justice Ministry. However, the authority of the former was reduced by the decentralization process, in favour of local government. The Education Ministry, which is directly involved in the education and re-education of children suffering from various forms of maladjustments (needing special classes and staff with various specific qualifications), is hardly represented at all in the departments.

The various responsible authorities (local government or state) entrust the children to services managed directly by them, or to institutions managed by private associations. In the vast majority of cases, these are institutions associated with the 1901 Act: non-profit making institutions, whose funding is exclusively public.

History and origins

In France, the history of placement in family foster care falls within the broader scope of the history of child welfare, which is often concerned with the protection of society from dangerous children and young people. Individuals and families have always intervened in order to rescue abandoned children or to take advantage of their situation: 'We can agree that placement into family foster care has been practised since high antiquity, if we mean by that phrase that a child is brought up by a family other than its own natural family' (Soulé et al., 1983, p.13). In France, it seems that even if similar systems existed prior to that period (especially in the form of charitable residential homes for abandoned children), organized placement in family foster care appeared in the twelfth century. The Order of the Holy Spirit of Montpellier is generally credited as having played a crucial role in the development of institutions for abandoned children. The younger children were first entrusted to the care of nurses, and then admitted to the local institution, which could house up to 600 children. This same religious order went on to found similar establishments in France and throughout Europe with the help of the Catholic Church.

In the Middle Ages, both abandoned children and the children of well-off families were placed in the care of nurses. Appalling transportation conditions caused the death of many infants, combined with the harsh living conditions of the nannies themselves. Many go-betweens – 'transporters', 'leaders', *'recommandaresses'* – set up an organization around family foster care, to the extent that some historians have spoken of a 'child fostering industry'.

Towards the end of the Middle Ages, the circumstances of foundlings seems to have deteriorated, as wars and famines hindered the work of charitable undertakings. Exposure under church porches, child trafficking and death, were commonplace. Indeed, at La Couche – a shelter for abandoned children established in Paris in 1570 – children were sold for 10 pennies a head to beggars, travelling acrobats or magicians. The death rate was very high: 100 per cent in some shelters. It was against this background that the endeavours of Saint Vincent de Paul succeeded in forging the beginnings of 'modern' child fostering methods. With the help of charitable brotherhoods, he sought to promote changes in people's perceptions concerning abandoned children, and most particularly illegitimate children. In 1638, he created the Oeuvre des Enfants Trouvés, a charitable organization for foundlings, which was later transferred to the authority of the Assistance Publique (state-run relief) of the Seine district in Paris. Tangible and technical changes in methods were developed: experiments were undertaken on feeding babies with cow's milk, attention was paid to the health of the children, and concern was expressed about their later social and professional integration into society. A system was developed whereby foster families were paid for caring for abandoned children up to 6 years of age. This system was associated with a closer monitoring of nurses or foster mothers, who had to be recommended by a parish priest in order to be eligible for payment.

The proportion of abandoned children rose dramatically during the eighteenth century due to three factors: a large increase in the number of illegitimate births; an improvement in living conditions among placed children (which led to an increase in placements), and the institution of the 'turn', a revolving, cylindrical platform in the wall of a shelter for children, on which the unwanted baby was placed, to be taken in by the organization on the other side of the wall.

The French Revolution secularized and brought about the reorganization of the relief system. Before the Revolution, the relief system had been organized by the Church, but afterwards, it became part of the duties of the state. Although secular relief measures were not standardized, the work of the revolutionaries in this field was of major importance, and was to shape attitudes, practices and legislation to come.

The nineteenth century was marked by an increase in financial support for child welfare, technological innovations and also, to a certain extent, by a rationalization of the administrative framework. The Napoleonic decree of January 1811 was an important stage in this development of child welfare, since it defined the eligibility criteria for admission to public institutions, the obligations due to placed children, and the amounts of money to be set aside for their care. It also established a system for monitoring placement conditions, appointing 'special commissioners', who were replaced in 1870 by 'inspectors for assisted children'. The benefits accruing to placement within a family were progressively expounded.

In the twentieth century, a national welfare policy developed regarding placement. After a period marked by the first educational experiments, by the principles of preventive action, and by the separation of abandoned or mentally deficient children from other types of 'marginals' or people in care, the development of increasingly sophisticated educational and preventive measures was intensified in the twentieth century. The decree of 29 November 1953 (as well as subsequent decrees between 1954 and 1956) modified the French apparatus of social relief measures. The term Aide Sociale à l'Enfance (ASE – Youth Welfare Service) was coined as a substitute for Assistance Publique (Social Relief).

Various legislative reforms marked the evolution of social policies regarding the protection of children, but as far as foster family placement is concerned, the most significant change was introduced by the law of 17 May 1977 which granted official status to the nurses, who consequently became paediatric assistants. The circular of 20 December 1979 detailed eligibility conditions for optional training. A new law of 12 July 1992, together with guidelines for its implementation, developed the professional dimension of the status of the paediatric assistant nurses.

Therapeutic placements in foster families have a short history, even though mentally deficient children have been cared for in families over quite a long period. A decree of 1952 legalized placement in family foster care for physically or mentally handicapped persons. Various experiments, in particular in Paris, were undertaken towards the end of the 1960s, with the result that foster family placements came to be considered part of the therapeutic process. However, it was the law of 10 July 1989, and the order of 1 October 1990 which provided a legal basis for therapeutic family fostering. Family foster care had now become a tool which could be used by local psychiatric services (Brunier, 1993, pp.47–8).

Administration and organization

Two placement systems co-exist in France – one involving institutions, the other involving families. Foster family placements are made for infants, teenagers and adults, including old people and families (for instance, taking into care a mother and child). Foster placements for adults are particularly concerned with the care of the mentally ill. For example, for over a century, two villages in the Centre region of France, Dun-sur-Auron and Ainay-le-Château, have carried on a tradition of caring for the mentally ill in a family environment. In general, foster placements are made in response to various social situations and problems related to physical and mental health or handicaps. The different types of foster family placements developed in response to living conditions inside residential institutions, which were often viewed as dehumanizing. Foster family placement appears a more appropriate solution: it is considered warmer and more 'normal', especially where young children are concerned. Nevertheless, it is still viewed as the focal point of tensions between a natural family-type environment and the demand for professionalization. It is a traditional care system which has evolved to a very large extent over the past twenty years.

Of particular importance in this evolutionary process is the Act of 12 July 1992 concerning assistant paediatric nurses, which alters the Code of the Family and Social Welfare, and the Code of Health and Labour. This law and the guidelines for its implementation have led to changes in the organization of family placements, and imply a genuine professionalization of foster parents. A clear distinction is made between certification and recruiting, a contract must be signed prior to employment, and monthly wages for nurses (foster mothers or, more rarely, fathers) and training obligations on the part of the employer are set out. The law recognizes assistant paediatric nurses as non-incumbent staff members (i.e. lacking the rights of the French civil servant) of public services under the local authority and the hospital services.

Three main categories of foster family placements can be distinguished: the category defined by the Aide Sociale à l'Enfance, specialized placements and therapeutic placements. These three categories apply in three different situations and are undertaken within three major areas: social, medico-social and sanitation. These three areas are not completely distinct, and the populations involved are very similar, but they are nevertheless financed and regulated along different lines, despite the fact that their evolution was similar (Oui, 1993, p.23). As will be shown later, there are discrepancies in the scale of these different types of placements.

Placement in foster family care involves a procedure which includes the certification, recruiting, training, follow-up and monitoring of the assistant paediatric nurses. Some of these tasks are the responsibility of the district authorities for child care, regardless of the type of foster family placement; others concern the employer, who can be a legal representative by public law (mainly the General Council, but also hospitals) or connected with private associations (services for maladjusted or handicapped children or adolescents).

Any paid person who fosters a child at home is required to have been certified as an assistant paediatric nurse by the president of the General Council of the department where the nurse resides. The district services for maternal and infant protection are responsible for the certification procedure. One of the aims of the 1992 Act was to prevent clandestine labour. Although economic factors also have a role to play, clandestine fostering was also caused by the lengthy procedures and long delays (a year, or sometimes two) between the application for certification and the official response. The law states that if no answer is received within six months (three months for fostering only during the day), the certification is to be considered as secured. Certification is intended to verify that 'fostering conditions guarantee the health, the security and the development of the children who are cared for' (law of 12 July 1992, Article 1). This certification procedure is identical throughout France, regardless of the type of fostering provided. Certification criteria are clearly stipulated by the law, but they allow a margin for interpretation by local authorities. The certification indicates whether permanent fostering is permitted, and details the number and the ages of the children allowed to be cared for by the assistant paediatric nurse, as well as the times at which the children will be looked after, if necessary. Unless otherwise authorized, no more than three children may be taken into one family at a time, even when siblings are fostered in the same family. The certification is valid for three years, with the possibility of renewal; renewal is not automatic, and the assistant paediatric nurse must submit a renewal application. The certification may be cancelled, modified or suspended if certain conditions are not met. In such cases, the president of the General Council must first confer with a joint consultative commission, including members of the district authority and assistant paediatric nurses.

According to the law, recruitment is now distinct from certification: this was not the case previously, since hiring an employee is involved. The conditions which apply in the case of dismissal are also detailed by the law.

The monitoring and counselling of the assistant paediatric nurses are nearly always associated with the monitoring of the children placed. These vary widely between one local government and another and according to different types of placement. As far as the Youth Welfare Service is concerned, various situations exist in different areas: 6 per cent of departments have a specific interdisciplinary team responsible for this work (Cébula and Horel, 1994), while other departments entrust this task to the Youth Welfare Services or to the interdisciplinary social service.

As for the other types of placement (specialized and therapeutic), the follow-up and monitoring of foster families, parents and children are crucial issues in the debate. Myriam David, an expert on the subject of placement in foster families and the author of an important book on the topic, reminds us that in 1965 the GELPS was founded (Groupe d'étude et de liaison des placements familiaux specialisés). David (1989) remarks that since 1965 – when the first symposium of the services dealing with such forms of placement took place – the majority of specialized placements have led to practical improvements which inspired those in charge of the Youth Welfare Services. This has a bearing on the conditions of admission (checking on the relevance of the indicators for placement), the regular follow-up of each case, the use of interdisciplinary teams, the reinforcement of the work accomplished with the foster families, collaboration with the parents, and the possibility of treating the child (David, 1989). Some heads of residential care units choose to integrate their establishments within the institutional framework of foster family placement, so that the carers are certified as foster families. Finally, it might be noted that the religious aspect which has been so significant in the field of child welfare in the past has, with few exceptions, almost completely disappeared today.

It is important to point out that the French situation is characterized by ample recourse to the 'private' sector – as it happens, it is not truly private, since its financing is entirely public, though mainly associative services conduct the practical work.

Who is placed in foster care?

No precise assessment of the number of children and young people placed in foster family care is available, partly because a number of censuses commissioned by the state were produced on the basis of unreliable data provided by local governments. The problem is also inherent to placement, since some children are boarders in residential care during the week, but are placed in foster family care at weekends and during holidays.

Foster family placement, as we have seen above, concerns various types of children and young people, but it is mainly used for those whose parents are temporarily or permanently unable to bring them up due to social or psycho-social problems.

The Youth Welfare Service is in charge of such situations. Of the 120,000 children and young people cared for by this office, approximately 57,000, or 47 per cent, are fostered in families (Cébula and Horel, 1994). Under the supervision of J.C. Cébula and C. Horel, the IFREP (Institut de formation, de recherche et d'évaluation des practiques médico-sociales) in Paris has recently released the results of a national survey on foster family placement, entitled *Le placement familial de l'aide sociale à l'enfance*. This survey shows that although there used to be a certain stability in the proportion of children fostered within families, there has been a decrease of more than 5 per cent over the last five years. It should be noted that the rates are quite different from one department to another: the proportion of children in foster family placement varies from 12 per cent to 97 per cent, with no clear explanations for this phenomenon, except perhaps the 'classical' interpretation, which is linked to history, and especially to the existence of a long tradition of foster family or institutional placement.

With respect to therapeutic foster family placement, a recent study carried out by the IFREP, in co-ordination with the survey concerning foster family placement in the Youth Welfare Services, has shown that 540 children are involved in this type of placement (Cébula and Horel, 1994). The number of children cared for in the context of specialized foster family placement is more difficult to evaluate, since these are independent services. There is, and in some cases there has existed over a long period, a limited amount of foster family care specially designed for populations other than abused and neglected children: drug addicts, for instance.

Care providers

The status of assistant paediatric nurses can vary according to the type of employer. If the employer is the state, the nurses count as non-incumbent staff either of the local authorities (this applies to the majority of assistant paediatric nurses) or of the state-run hospital system (therapeutic placements). If the employer is a private service, the nurses are employees under private law, and are governed by current collective agreements.

In 1977, legislation granted professional status to nurses who had become assistant paediatric nurses. Recently, this law was revised to take into account social evolution and increasing professionalization. The functions of the assistant paediatric nurses are many and varied: children may be fostered permanently or temporarily, 24 hours a day or only in the daytime, various types of employers are involved, and so on. Nevertheless, the specific characteristics of the profession are maintained. In the legal texts, the wording is such that an assistant paediatric nurse may be male or female. However, male paediatric nurses remain a tiny minority. Data collected in 52 departments have shown that just over 1 per cent of assistant paediatric nurses are men: 209 out of 18,287 (Oui, 1993).

The number of foster families is difficult to assess. Fewer professionals are involved in permanent fostering today than was formerly the case: approximately 40,000 at the beginning of the 1990s, compared with 70,000 in 1979. The decrease has been caused by the falling numbers of children being placed in foster care, especially in the Youth Welfare Service. However, the types of services provided by foster care professionals have diversified:

- approximately 36,000 work for the Youth Welfare Service, including public social and medico-social establishments;
- 2,000 work within private social services (foster family homes, regulated by the 1975 Act);
- 1,500 work in specialized foster family homes, under the jurisdiction of the 24th amendment of the decree of 27 October 1989;
- 500–700 work in therapeutic foster family services, under the decree of 1 October 1990. (Oui, 1993, p.23).

Professional training has become compulsory and must amount to at least 120 hours during the first three years of practice. A decree of 27 November 1992 outlined the major areas to be covered in training: child development, the special factors relating to the separation of children from their families, the profession of the assistant paediatric nurse and the institutional and legal framework. The assistant paediatric nurse is paid during his or her training period. Funding for his or her wages and for the training is covered by the employer, who must also provide for the care of the foster children during his or her absence. It should be borne in mind that the 1992 Act specifies that 'all those persons living at the home of the assistant paediatric nurse certified to care for children on a permanent basis constitute a foster family'. Thetraining curriculum and process is entrusted to the Maternal Protection Services or the Youth Welfare Service, by local social workers' training colleges or by other educational institutions: these must obtain their certification from the regional head of the social and sanitary services.

In addition to the notion of an employment contract specific to the function of foster carer, a separate contract is drawn up between the assistant paediatric nurse and her employer with respect to each child or young person cared for on a permanent basis. This contract details the role of the foster family and of the service responsible for the placement, conditions of admission and departure of the child from care, the timetable, and the procedure for contacting the service in case of emergency.

Recent legislation takes into account the need to monitor the performance of assistant paediatric nurses, as well as the importance of considering them as full partners in the contract rather than merely as employees, so local government is in charge of the professional monitoring of the assistant paediatric nurse. Moreover, the nurse must be consulted about any decision relating to the foster child taken by the representative of the service which employs him or her. Assistant paediatric nurses also take part in the regular assessment of the foster child's situation. Practices vary from one department to another: in some cases, the monitoring is performed by the local social services, or by the Youth Welfare Service, or by both services together. This monitoring is usually carried out by social counsellors or community workers, who may, if necessary, by assisted by psychologists or community workers. Generally speaking, assistant paediatric nurses do not collaborate outside the training context.

Financial support

Funding differs according to the situation of the children and families: the departments are in charge of placements for social reasons, while the national health service (Sécurité Sociale) looks after placements for sanitary or medico-social reasons. Foster family placement has often been favoured because it is less costly than residential placement. However, in addition to the wages of the assistant paediatric nurses, an accurate evaluation of the cost of foster family placement ought to take into account those expenditures related to the certification, professional training and monitoring of nurses. Such an assessment proves complex, since these costs are not distinguished from the other costs of the services concerned. In this context, it is appropriate to mention one of the few works on the issue which takes a social and economic approach, even though it mainly deals with institutions: Fenet's 1989 book, *L'aide sociale à l'enfance, stratégies et redéploiement*.

The assistant paediatric nurse's wages are guaranteed during the fostering period: therefore, temporary absences of the child have no financial consequences for the carer. If fostering is periodic (for a period less than or equal to 15 consecutive days), a day is paid inclusively at a rate equal to three times the minimal legal hourly wage. If fostering is continuous, the monthly rate is equal to 84.5 times the minimal legal hourly wage by month, which amounts to about half a month's pay at minimum wage per fostered child (2,350 francs, approximately $US486). In addition to this, money is paid for the child's keep. Payment ceases when the child leaves care, but compensation is paid for three months if the employer is unable to place another child in the care of the assistant paediatric nurse.

Major problems

A number of problems, especially material, have emerged due to the 12 July 1992 Act, which is related to assistant paediatric nurses. In the present transitory period, some difficulties have yet to be resolved, for instance in relation to the retirement of assistant paediatric nurses who have been involved in the work of fostering for a long time. Other difficulties are inherent to foster family placement, although recent legislation has introduced a few significant measures which make it easier to address certain problems. For instance, the role of the assistant paediatric nurse is not always easy, and his or her own children may also find it difficult to assume the role of foster siblings. On the other hand, there is a risk that the foster family may attempt to claim the fostered child as its own. However, nowadays, it seems that such problems less often lead to outright conflicts between the administration and assistant paediatric nurses who refuse to allow foster children to be withdrawn from care than was formerly the case. A few years ago, the media reported such incidents regularly. Nevertheless, it is obvious that tensions exist over whether the child should draw his or her feelings of identity from the natural or the foster home, and these tensions are manifest in the difficulties encountered in contacts with the natural family and the attachment felt by the foster family to a child who lives permanently in their home.

With respect to the natural family, it is difficult to avoid the parents feeling that they are considered to be 'bad parents' since another family has shown a better ability to care for the child. As in any situation where placement is concerned, there always remains a risk that the natural parents will relinquish their parental role.

A few years ago, finding foster families proved difficult, but today, demands for certification are abundant, except in the very large cities, and especially in the Parisian area, where housing conditions often lead to lack of space. It is likely that the economic situation and problems due to unemployment have played a significant role in this change. Nevertheless, some needs of children requiring placement may still not be met at any given time or place, particularly because of the growing concern over placing children in reasonably close proximity to their natural parents.

There is no doubt that the relationship between foster families and social institutions or services is one of the most important issues at stake with regard to the assistant paediatric nurses' new status. Social workers eventually become senior staff, and are required to become supervisors and assume monitoring responsibilities – a role which they find hard to fulfil because of lack of training. It will probably require a few more years for relationships to change before assistant paediatric nurses, the social services and social workers can collaborate fully.

In conclusion, reference should be made to the national survey on foster family placement conducted by IFREP (Cébula and Horel, 1994). As the IFREP report emphasizes, many problems are caused by that fact that there are few or no genuine foster family services within the Youth Welfare Service administration:

> It seems that few high-level decisionmakers in any area (financial, organizational, technical) have viewed Youth Welfare Service foster family placement as a specific type of care, likely to generate specific effects and problems. Only in exceptional cases has this issue been dealt with in a structured manner (Cébula and Horel, 1994, p.34).

Major trends

The major trends are partly due to the new legislation:

- the professionalization of the assistant paediatric nurses;
- the development of teamwork including the other institutional partners involved in the placement.

Some trends concern the evolution of perceptions concerning placement: emphasis is laid upon the specific needs of each placed child. This emphasis is reflected in the legal obligation, which has existed since 1990, to prepare an individualized case plan for each child placed outside his or her home. The case plan includes placing children with relatives whenever possible, placing them in close proximity to the natural family where possible, and making parents aware of their continuing responsibility.

Finally, I should mention a trend which is not new but is perhaps particularly strong in France: the increasing role played by psychologists, mainly psychoanalysts, in the monitoring and follow-up of service staff, assistant paediatric nurses, children and parents.

Role of national foster care associations

Local associations and the private assistant paediatric nurses belong to one of two national federations: the Union Fédérative des Associations de Familles d'Accueil et Assistantes Maternelles, which has 13,750 members scattered in 82 departments, publishes a quarterly periodical *L'arc*, and runs an information centre which caters for foster families (through a hotline and a periodical) and training (two annual symposiums); and L'Amicale Nationale des Familles d'Accueil et Assistantes Maternelles sans Frontières. These two associations are concerned both with registered carers (foster family care) and with day care services. Their roles are identical: their purpose is to inform their members, to play a role in their training, to represent them in collective procedures and to promote the position of assistant paediatric nurses. These federations were involved in the debate which shaped the recent legislation. Also worthy of note is the publication of a periodical called *Familles d'Accueil* (B.P. 6 83330 Le plan du Castelet, contact: Jean-Baptiste Pages). A specific union has been in existence for a number of years, called the Syndicat National Professionnel. The unions have a foster family unit in their federation, which includes the staff of local authorities.

Contacts: Union Fédérative des Associations de Familles d'Accueil et Assistantes Maternelles, *Headquarters*: 47 rue de l'Université, 75007 Paris, France; *Administrative Secretariat*: Kernevez Huella, 29470 Plougastel Daoulas, France *Telephone*: (+33) 98-40-34-20. L'Amicale Nationale des Familles d'Accueil et Assistantes Maternelles sans Frontières, 239 rue des quatre roues, 83000 Poitiers, France *Telephone*: (+33) 49-88-23-06 *Fax*: (+33) 49-52-21-91. Syndicat National Professionel, 16 rue des quatre roues, 86000 Poitiers, France.

Research

Research regarding placement in general in France is quite scarce, particularly that which is undertaken on the basis of 'academic' scientific criteria (Corbillon, 1993). The weakness of these works is even more pronounced concerning foster family placement. Nevertheless, it should be noted that the Office of Childhood of the Head Department of Social Welfare (at the Ministry for Social Affairs) has set a priority on following and sponsoring 'studies, research and practical ground research on the different aspects of (permanent foster family) care' (Oui, 1993, p.32).

Many of the works which have a practical orientation focus on foster family placement, covering such topics as the recruitment of assistant paediatric nurses, their training and status, and the relationships between foster families and natural families. In these studies, the organizational aspects of foster family placement and the professional issues are seldom addressed. In most cases, they are studies conducted by specific services, and their conclusions relate only to the local context.

On the other hand, one must bear in mind that over the past thirty years, numerous authors, influenced by psychoanalytic trends, have emphasized the trauma experienced by children separated from their parents. These authors have generally been far more critical of residential fostering. In particular, an important book by David (1989) draws on the long experience of the author in the field. On the basis of her observations, David accounts for the difficulties encountered by the various actors involved in foster family placements. She concludes that it is necessary to 'combine with social and educational measures, a permanent and specific therapeutic follow-up' centred on the child.

Two recent studies also deserve to be mentioned:

- research on the adult futures of subjects who were placed in foster families (with the Oeuvre Grancher institution) between 1960 and 1984 (Coppel and Dumaret, 1995). The survey examines the development and adaptation mechanisms of 63 persons who came from families suffering from severe psychological and social difficulties. It bears testimony to the positive effects of stable foster family placement: in terms of health and social integration, for example.
- the previously mentioned national survey conducted by the IFREP (Cébula and Horel, 1994), which aimed to assess practices involving foster family placement in the different French departments. This survey offers a minute description of the organization and functioning of foster family placement as performed by the Aide Sociale à l'Enfance. It reveals the wide diversity in practice which exists from one department to another.

Bibliography

Bezat, J.M. (1995) 'Dossiers et documents', *Le Monde*, No. 232, May.

Brunier, J. (1993) 'En France', in Wetsch-Benqué, M. et al. (eds) *Les interactions en accueil familial*, Toulouse: Erès.

Cébula, J.C. and Horel, C. (1993) *L'Accueil familial organisé à l'hôpital*, Paris: IFREP (Institut de formation, de recherche et d'évaluation des pratiques médico-sociales).

Cébula, J.C. and Horel, C. (1994) *Le placement familial de l'aide sociale à l'enfance*, Paris: La documentation française.

Coppel, M. and Dumaret, A.C. (1995) 'Placement familial et devenir: une triple approche', *Informations sociales*, January.

Corbillon, M. (1993) 'France', in Colton, M. and Hellinckx, W. (eds) *Child Care in the EC*, Aldershot: Arena.

Couet, C. (1995) 'Bilan démographique 1994', *INSEE Premiere*, INSEE (National Institute of Statistics and Economic Studies), No. 359, February.

David, M. (1989) *Le placement familial de la pratique à la théorie*, Paris: Editions Sociales Françaises.

Fenet, F. (1989) *L'aide sociale à l'enfance, stratégies et redéploiement*, Vanves: CTNERHI (Centre technique national d'études et de recherches sur les handicaps et les inadaptations).

Lévy, M.L. (1995) 'La population de la France en 1994', *Population et sociétés*, INED (National Institute of Demographic Studies), No. 229, March.

Oui, A. (1993) 'Le placement familial, un concept en évolution', in *Le placement familial, un lieu commun?* Toulouse: Erès .

Soulé, M., Noël, J. and Bouchard, F. (1983) in *Le placement familial*, Paris: Editions Sociales Françaises.

Thévenet, A. (1989) *L'aide sociale aujourd'hui* (7th edn), Paris: Editions Sociales Françaises.

7 Germany

Jörg Maywald and Peter Widemann

Jurisdiction

The German Federal Republic is situated in Central Europe and is part of the European Union. Since the reunification of the two German states (the Federal Republic of Germany and the German Democratic Republic) in 1990, Germany has become a medium-sized country with an area of 357,000 square kilometres and a population of 81 million (227 inhabitants per square kilometre). Although in Germany, more people die each year than are born, the population is still increasing slightly due to the considerable number of immigrants. Each year, 1.5 million immigrants enter the country, more than twice as many as emigrate from Germany.

The age distribution is characterized by a great increase in the number of old people in comparison with young people. Since the 1980s, the number of people aged over 60 (mainly women, because of their higher life expectancy and because of the large number of soldiers killed in the Second World War) has exceeded the number of children and young people up to the age of 18. In Germany, there are 15.7 million minors, 12.4 million of whom are under the age of 14, and 3.3 million of whom are between the ages of 14 and 18. Approximately 6.5 million people living in Germany are foreign nationals – about 8 per cent of the population. Turks make up the largest group with 29 per cent, followed by nationals from other European Union member states with 27 per cent, and 12 per cent from the former Yugoslavia.

The average number of people living in one household has decreased continually in the last few decades, and is now approximately 2.26 persons per household. The strong shift towards individualism and the low birth rate (1.2 children per woman) have led to a great increase in the number of one-member households (34 per cent) and childless households (60 per cent). The number of minors living with one parent (in 88 per cent of the cases, with the mother) totals 14 per cent.

Approximately 6 per cent of the population in Germany is partly or entirely supported by the state (welfare aid). The unemployment rate is 9 per cent nationally, and in some regions is greater than 20 per cent. The economic recession has seen an increase in the number of people receiving social security benefits, and the gap between rich and poor has widened. A new level of poverty among the lower third of society has been described (Statistiches Bundesamt, 1995).

Social system

According to its constitution (*Grundgesetz*), the Federal Republic of Germany is a democratic and social federal state. Maintaining the welfare state – with the task of ensuring social justice and establishing and maintaining social security for its citizens – is one of its fundamental aims. The principles of solidarity and subsidiarity are the socio-political pivots of social work structures in Germany. Subsidiarity is the principle whereby self-help and help from independent agencies take precedence over state aid. According to the supreme court in Germany, the German Constitutional Court, subsidiarity means 'that firstly the smaller community should act and state resources should only be used when it is unavoidable'. If the individual cannot help him or herself, then first of all the family, neighbours, a self-help group, or independent social work organizations should give active assistance; if all else fails, only then should state institutions intervene.

The system of social welfare in Germany is divided into three areas:

- social security (covering health, accidents, pensions, nursing care and unemployment) is mainly financed by contributions paid by employers and employees;
- care and social balance (child allowance, allowances for parents with children under 2 years of age, housing benefit, the pension scheme for war victims, assistance for victims of crime, and so on) are financed by state taxes;
- welfare (youth welfare, health aid, welfare aid) covers cases of need which arise from the plight of the individual; such aid is largely financed by local taxes.

In accordance with the principle of subsidiarity, there are a number of independent organizations active in the welfare field, in which youth welfare and full-time foster family care hold an important position. Apart from the state-run organizations active at national, regional and local levels, there are six national associations for social work, as well as many small, independent organizations and self-help groups which were established within the framework of civil rights movements. Whereas the small, non-profit youth welfare organizations must apply for recognition as organizations deserving aid, such recognition is bestowed upon the charitable organizations working at the national level by virtue of law. In particular, this refers to the following organizations:

- Workers' Welfare Association (Arbeiterwohlfahrt – AWO);
- Social Welfare Association of the Protestant Church in Germany (Diakonisches Werk der Evangelischen Kirche in Deutschland – DW);
- Social Welfare Association of the Catholic Church (Deutscher Caritasverband – DCV);
- Umbrella Association of Independent Charity Organizations in Germany (Deutscher Paritätischer Wohlfahrtsverband – DPW);
- German Red Cross (Deutsches Rotes Kreuz – DRK);
- Jewish Charitable Organization in Germany (Zentralwohlfahrtsstelle der Juden in Deutschland – ZWStdJ).

History and origins

Terminology

In Germany, full-time foster family care is defined as the temporary or permanent placement of a child or young person day and night in a private household outside the child's natural family. In this way, full-time care differs from day care, which is the care of children under the age of 6 in private households during part of the day. (Institutionalized day care in Germany, which is a state-financed alternative to day care nurseries, is not considered in this chapter.)

History

The history of full-time foster family care is closely connected with the history of children's homes. Depending on the state and institutional circumstances and financial interests, a choice is made between placement in homes or the much cheaper alternative of care in families. Well into the twentieth century, the care of children in homes and of foster children was hygienically, pedagogically and materially inadequate. Particularly in rural areas, many children were exploited, suffered from diseases, and died. This led to the establishment of state supervision of foster children during the nineteenth century, at first administered by the police. Later, in some big towns, central offices for the protection of foster children were set up in which *Waisenpflegerinnen* (women who cared for orphans) were employed full-time or in an honorary capacity to select, supervise and advise foster families. After the First World War, the supervision of foster children was nationally regulated for the first time in 1922 by the Imperial Law for the Wellbeing of Youths (*Reichsjugendwohlfahrtsgesetz*). As a result of this law, foster children as well as illegitimate children came under the control of local youth welfare departments. The establishment of these offices was mandatory for all towns and districts. When the National Socialists took over power in 1933, the wellbeing of the individual child became a thing of the past. National Socialist welfare served the 'wellbeing of the nation' and was, in addition, 'a service to the race'. Based on the racist principle of selection, children of 'healthy heritage' whose upbringing was at risk were placed in open homes, whereas those children who were classified as maladjusted and of 'inferior heritage' were placed in closed reformatories. Placement of children into foster families was preferred, but owing to the political demands on foster families, not enough placements were available.

After the Second World War and the division of Germany, East and West Germany went their own ways in the field of foster care. In the German Democratic Republic, the idea of collective upbringing was in the forefront. Children and young people who were unable to live with their parents were mostly (in 90 per cent of cases) placed in homes. Only a small number of children were put into the care of foster parents, normally into the care of relatives, for the long term and in connection with the withdrawal of parental custody. Day care was almost unknown. For children with working mothers – the majority – there were ample places in creches and kindergartens.

In the Federal Republic of Germany, children's homes continued to exist side by side with full-time family foster care. Through civil rights movements and the influence of research into bonding and institutionalization, criticism of the inhuman conditions in the 'total institutions' into which children had traditionally been placed became louder. In some places, this criticism led to professional approaches in the area of foster care, mostly on the initiative of the regional youth welfare departments. Parallel to this, institutions were restructured (reduction in the size of home units, the establishment of age- and sex-mixed groups, greater autonomy for the individual groups, and additional training and supervision of staff). Around the time of German reunification, a new Child and Youth Welfare Act (*Kinder- und Jugendhilfegesetz* – KJHG) came into effect in 1991, covering the entire country. Despite the different traditions, this Act laid down the same norms for child care in east and west Germany.

Legal regulations

The German Constitution which was passed in 1949 places the family under the special protection of the state. Children can only be separated from their parents against the will of their legal guardian through a decision made by the *Vormundschaftsgericht*, a special court dealing with matters of guardianship, 'if the legal guardians have failed to carry out responsibilities or if for other reasons the children are at risk of being neglected' (s. 6, para. 3). According to the Civil Code, separation of the child from the natural family is only allowed as the last resort if the danger the child is in cannot be combated in any other way: for example, through non-residential care (Section 1,666a in conjunction with Section 1,666 of the Civil Code).

If custody is partly or entirely withdrawn from the parents by a court order, then the court appoints an official or private (honorary) guardian for the child – this is the case with 1 in 3 foster children. Because of possible conflicts of interest, foster parents are rarely appointed as the guardians of the foster child. It is possible for the natural parents of the foster children to apply for the appointment of the foster parents as guardians. In practice, however, this is rare.

According to the legal practice which was first explicitly and legally set out in the Child and Youth Welfare Act (1990), foster parents can exercise parental care on the basis of a written foster care contract: they take care of, raise and supervise the child and conduct the legal affairs of daily life. Important decisions, such as consenting to operations, selecting the type of school and vocational training for the child, as well as the determination of the child's place of residence, do not come under their authority. Therefore, a child can be removed from the placement at any time by a parent with custodial rights, unless the child has been living in the family 'for a long time'. The foster family can apply for a court order to decide whether the child should remain with the foster family for its own wellbeing (Section 1,632.4, Civil Code). The law is not very precise on this point: much depends on individual verdicts, which have not been very consistent so far. While in some verdicts, changes in the natural family are taken into account in deciding for or against returning the child to its natural family, other verdicts concentrate on the positive and negative consequences for the child. According to socio-economic findings, in the last few years, the courts have decided more and more on the basis of the needs of the child.

Since the Custodial Rights Reform of 1979 (*Sorgerechtreform*), if a child has lived in full-time foster family care for a long time, the foster parents have the right to a hearing and a right of appeal in court on all matters concerning the child's welfare (Section 50c, FGG Law Concerning Interests of Voluntary Jurisdiction – *Gesetz über die Angelegenheiten der Freiwilligen Gerichtsbarkeit*). The Child and Youth Welfare Act lays down the rights of the Youth Welfare Department to intervene. The Youth Welfare Department is obliged to place a child or young person temporarily into care (for example, in a foster family), if the child or young person makes this request, or if there is a danger to his or her wellbeing. The legal guardians must be informed of this immediately. If they cannot be contacted, or if there is conflict with them over the place of residence of the child, then on the second day at the latest, the court must decide what further action is to be taken (Section 42, KJHG). If delay could place the child in danger, then the Youth Welfare Department has the authority to remove the child from foster care, even without the consent of the persons who have custodial rights, and to place the child temporarily in another family or home. If the guardians do not agree, then the Youth Welfare Department must immediately obtain a court order (Section 43, KJHG). According to the KJHG, full-time foster family care has social and pedagogic ramifications, which are the legitimate concern of the legal guardians 'if the correct upbringing for the wellbeing of the child is not being provided, and assistance for the child's development is suitable and necessary' (Section 27, KJHG). Furthermore, the following special conditions also exist:

- Type of placement – the placement with a foster carer can be temporary or long-term. For developmentally disabled children and young people, suitable and formally qualified forms of full-time care must be enforced (Section 33, KJHG).
- Finding a placement – the legal guardians and the child or young person must be included in choosing the appropriate form of assistance and selecting the placement. Their wishes and choice must be complied with as long as excessive extra costs are not involved (Section 36, KJHG).
- Counselling and support – foster parents have access to advice and support before they take a child in, and during the time the child is in their care. This also applies to foster parents who have grouped together (Section 37, KJHG).
- Payment – the youth welfare departments have to guarantee the upkeep of the children or young people they have placed into care on the basis of actual costs. Maintenance also includes a fee for the foster carers for looking after and raising the children, and where necessary, for medical costs (Sections 39 and 40, KJHG).
- Foster care licences – all applicants are assessed to determine their suitability (Section 37.3, KJHG). The small number of foster parents where the Youth Welfare Department is not involved in the selection process and who receive no financial support from the state require a special licence for care outside the extended family and for periods over eight weeks (Section 44, KJHG).

Administration and organization

For historical reasons, in the area of foster care, even today, there is a great concentration of responsibility in the local Youth Welfare Department.

However, the work of independent organizations is gaining increasing importance in the field of foster care, in light of the Child and Youth Welfare Act, which is service- and not intervention-oriented, and which approves of the right of legal guardians to choose between different organizations and offers of support.

State-run as well as independent youth welfare organizations offer services in the field of foster care. State-run organizations are obliged to provide assistance, and they have overall responsibility, especially for planning. Some executive-level activities (for example, issuing licences to foster parents in special cases, removing children, and temporarily placing children and young people when they are at risk) can only be carried out by state-run organizations.

State-run organizations

Government youth welfare agencies comprise the local Youth Welfare Departments and the regional Youth Welfare Departments. Regional departments consist of a specialized socio-pedagogic/administrative authority, as well as an elected Youth Welfare Committee, through which fundamental questions of concept, finance and administration are decided. Full-time staff (social workers/social pedagogues) are employed in Youth Welfare Departments. Apart from the general social services, or integrated within them, there are foster services with a regional responsibility. The number of cases per social worker varies from region to region, and may be anything from 30 to 150 cases. The responsibilities of the foster care services include preparing and selecting applicants, placing children with suitable families, participating in planning assistance procedures in co-operation with the natural family, foster family and other social services, working with and counselling foster families, helping foster families with applications for financial and other assistance, as well as advertising and public relations work.

Independent organizations

In some places, the charitable organizations of the large Churches have set up counselling and foster agencies which are mostly connected to adoption agencies, and which are involved in the selection of foster families.

In the 1970s and 1980s, two national foster care associations and a large number of regional and local foster care groups were set up. Their duties include the counselling and exchange of foster families, the preparation of placements, and the representation of foster parents in politics and in professional discussions, as well as public relations work.

In some cities, the independent organizations have taken on a special form.

With public funds, they have employed professional staff for specific tasks and projects: for example, placement and work with HIV-infected children in foster families, and setting up emergency foster care. Finally, under the title 'special care', there is a nationwide organization which employs pedagogically qualified foster parents. The organization provides these foster parents with counselling, supervision and further education if they take in a child who is developmentally disabled.

Who is placed in foster care?

Empirical findings

On 1 January 1993, 52,000 young people in Germany were living in full-time foster family care, 13,000 with grandparents or other relatives and 39,000 in a foster family. This does not include those living with relatives of whom the Youth Welfare Department is unaware. In contrast, at this time, 73,000 young people were living in some kind of institution. Not included in this number are those children and young people living in health care institutions such as rehabilitation centres.

The proportion of those under the age of 18 living outside the natural family and in care is 0.7 per cent. On 1 January 1993, 21 per cent of the foster children were under the age of 6, 50 per cent were between the ages of 6 and 15, 19 per cent were between the ages of 15 and 18, and 10 per cent were over the age of 18 (young adults between the ages of 18 and 21 can, in special cases, remain in care for longer, if their situation requires this).

In contrast to children's homes, where adolescents are the dominant age group, foster children are mainly of preschool and primary school age.

About 2 out of 5 foster children were born to unmarried parents, 3 out of 4 come from single-parent families, and 6 per cent are of foreign origin.

In the case of 70 per cent of foster children, other forms of care had been the first step: 16 per cent were fostered from children's homes, and 6 per cent were fostered from other forms of care. By comparison, 6 per cent of the young people in institutions came from foster families and other forms of care. One in three foster children comes into family foster care via custodial court decisions. The average length of time spent in a foster family is 5½ years, 13 per cent of children spend less than two years in family care, and 32 per cent spend more than seven years in foster care (Statistiches Bundesamt, 1995).

Different trends in child placement

At present, about 2 out of 3 officially registered foster children are placed in homes (Statistiches Bundesamt, 1995). In the last few years, the borders between homes and foster families have become more open. There are children who are eligible for both, but who, for practical reasons, are placed in one or the other. The heated debate in Germany in the early 1970s about 'getting children out of homes' gave way to less emotional consideration of the risks and possibilities of the different options.

What is remarkable is that the placement procedure varies from region to region. The number of placements in foster families varies regionally from 6 per 1,000 to 16 per 1,000 children and young people. The percentage of placements in full-time care, compared with placements in children's homes, ranges from 40 to over 60 per cent. In a more precise analysis, neither the differences between urban and rural regions nor regional structures suffice as an explanation. Therefore, fundamental causes must be sought in the different policies of the Youth Welfare Departments responsible for the placement of children, or in the amount of care taken in decisionmaking.

Forms of full-time foster family care

About 90 per cent of all foster children are in the most economical form of permanent care. At the same time, some Youth Welfare Departments have developed special forms of care:

- short-term or emergency care for children whose parents (or single parent) cannot take care of them for a short time because of illness, or the mother's confinement and similar situations, or because the children are temporarily at risk;
- remedial education care or professional foster care for developmentally disabled children and/or handicapped children and young people, where the carer is required to prove that he or she is qualified to take care of the child; in Berlin, it is possible for experienced parents to gain the appropriate training by attending a 'foster parent school';
- foster care during the week, mainly for children whose mothers work and who cannot take care of their children on several consecutive days (because, for example, they work shifts);
- large foster families, in which there are normally three to five children or young people who can benefit from the advantages of a stable peer group; the foster parent must be specially qualified, and receives assistance in the home.

Apart from these types of care, special placements similar to full-time care have been created by institutionalized homes: for example, as part of his or her contract of employment, a qualified educator or socio-pedagogue takes a child or young person into his or her home – in most cases, one who is developmentally disabled.

Care providers

Foster care providers can be married or unmarried couples, single people, or people in a long-term relationship.

Before the child or young person is placed with a family, the prospective foster parents are informed of the background and characteristics of the child or young person and of his or her natural family. In order to ensure that children are placed in families which will meet their needs, in the last few years, social workers have increasingly started to make the foster family and the natural family acquainted before placing the child into care, so that special requests and reservations can be expressed and considered at an early stage.

The amount of counselling and support which the foster families receive during the placement of the child differs. It ranges from intervention in situations of crisis to the offer of regular individual and group counselling or further training in specific areas. Usually, only a small amount of counselling is available, and an important reason for this is the inadequate provision of support in foster care services, and the lack of independent counselling facilities.

Financial support

The limits and conditions of financial support are generally determined by the appropriate regional minister. There is a flat rate for the boarding-out allowance, which depends on the age of the child, and which covers board and lodging, clothes, pocket money, school expenditure and personal liability insurance. It varies from one region to another, and in 1995 amounted to approximately $US400–670 per child per month. Some Youth Welfare Departments pay a higher rate for developmentally disabled children and for handicapped children. The payment of a one-off grant and allowances (for example, for initial costs, for important personal reasons, for private tuition and music lessons, or for holidays and excursions) are made at the discretion of the Youth Welfare Department and social workers, and often do not cover the full amount.

Despite the fact that the costs involved in children's homes are five or ten times higher, there is no adequate remuneration for the work of the foster parents in raising and supervising the children. Child benefit in most areas amounts to approximately $US220 per month, and is sometimes even less.

Only in 5 to 10 per cent of special care cases with mainly (semi-)professional demands is $US400 paid, and very rarely is payment more than $US700. Not only does the state provide for children in care, but natural parents are also required to contribute towards the upkeep of their children, the amount depending on their income (calculations based on recommendations from the German Lander and the Deutscher Verein für Öffentliche und Private Fürsorge).

Major problems

Public attention

Foster care receives little attention in public from the media or in politics. It is still associated with the charitable activities of housewives. Foster parents are mostly isolated. So far, they have not developed a powerful association to represent their interests. Their lobbying power in public and in politics, especially when confronting financial interests, is weak. Local public relations initiatives have shown that information and advertising strategies have to be created professionally, and planned over the long term.

Qualification of foster carers

Foster parents are often inadequately prepared, and receive too few opportunities for further training. Better counselling and further training is necessary, independent of the possible crises in the relationship between foster child and parent. For some foster parents, qualifications must also be connected with all the benefits of a contract of employment. The Berlin foster parent school has shown good results with new methods in the further training of foster parents. Those who are interested can take a course and receive a certificate on completion, which allows them to take in a child or young person who is handicapped or developmentally disabled. They are then remunerated accordingly.

Professional qualifications

After basic training in colleges for social work and social pedagogy, there are no systematic training programmes which specifically prepare professionals for work in foster care. In particular, there is no guidance or how to deal with natural and foster families, nor for the management of placement procedures. The first programme to train people in foster care was set up by the Ministry for Women and Children, for social workers in the new federal states.

Type of placement

The different forms of foster care and how they are financed must fit the needs of the individual child. There is often a lack of imagination. Only a few areas have special temporary programmes to clarify prospects (temporary foster families) and to place children into care, in some cases in co-operation with children's homes.

Allocating costs

The difficult legal and bureaucratic problems of determining who should carry the costs mean that programmes for the placement of handicapped children in foster care are still in the early stages.

Support for independent organizations

Innovative projects are often developed by small, independent organizations dealing with youth welfare. However, in comparison with other fields of social work, in foster care there is still a strong concentration of work in the hands of the Youth Welfare Departments. State-run agencies fear that delegation of their tasks could undermine the traditional domain of their work, and furthermore, they are wary of the legal implications. Independent organizations are inadequately funded. On the other hand, experience in some areas has shown that the participation of independent organizations in central tasks (recruiting foster parents and preparing for the placement, creating a plan of assistance, counselling and further education) can improve the efficiency and quality of the work.

Legal regulations

There are initiatives to improve the legal representation of the child in custody battles. In addition, there are moves towards granting those foster parents who have taken in a child permanently similar rights to those of the parents, so the boundary between foster care and adoption is becoming blurred.

Finance

There is no guarantee of a pension for foster parents. They must pay their own contributions into a pension scheme. In most cases, child benefit does not meet the cost of the service provided. The system of flat-rate payments excludes flexible decisions based on individual cases. One particular problem is that the money paid for special care varies from region to region.

When parents or foster parents move into another region, the amount of money paid is reassessed. Foster care services and independent organizations are often understaffed. For certain tasks (for example, further training or public relations work), there are not enough resources.

Role of national foster care associations

In Germany, two associations are active at the national level; the Federal Association of Foster and Adoptive Parents (Bundesverband der Pflege- und Adoptiveltern e.V.) and the Federal Association of Handicapped Foster Children (Bundesverband behinderter Pflegekinder e.V.). Both associations receive state subsidies, but above all, they are dependent on the voluntary efforts of their members. The focus of their work lies in the counselling of foster parents, in representing their interests in politics and in professional discussions, as well as public relations work. In the last few years, particularly in the area of further education, there has been an increase in contact between various professional groups, as well as moves towards more professionalism in the work of the associations.

The Federal Association of Foster and Adoptive Parents, founded in 1976, has eight regional branches and about 750 individual members. It publishes the quarterly magazine *Kindeswohl*.

The Federal Association of Handicapped Foster Children represents the interests of families with handicapped foster children. It was founded in 1983, and has about 800 members. The association plays an active role in the placement of handicapped children in foster families. It publishes the bi-monthly magazine *Mittendrin*.

Contacts: Bundesverband der Pflege- und Adoptiveltern, Roggenmarkt 9, D-48143 Münster, Germany *Telephone*: (+49) 251-45940. Bundesverband behinderter Pflegekinder, Große Straße 100, D-26871 Papenburg, Germany *Telephone*: (+49) 4962-103 *Fax*: (+49) 4962-66.

Research

Interest in research into the problems of foster care in Germany is relatively small. In particular, there is a lack of up-to-date, empirically broad, cross-sectional research into relations between the child, the family of origin, the foster family and social services. On the other hand, there are a number of dated studies concerning individual questions: the relationship of the development of foster children and children in homes (Dührssen, 1955); the role definition of the foster parents (Blandow, 1972); a conceptual stock-taking (Bonhoeffer and Widemann, 1974); the position of foster children at the end of the 1970s (Junker et al., 1978); foster care by relatives (Deutscher Verein für Öffentliche und Private Fürsorge, 1980); the practice of decisionmaking by the youth welfare offices (Schrapper et al., 1987); the reasons for and consequences of ending foster care (Güthoff and Jordan, 1991); as well as the forms of professional care in private households (Internationale Gesellschaft für Erzieherische Hilfen, 1995).

While there is a lack of empirical data in the field of foster care, there has been an animated theoretical discussion over the last ten years, which has partly led to a polarization between the concepts of the substitute family and the 'supplementary' family. The first psychoanalytically oriented approach (Nienstedt and Westermann, 1990) assumes that a child who has lived in a foster family for a relatively long period (about two years) develops ties to his or her foster parents through which social parenthood is established. These newly-emerged ties to substitute parents should be protected by the state through legislation (Salgo, 1987). In the practice of child welfare, this approach has resulted in the fact that the main interest lies in long-lasting foster care and the relationship between the foster family and the child. There is little or no interest in the natural family.

The second approach is oriented towards family systems (Deutsches Jugendinstitut, 1987; Wiemann, 1994), and assumes that when the child is put into care, two families are created. It is therefore important for the child's wellbeing that the natural family and the foster family form one ecological system, respect each other and co-operate as far as possible.

The following texts are recommended:

Deutsches Jugendinstitut (1987), *Handbuch Beratung im Pflegekinderbereich*, Munich: Juventa.
Güthoff, F., Jordan, E. and Steege, G. (eds) (1990) *Mut zur Vielfalt. Dokumentation des Hamburger Pflegekinderkongresses*, Münster: Votum.
Maywald, J. and Weissmann, R. (1995) *Fachkräfte im Pfegekinderbereich. Ein Handbuch zur Weiterbildung*, Berlin: Arbeitskreis zur Förderung von Pflegekindern e.V.
Wiemann, I. (1994) *Ratgeber Pflegekinder*, Hamburg: Rowohlt.

Bibliography

Blandow, J. (1972) *Rollendiskrepanz in der Pflegefamilie*, Munich: Juventa.
Bonhoeffer, M. and Widemann, P. (eds) (1994) *Kinder in Ersatzfamilien*, Stuttgart: Klett.
Deutscher Verein für Öffentliche und Private Fürsorge (1980) *Grosselternpflegeverhältnisse*, Frankfurt.
Deutsches Jugendinstitut (1987) *Handbuch Beratung im Pflegekinderbereich*, Munich: Juventa.

Dührssen, A. (1955) *Heimkinder und Pflegekinder in ihrer Entwicklung*, Göttingen: Vandenhoek und Ruprecht.

Güthoff, F. and Jordan, E. (1991) *Gründe und Folgen der Beendigung von Pflegeverhältnissen*, Institut für Münster: soziale Arbeit e.V.

Güthoff, F., Jordan, E. and Steege, G. (eds) (1990) *Mut zur Vielfalt. Dokumentation des Hamburger Pflegekinderkongresses*, Münster: Votum.

Internationale Gesellschaft für Erzieherische Hilfen (1995) *Erziehungsstellen – Professionelle Erziehung in privaten Haushalten*, Frankfurt.

Junker, R. et al. (1978) *Pflegekinder in der Bundesrepublik Deutschland*, Frankfurt: Deutschen Verein für Öffentliche und Private Fürsorge.

Nienstedt, M. and Westermann, A. (1990) *Pflegekinder*, Münster: Votum.

Salgo, L. (1987) *Pflegekindschaft und Staatsintervention*, Darmstadt: Verlag für Wissenschaftliche.

Schrapper, C. et al. (1987) *Welche Hilfe ist die richtige? Historische und empirische Studien zur Gestaltung sozialpädagogischer Entscheidungen im Jugendamt*, Frankfurt: Deutscher Verein für Öffentliche und Private Fürsorge.

Statistiches Bundesamt (1995) Wiesbaden.

Wiemann, I. (1994) *Ratgeber Pflegekinder*, Hamburg: Rowohlt.

8 Hong Kong

Christopher Bagley, Grace Po-chee Ko and
Charles O'Brian

Jurisdiction

Hong Kong is a small territory in both area and population (its population was 6.5 million in 1995). Its GNP per capita ranks Hong Kong as the eighth richest country in the world, but wealth is distributed unequally, and indicators of income inequality between the very rich and the very poor in Hong Kong are high (Toshiyuri and Takayama, 1984). There are many US dollar millionaires in Hong Kong, and a large number of people, including the elderly and young families, earn less than $US500 per month. Twenty-five per cent of the population earn less than $US1,665 a month (Lee, 1995).

Because of the population density and lack of building space, accommodation in the open market is very expensive, and a 74 square metres apartment cost about $US500,000 in 1995. Because housing in the open market is too expensive for most people, publicly-subsidized housing is available to nearly 50 per cent of Hong Kong families. In 1995, the waiting list for public housing contained 140,000 people, with another 50,000 living in very crowded conditions in public housing, waiting to move to larger accommodation. One-roomed shanty dwellings built on waste ground are a common sight. Hong Kong people are used to living in crowded housing, and many families who might accept a foster child simply do not have enough space in their homes. The combined impact of extreme crowding, financial stress and social isolation is illustrated by a recent case of an immigrant family from China. Two adults and three children aged 1–6 years slept, cooked, ate and washed in an 8 square metre room. The arrival of a relative from the People's Republic of China (PRC) brought matters to a head, and one of the children died from head injuries after allegedly falling from a bunk bed. The coroner was told that the child's body was scarred from beatings, and the mother admitted to beating the 2-year-old with a coat hanger (Parsons, 1995).

Hong Kong will remain a British territory until 1997, when Hong Kong, Kowloon and the New Territories will become a semi-autonomous region within the PRC, relying on it for external defence and diplomacy, but with some autonomy which will ensure the continuance of a system of highly individualized capitalist enterprise.

The extreme spirit of independence of Hong Kong people is one reason why supportive social service development has not kept pace with the amount of national wealth. Traditional Chinese culture also emphasizes reluctance in asking strangers (or social service bureaucracies) for help (Chow, 1987). The authority of the father and the importance of sons and their families in providing care, control and support are crucial in a culture in which the majority of individuals engage in regular worship of their ancestors. Accepting an unrelated child into one's household is foreign to this concept of lineage and continuity of ancestral lines.

Hong Kong's administration system has also been paternalistic, and has not traditionally been informed by democratic values. Rather, a system of colonial administration has ruled according to principles of public order and facilitation of individual capitalist enterprise. Only since the arrival of Chris Patten, Hong Kong's final colonial governor, in 1992 have attempts been made to construct representative democracy at the local level. It is uncertain whether these changes will continue after 1997.

The colonial administration in Hong Kong has been reactive to perceived threats to public order, rather than humane or consultative. This is illustrated by the history of social service and public housing development. In 1953, a massive fire destroyed many traditional dwellings, and the government responded to the problem of 10,000 homeless people by erecting public housing – a policy continued when it was seen to provide a solution to the potentially troublesome demands of low wage-earners for basic accommodation. Another example of reactive social policy development is the government's response to the riots of 1966–67. Influenced by the cultural revolution in the PRC, there was a ten-month period of strikes, large-scale public demonstrations and rioting. In partial response, the government expanded the embryonic Social Welfare Department (SWD) and initiated programmes of welfare for the elderly, destitute families, and children without proper home care. Previously, these programmes had been provided by religious foundations, with minimal government support.

There has been a gradual development of social work services from the 1970s, based on the principle of 'positive non-intervention' (Chow, 1989), including income support for the very poor, introduced in 1971. In 1995, a single parent with four children would receive about $US650 a month in public assistance, an allowance which includes $US300 per month for rent. This would enable a single parent with four children to rent a room measuring 2 metres by 3, in a building with a shared toilet and no bathing facilities. The room might be windowless, but it would have a piped supply of cold water. Teenage children of different sexes often have no alternative but to sleep in shared bed space (information supplied by Cheung Kim Fung of the SWD).

Rapid economic and population development from the 1970s onwards brought new migrant populations, divided families, higher rates of broken families, and problems among young people whose families were caught up in the rapid rush to achieve prosperity. Youth gangs, drug abuse and teenage suicide are now seen as major problems in Hong Kong (Tse et al. 1994).

The wealth of Hong Kong is illustrated by the 1995 welfare budgets, which announced a 13 per cent real increase in welfare spending, including programmes for family support, and preschool day care (1,400 new places) and 12 new group homes. The total amount of social service spending in 1995 was US$1.61 billion, the large majority of which was to be spent on providing public housing and income support. About 9 per cent of total public spending is allocated to welfare services, which many observers regard as entirely inadequate. In the same budget announcement, the basic rate of taxation was cut, so that 62 per cent of wage-earners will pay no tax at all, the highest rate of marginal tax being 15 per cent of income. By the time of the 1997 handover, the budget surplus is projected to be $US44.4 billion. Certainly, if the political will were available, Hong Kong could afford to fund an excellent array of social services, including high-quality foster care delivery.

History and origins

In traditional Chinese society, the extended family would care for children whose biological parents were unable to do so. In times of civil disruption and rapid social change (which have been a feature of Chinese history over the past fifty years), unwanted or abandoned children in Hong Kong (as in China) have been housed in large institutions with poor-quality, overcrowded conditions and a low ratio of untrained and poorly-paid staff to children. A glimpse into conditions in such institutions in southern China was given by Bagley (1993): a large number of infants were tied to their cribs, sitting among soiled bedclothing, unchanged for many hours, the children rocking and headbanging in listless despair. Many previously healthy children were 'waiting to die' (Ralston, 1993). Fortunately, the two large children's homes which still exist in Hong Kong have much better conditions than those in the PRC.

The introduction in Hong Kong of the Public Assistance Scheme in 1971 allowed voluntary and charitable organizations to begin providing direct social welfare services, including foster care, to the public. Under these provisions, private agencies received government subsidy from the Social Welfare Department. Responding to this government initiative, the Hong Kong Lutheran World Federation (now called Hong Kong Christian Service) set up Hong Kong's first formal fostering service in 1972 for children of impoverished parents who, for a variety of reasons, were unable to provide adequate child care (Chung et al., 1989).

In 1982, the SWD established the Central Foster Care Unit, responsible for the recruitment, screening and early assessment of foster home applicants, as well as continued inspection and training of foster parents. By 1990, family-based foster care was offered by the SWD and five voluntary agencies. These were the pioneering Hong Kong Christian Service, the Hong Kong Family Welfare Society, Save the Children Fund, Mother's Choice, and International Social Service (specializing in care for children separated from parents by international boundaries). By 1994, further funding was allocated in order to increase the 320 foster care places by 160. However, the projected number of 480 foster care places (which had not been implemented by 1995) is less than a fifth of the estimated 2,870 children in the care of the SWD and the voluntary societies. The remaining children are accommodated in group homes or larger institutions housing up to 165 children each (SWD, 1995).

Administration and organization

The Central Foster Care Unit has produced a manual of procedures guiding all aspects of foster care (SWD, 1995). A steering group on the development of residential services was established in 1987, and its findings were published in 1989 (SWD, 1989). Acknowledging the harmful and long-lasting damage caused by institutionalization, the group proposed that the future development of services should be conducted on the basis of four principles:

1   Wherever possible, a child should remain with his or her own family.
2   A family setting meets the needs of a child in care better than an institutional setting, particularly for younger children.
3   In an institutional setting, smaller residential units are preferable to larger ones.
4   A comprehensive programme of planning and regular assessment for the family and the child is essential from pre-placement to after care.

Following the acceptance of this report, the SWD began a policy of breaking up large orphanages into smaller units run on group home principles, together with an expanded programme of recruitment of foster homes; before 1989, most of the foster homes available were provided by the voluntary societies, and the process of recruiting foster homes has been slow.

In part, this reflects the fact that the practice of foster care by a family unrelated to the child has had little place in Chinese culture. Only 5 per cent of the population in Hong Kong are members of Christian Churches, so Christian families have been disproportionately involved in providing foster care, through their links with Churches affiliated to voluntary social services societies (Poon, 1992).

Who is placed in foster care?

Because of the importance of the extended family in Chinese culture, alternative care has been given only in the most extreme cases of abandonment, severe and chronic neglect and abuse. However, as more places become available, social workers are increasingly using foster care as an alternative form of care in less urgent cases where single parents are struggling with work and child care, or where there is prolonged illness without extended family to help (Lam, 1992).

The only recent research on the nature of children in foster care comes from a study of 92 children placed by the Hong Kong Family Welfare Society (Lam, 1992). Two-thirds of the children placed were under 6, reflecting the policy of placing young children in group homes; 51 children were male, and 49 per cent had been living with their natural families in Hong Kong. A third of the children placed had been admitted to care and later discharged prior to their placement. The social background of the biological parents indicated fewer years of education, and lower income and occupational status than would be expected of the average family in Hong Kong; some were very poor. Half of the biological parents had been born outside Hong Kong, and less than half spoke Cantonese (the local language). The 92 children studied had 134 siblings, 40 of whom were also placed in foster care. Eighty per cent of these were placed in the same foster home as their siblings. Eleven children in the study had experienced more than one change of foster home during their current period in care. In 35 per cent of the cases studied, foster parents requested that the child be removed, for a variety of reasons.

Care providers

Recruiting foster parents in Hong Kong since the major policy changes of the late 1980s (which emptied the very large orphanages) has been a difficult and slow process, and most children still go to group homes, small orphanages or institutions. In 1988, 162 active foster parents were identified, compared with 240 in 1994 (SWD, 1995). The difficulty in recruiting foster parents reflects the novelty of this practice within traditional Chinese culture; but social work bureaucracies must also bear part of the blame.

Lam's (1992) study of 92 foster parents showed that couples had to wait between six and nine months for their application to be approved before any matching process could begin. More than half of those surveyed thought the process took too long. This waiting time resulted in many potential foster parents losing interest. The shortage of social workers in the Central Fostering Unit was the prime reason given for the lengthy waiting period. The effect of these delays was a rather small pool of foster parents with whom children could be placed, and a long waiting list of children awaiting placement.

When a child returned from foster care to his or her biological family, 22 per cent of the foster parents in Lam's survey had to wait between three and twelve months before another child was placed with them. This clearly implies an inefficient use of a scarce social service resource.

Reasons for discontinuing fostering given by the couples in Lam's survey were: problems of conflict with biological parents over the child's care; personal circumstances (pregnancy, illness or adopting their own child); dissatisfaction with the level of the fostering allowance, and difficulty in forming and maintaining a relationship with a foster child. In these latter circumstances, social workers were rarely available to give support and consultation. One reason for the apparently frequent conflicts between biological parents and foster parents may be the guilt felt by the biological parents, who have been unable to fulfil traditional family obligations towards their children.

Financial support

The allowances for foster children are only meant to cover the child's daily needs: no element of reward or salary is involved. In 1995, the allowances were the equivalent of $US150 on taking the child into care, with a monthly allowance of $US150 per child. For the service providers, this compares favourably with the $US650 cost of keeping a child in an institution. Children are supported at this level up to the age of 15 (the normal school-leaving age), but foster care allowances can be paid up to age 21 if the child remains a full-time student.

One third of the foster parents in Lam's (1992) survey complained that the allowance was too low. One problem is that the crowded conditions of many families mean that there is usually no room for an extra child; the fostering allowance merely covers the cost of food, clothing, school books and so on, but is quite insufficient for acquiring extra accommodation. Because of this, most of the foster parents are middle-class people with the necessary income to own or rent housing in the open market.

Major problems

A major problem in delivering good foster care in Hong Kong results from the slow, understaffed and bureaucratic social work practices, which mean that screening of foster parents is painfully slow and is often followed by an inexplicable wait of several months before a child is placed. Foster care is used as a haphazard resource in casework planning, and the idea of permanency planning was only adopted as official policy in Hong Kong in 1995 (SWD, 1995). The concept of treatment foster care is still unrecognized in official practice.

One policy dilemma concerns the government's well-intentioned declaration of intent to move from institutional to family care (SWD, 1989). The Director of Social Welfare in Hong Kong implied in a public statement (Strachan, 1993) that the government regarded group homes as a form of family care, fulfilling the policy mandate set out in 1989. In 1990, three agencies ran 14 small group homes, accommodating 112 children. By 1993, six more agencies began establishing these homes to house children who had been in large institutions. Small family group homes emphasize a family atmosphere, and are staffed by a married couple who act as houseparents, assisted by a domestic helper and the support of a social worker. The houseparents are employed at welfare worker grade, and do not have social work or child care training.

Each home contains about eight children aged 4–18, including sibling groups. However, children under 4 (including siblings of older children in the group home) will be placed in one of a number of residential creches, two of which house 120 babies each (SWD, 1995). Six large children's homes remained in Hong Kong in 1995, catering for more than 100 children each; the largest home housed 165 children.

The dilemma of advocating a family atmosphere for child care settings is illustrated by the recent acquisition by the SWD of an apartment block (formerly housing medical doctors), and the conversion of this large block into over 50 'group homes' – this is a large child care institution in all but name (O'Brian, 1995).

Major trends

Despite the declared policy intention, Hong Kong has moved slowly from a system of institutions to a system of temporary foster care for children whose biological parents are unable to care for them. Similar slowness of policy and practice development can be found in the field of adoption (which could, in theory, provide permanent homes for some of the previously institutionalized children). A high proportion of adoptions in Hong Kong are transracial, involving an expatriate or mixed-marriage couple adopting a Chinese child (O'Brian, 1994).

While it is known that foster children often have special mental health needs (Chung et al., 1989), there have been few developments in the field of training or supporting foster parents to address the mental health of the children placed with them. Apart from useful descriptive studies (e.g. Lam, 1992), there is no research available on foster care in Hong Kong. The foster care system in Hong Kong is still embryonic in its conception, planning, administration and development. The future of foster care, like the future of Hong Kong after 1997, is uncertain.

Bibliography

Bagley, C. (1993) *Transracial and International Adoption: Mental Health Perspectives*, Aldershot: Ashgate.

Chow, N. (1987) 'Chinese and Western ideas of social welfare', *International Journal of Social Work*, Vol. 30, pp.31–41.

Chow, N. (1989) 'Social welfare', in Tsim, T.L. and Luk, H. (eds) *The Other Hong Kong Report*, Hong Kong: Chinese University Press, pp.109–23).

Chung, S.Y., Wong, W. and Mak, F.L. (1989), 'Foster care in Hong Kong', *Hong Kong Journal of Mental Health*, Vol. 18, pp.28–34.

Lam, G. (1992) *Foster Care Service in the Hong Kong Family Welfare Society: Client Profile and Operational Procedures*, Hong Kong: Hong Kong Family Welfare Society.

Lee, E. (1995) 'A miserable future for old and poor', *Eastern Express* (Hong Kong), 26 February, p.2.

O'Brian, C. (1994) 'Transracial adoption in Hong Kong', *Child Welfare*, Vol. 73, pp.319–30.

O'Brian, C. (1995) 'An end to institutionalization? Foster care and small group home development in Hong Kong', *Asia Pacific Journal of Social Work*, Vol. 5, pp.1–11.

Parsons, C. (1995) 'Cramped flat "led to child abuse"', *South China Morning Post*, 14 March.

Poon, R. (1992) 'A brief introduction to foster care: Hong Kong Christian Service and Save the Children Fund', *Prolife News Quarterly*, Vol. 7, pp.20–7.

Ralston, M. (1993) 'Children condemned to die', *South China Morning Post*, 23 May.

Strachan, G. (1993) 'Family action plan: Speech delivered by the Director of Social Welfare', *South China Morning Post*, 21 May.

SWD (1989) *Report of the Steering Group on Residential Services*, Hong Kong: Social Welfare Department.

SWD (1995) *Manual of Procedures for Foster Care Services*, Hong Kong: Social Welfare Department.

Toshiyuri, M. and Takayama, N. (1984) *Equity and Poverty under Rapid Economic Growth: The Japanese Experience*, Economic Research Series No. 21, The Institute of Economic Research, Hitotsubashi University, Tokyo: Kinokuniya.

Tse, J., Bagley, C. and Mak, H.W. (1994) 'Prevention of teenage suicidal behaviour in Hong Kong', *School Psychology, International*, Vol. 15, pp.99–114.

9 Hungary

Maria Herczog

Jurisdiction

Hungary is located in Central Eastern Europe, surrounded by Austria, Slovakia, the Ukraine, Romania, Serbia, Croatia and Slovenia. Its territory covers 93 square kilometres, and there are about 10.25 million inhabitants. The number of children under the age of 14 is 1,871,000 (720,000 under 5), 1,619,000 of the population are aged between 15 and 24, 4,750,000 between 25 and 59, and 2 million over 60. Roughly half the inhabitants are women, but above the age of 55, the number of men decreases dramatically (Statistical Yearbook of Hungary, 1994).

In Hungary, there are a number of ethnic minority groups. The largest group is the Gypsies (Romanies), numbering approximately 500,000–600,000. Slovaks, Germans, Croatians, Serbs and Romanians are also present in relatively small numbers. With respect to religion, the population is basically Roman Catholic, but there are Protestants and Jews as well. The exact numbers are not known nor registered in any way.

The economy is based on the principles of the social market. Since the political transition in 1989, the policy is to follow the 'European way'. Heavy industry and other large state-owned concerns are being privatized and becoming more flexible, providing the opportunity for a transition towards other fields of production less demanding in terms of resources, and especially to the traditional strength of Hungary: its agriculture and food industry.

Social services and health care in Hungary are the responsibility of the Ministry of Welfare. The ministry prepares legislation, provides professional direction, gives grants, runs research programmes and administers a number of institutions. With respect to children's services, there are nine institutions belonging directly to the ministry, including three detention centres for young offenders and four special residential homes for children with behavioural disturbances. The largest of these is the former 'children's town' located at Fót, which represented in the past the 'ideal' model of the socialist way of bringing up children in state care. Over 1,000 children used to live in this home, and it still accommodates 350. The National Centre for Babies' Homes is also a symbol of the former ideological and professional ideas related to caring for children under the age of 3.

Hungary comprises 19 counties plus Budapest. County municipalities direct social services, and most of the children's institutions belong to them. First, there are the County Institutions of Child and Youth Protection, which make unilateral decisions about children's placements. Children come into care through reports and orders made by the 3,300 local governments who should provide all kinds of social services to families and children. However, social work education did not exist in Hungary prior to 1986, and children's services were handled as a pedagogical rather than as a social matter: hence, there are very few professionals in the field.

At the local level, the professional requirement is a degree in law, since decisionmaking in matters relating to families and children is regarded as falling within the legal sphere. The lack of social service institutions and social workers has created a very confusing and unsatisfactory situation where there are no clear duties for the different actors working in the field. Visiting nurses, teachers and doctors work according to their own capacities and beliefs, and local customs play a major part in decisionmaking. There are 150 Family Help Centres and 20 Advisory Centres for parents, all funded by the municipalities, which, together with the growing number of foundations and associations, try to support families. Problems arise because there are very few private facilities and the system is too centralized. Also, in most cases, employers want fewer problems and demands, not increasingly knowledgeable and demanding clients. For example, mothers have been eligible for the three-year maternity allowance since 1967, but until 1988, only those who had been employed for at least one year were eligible. Since 1988, every woman who gives birth has been eligible. Between 1992 and May 1996 only families earning less than a certain monthly income were eligible to receive this allowance. In 1992, a new scheme was introduced for families which have at least three children, with the youngest under 6 years old. Mothers in these situations were 'employed' as full-time caretakers, and were eligible for pensions and all social services. In 1996, this scheme was restricted to families earning less than a certain income.

The family allowance system is also changing. Until now, with periodic changes in eligibility over the last 40 years, almost all families with dependent children received a monthly sum, differing according to the number and ages of the children. Single parents and families with handicapped children received a slightly higher amount.

Children under the age of 3 can go to creches or nurseries which are run by local government, and have formerly been run in great numbers by companies for their employees. These nurseries operate from 6 o'clock in the morning until 6 o'clock in the evening, but they can accommodate less than 10 per cent of the children needing spaces. Full-time kindergartens are very widely used, and over 90 per cent of children aged between 3 and 6 attend them. The children receive three meals a day, and the parents pay different amounts depending on their income and the decision made by the local government. In earlier decades, these institutions were very highly subsidized to enable all children to attend, though there has been a constant need for more places over the years. In recent years, more and more nurseries have been closing down, since municipalities are only obliged to run children's services related to kindergartens and schools. There have been many public and scientific discussions about the aims of these kinds of services and about the needs of children. Two-income families have been the norm over the last forty years, but ideological changes, new attitudes towards family life and questions surrounding the responsibilities of the community and state have made this a very complex issue.

Families and children who need emotional as well as financial help cannot easily obtain appropriate and satisfactory services. One explanation for this is a lack of resources, but lack of knowledge is also a factor, and there is a tradition which militates against asking for such help. In cases of abuse, there is still a gap between everyday reality and the ideas of researchers, psychologists and educators in social work. Not even professionals working with families, such as teachers, visiting nurses, doctors, administrators and the police, are aware of the emotional needs of families and the importance of professional standards and protocols.

Widespread unemployment, poverty affecting mainly the elderly and families with children, homelessness, harsh cuts in social expenditure, recession, and the relatively incomprehensible changes in policies are leading to frustration and depression for many. Alcoholism is the most serious substance abuse problem, followed by smoking. It is estimated that there are 700,000 alcoholics and more than 4 million smokers (*Statistical Yearbook of Hungary*, 1994). Drugs are a growing problem. All kinds of drugs are used, but they are very expensive, so glue-sniffing is more prevalent among young people.

Until recently, non-government organizations (NGOs) have not played an important role in social services and in the life of Hungary in general, as this went against the political will. In the last six years, there has been a rapid increase in the number of NGOs, and thousands of foundations and associations are looking for a role, but many authorities still do not trust them as service providers.

History and origins

Foster care in Hungary started with conscious attention to abandoned, neglected and orphaned children in the nineteenth century. As was the case in many other countries, communities were obliged to take care of their 'miserables', as Maria Teresa called them in her order. This obligation was repeated in the XIV Law on the Communities (1876), although financial provision for enforcing it was not made, nor were there concrete regulations to control methods of caregiving. In some areas, children were allowed to beg, while in others, well-off farmers were obliged to feed and accommodate them on a daily basis, or charities, Church organizations or the magistrates helped them. According to the XIV Law, the behaviour of nurses (maids) who were caring for children younger than 7 years old was supposed to be monitored and controlled, but this remained a principle only, not a practice. The so-called 'wetnurses', similar to those who worked for baby farms in Anglo-Saxon countries, were paid for taking care of babies, those who asked for least money being given preference.

The Orphan's Courts, set up in 1877, handled only financial and property cases at first. In 1898, a law was passed establishing a Sicknursing Fund, whereby children under the age of 7 could be cared for using the fund's money.

In 1901, two pieces of legislation linked with the name of the Prime Minister of the time, Kálmán Széll, represented a revolutionary step forward compared to earlier times. According to the first piece of legislation (the VIII Law), every child under the age of 15 had to be provided for by the community if the parents were not capable. The implementation of this legislation was very successful, and this was recognized by many other countries in the developed world.

The second piece of legislation (the XXI Law) stipulated that children should preferably be brought up and cared for within families. Children coming into care had their health checked and administrative matters attended to in an asylum, and then, following an Orphan's Court Order, they were placed with foster families. Only children with a severe handicap or serious illness stayed in the institutions. For health and educational reasons, children were placed with farmers and craftsmen who lived in a healthy environment. The idea behind the legislation was not only to provide favourable surroundings for children but also to provide them with an environment which was closer to normality than that in an institution.

Settlements were organized in selected communities where there were at least 30 families willing to become foster carers. It was required that there be a school and a doctor as well. In 1905, 18 asylums and 351 settlements were organized, containing 23,098 children, 80 per cent of whom lived in foster homes. In 1926, out of 38,000 children living in state care, 35,000 lived with foster families (Statistical Yearbook of Hungary, 1994). Settlement Committees were set up, comprising a number of the local inhabitants and the local doctor. Activities were supervised through twice-yearly visits from state personnel. Allowances for the children, clothing, health care and school equipment were provided by the state.

Families who wanted to become foster carers were checked for suitability by the local authorities, and received a certificate. This method of selecting foster families did not work very well, since municipalities were too busy to apply rigorous selection criteria, so some institutions set up their own standards and selection methods. This led to the development of a network of settlement supervisors. In principle, the supervisors were supposed to be experienced, trained nurses or caretakers, but because of the great demand, 170 women were trained on a short-term basis in 1909 to begin this kind of work: 'Among them were 30 teachers and 30 kindergarten teachers, and most of them had a high school education. Many of them were the daughters of doctors, teachers and pastors' (Csorna, 1929).

There was a special form of care, whereby a single mother was placed in a foster home together with her child. The young mother was required to help with the housework, but the main purpose was to enable her to breastfeed her baby. Children guilty of minor offences or with behaviour problems were placed in a type of foster home which today would be called a group home. There were 8–12 children in each group with a married couple as foster carers. The housing was provided by the National Child Protection League, and all the families lived in one settlement. Children had to work on the institution's farm and study at the same time. After one year, if they made sufficient progress, they were put into 'real' foster homes. In the first year of the programme, 1929, 927 children were in the care of the league.

After the Second World War, mainly for political reasons, but partly because of new ideas among professionals, foster care became less popular. Immediately after the war, foster families looked after their foster children despite the shortage of food and the lack of payment. In 1946 a one-month training course was held for would-be foster mothers, and six to ten babies were placed with each family. Milk powder was provided, and once a week, a paediatrician and a nurse visited the family. Soon afterwards, the first babies' homes were established, accommodating children from birth to the age of 3. Twenty-nine of them still exist, caring for some 1,850 children. The former system was virtually destroyed by adherence to ideas of equality and equal opportunity, higher professional standards for caretakers, and notions about the advantages of institutionalized care. Part of the myth lay in the idea that in a socialist state, there would be no families and children in need, since all their problems had been caused by political and economic mismanagement, which would soon be reversed. It seemed to be very fair and efficient for orphaned, abandoned and neglected children to receive a 'fresh start' in institutions which were set up to provide a better life. By 1955, only 50 per cent of children in care lived in foster families, and from then until the late 1970s, this proportion decreased to around 20 per cent (Hanák, 1983).

As was the case in all areas of the economy, health and social services care, children's services were nationalized. No private or charitable organizations were allowed to be involved, because taking care of children was thought to be the state's responsibility, and all other forms of care were considered dangerous and damaging. Only a few Church-run institutions remained active, looking after handicapped children and old people.

Foster care symbolized a private, individual way of handling problems by lay people. The aim was to find generalized answers for private difficulties. On the other hand, every mistake made by individuals was interpreted as political resistance: an action against the community's interest.

As a consequence of the industrialization of the country, forced development, the prevailing ideology and low wages, more and more women started to work full-time in the 1950s. Staying at home as a housewife and mother ran contrary to the political will. The idea was that it was best for children to spend their days in day care centres, nurseries, kindergartens and centres for after-school care.

Children in state care were mostly placed in institutions, where they were looked after according to their gender and age. Very few efforts were made in the areas of prevention, family preservation or review of former decisions. Until the mid-1980s, little attention was paid to children in care, apart from reports from the institutions and 'socialist brigades'. Groups of people working together and forming a brigade had an obligation to do things together after work, such as going to the theatre, inviting writers to speak, or acting as patrons to children in state care or older people. Many of these people wanted to adopt or foster the children whom they met in the institutions. It was not easy, but many of them became foster carers, or at least took the children home for weekends and holidays.

Nevertheless, there are areas all over Hungary where fostering has remained a tradition, part of the culture. Foster carers received an allowance to cover the children's basic needs, and they were eligible for free services at kindergarten and free after-school care, together with free transportation, and so on.

In the late 1960s, Hungary became much more open, people travelled more, acknowledged foreign experiences, and professionals started to obtain information and books from abroad. Although sociology and psychology were developing very quickly, child welfare and child protection were not. Poverty, deprivation, unemployment and addiction could not be investigated or even mentioned, as this would have acknowledged a failure of the socialist state and ideology, but they became more and more evident.

There have been many new developments, and the political and economic environment has been much more flexible since the 1960s, but institutionalization and ways of thinking about the 'best interests of the child' have been slow to change.

A three-year maternity allowance was introduced in 1967, enabling mothers to stay at home with their children. This has been a great achievement, though its evaluation is very controversial.

During the second half of the 1970s and the beginning of the 1980s, economic difficulties and the first series of research studies undertaken on families and child care started to alter views about the role of the family and its importance for children. The cost and efficiency of institutions were questioned, and many experts demanded a greater role for foster care. Resistance on the part of staff from the institutions and lobbyists has been, and still is, enormous. No general overview or research has been undertaken on Hungarian theory and practice, so arguments are based on emotion and belief, rather than on facts and the results of research and evaluation.

Because almost all women are in employment, a new, 'professional' foster care scheme was introduced in 1986, whereby mothers can be employed by the county child protection institutions and are obliged to care for at least five children – or only three in cases where the children are severely handicapped or have behavioural difficulties – as well as their own. Another family member, usually the husband, is employed part-time to take care of the children.

A new Child Protection Bill has been under preparation over the last ten years, but the authorities still do not seem ready to establish regulations, for the first time since 1901, on all questions related to children in care.

Administration and organization

In Hungary, one child and youth protection institution in each county and one in Budapest are eligible to run foster care services. These institutions are administered by the county councils. It is not illegal for another organization to set up a foster care service, but such an organization would be hampered by the fact that, with very few exceptions, the county institutions prefer to place children with foster carers employed by themselves. There is one experimental scheme in Fejér County, where the county council has agreed to co-operate with the Association for Fostered Children, giving them the right to run their own service but still gaining access to children through the county institution. This scheme includes about twenty-five children in seven families. All the carers are employed by the association; they receive a salary as well as allowances, each has two supervisors, they attended monthly meetings and are given training. There are some religious groups which wish to run an independent service, but they have not achieved this yet. In the past, no licensing procedure has been required for any of these organizations, but the Child Protection Bill, which came before parliament in 1996, provided for a detailed description of licensing criteria. Anyone will have a right to run a foster care service after being licensed.

Who is placed in foster care?

At the end of 1994, 22,377 children were in state care. Of these, 8,541 children (38 per cent) were in foster care, 6,120 in 'traditional' homes and 1,884 in 'professional' foster families, while 537 were older than 18 but were still living with their foster parents. The children fostered are mostly the less problematic ones. Foster carers usually prefer younger children with no serious problems, but obviously, handicapped, sick and disturbed children are also placed in foster families, and are welcomed there.

A special experimental programme was introduced in 1994 in Budapest, where Gypsy families were selected and trained to foster Gypsy children. The first 13 carers are already employed by the Budapest Institution for Child and Youth Protection, and 20 children have been placed. There is a supervisor, a sociologist and a former teacher, who has much experience of carrying out research into and running programmes for Gypsy families. This is the first time that the child's right to maintain his or her identity and culture has been recognized, in accordance with the United Nations Declaration on the Rights of the Child.

In Szabolcs-Szatmár-Bereg County, in the eastern and most deprived part of the country, there is a scheme whereby young, teenage mothers are placed in foster homes together with their babies. So far, there are three such placements, all working very well. The White Cross Foundation, at least in principle, aims to provide temporary, crisis care for children whose parents are troubled, sick or unable to care for them for some other reason. This foundation has been running courses for prospective foster carers and holds regular meetings for them, but there is no evidence of children or families coming into their care: the plan has not yet become reality.

Care providers

There are approximately 5,500 foster care providers in Hungary. Most of them have primary school and some vocational education, but there are also foster carers with college and university degrees. While they vary in age, the average age of traditional foster carers is close to 50, and many of them are quite old. Professional foster carers are usually younger, often in their 40s (Aczél and Somorjai, 1996).

There is no national standard for assessment or approval, and there is no right to appeal. In most counties, there is an initial interview, and potential foster carers must fill in a form. The investigation takes into account their living and housing conditions, their job and place of work, their children, their health and their police record. Supervisors, who generally hold a diploma in teaching, visit the family and write a report on their impressions, but generally, this report is not shown to the applicants. It is very subjective, depending on the supervisor's own tastes, beliefs and experiences, since there are no written guidelines on which to base the report. In many counties, there are training courses for future foster carers. These differ widely in length and content. Some last for two to four hours, while the course in Budapest lasts for four months. It should be noted that the Budapest programme applied to the Ministry of Labour for a grant to retrain unemployed people, and was obliged to follow the regulations stipulating the number of hours of training, including an examination to assess the results. The preparatory courses cover general knowledge in bringing up children, and information on legal and financial rights and duties. Information about the special needs of children in care is also provided.

In county institutions, there are supervisors, in most places called 'foster parent inspectors', whose role is unclear. These supervisors monitor the activities of foster carers and have to write regular reports. Each supervisor is responsible for too many families to allow him or her to monitor them adequately. The number of families allocated to each supervisor varies, but in general it is 50 or more. This often means that depending on their professional and personal devotion to duty, they concentrate on the problematic families and hope that the others are all right. They are also burdened by much administrative paperwork. According to research conducted by the author and her colleagues, 40 per cent or more of their time is spent on paperwork: for example, writing official letters to the Health Insurance authorities and to municipalities requesting various allowances for the children or the foster parents. As there are no separate caseworkers for children, it is unclear who the supervisors represent and who the client is. Not only do they try to represent the institution by monitoring and controlling the foster carers, they provide advocacy for the child as well.

Financial support

Foster carers receive reimbursement for children in their care. This varies from county to county, but the average sum is approximately 6,000 forints ($US45) per month. The average income in Hungary is approximately

$US250 per month. The family allowance depends on the number of children in the family, and amounts to $US25 per month per child. Twice a year, foster carers receive approximately $US100 to buy clothing, and once a year, they receive money for school supplies. The amount of money given to the foster carers depends on the institution's financial situation, and can vary depending on the child's age or special needs. There are no resources to finance music lessons, spectacles, travel and so on, except in very special cases. Families caring for severely handicapped children receive a somewhat higher allowance.

'Professional' foster carers are employed by the institutions, and their salary depends on their previous work experience, age and educational level. In Hungary, everyone employed in the public sector receives the same amount, calculated on a generalized basis and provided by the Ministry of Labour. On the basis of this generalized calculation, the average monthly salary of professional foster carers is approximately 22,000 forints ($US150). They do not receive any extra payment for overhead expenses, travel costs, and so on.

Major problems

The major problems in foster family care in Hungary are common in other countries, such as difficulties in finding sufficient numbers of adequate foster homes, the prolonged length of stay in foster care, low levels of payment to foster carers, inadequate training and support for foster carers, and lack of involvement of natural parents.

There are still debates on what the best interests of the child are once he or she is in state care. The children's homes are very influential, the institutional lobby is powerful, and it is much harder for authorities to work with foster families than with institutions. The residential homes work in relative privacy, while problems and outcomes are much more visible in foster care, and are viewed with much more suspicion by the public.

Children coming into care in Hungary at present are older and have more severe problems than was formerly the case. The existing system is ill equipped to deal with this situation, and foster parents either refuse to care for these children, or very often fail in the attempt, because their circumstances are inappropriate and they receive no preparation or support. The birth rate and the number of children in care are decreasing, but there are also fewer foster care applicants. People feel that they cannot afford to foster, as the work is very badly paid and has low prestige. Since the family allowance is estimated to cover 15 per cent of the total cost of raising a child, the reimbursement is worth less and less, particularly in light of the fact that today, money and status seem to be the major ways of measuring success in life.

Reviews of the progress of children in care are more formal than meaningful, and many professionals argue against reuniting children with their natural parents. Hence, most children grow up in their foster homes once they have been placed there. Many foster carers consider fostering as a means of adoption, and do not want their foster children to return to their natural home, nor do they want them to have contact with parents, siblings or other relatives.

There are no specialized foster carers, the training is far from adequate, and the inappropriate knowledge levels and attitudes of supervisors are frequent problems. Supervisors tend to regard foster carers as clients rather than partners, and this causes tension.

In addition, public opinion is not very supportive. People feel that foster parents should care for children for love, not for money, and therefore should not receive payments or salaries. In the case of employed carers, there are debates over the number of children placed in one family. The author and many of her colleagues would personally not place more than three children in one family, and would prefer to place only one or two, depending on their age, their level of functioning and the number of natural children in the foster family. However, many others would argue against this, wondering why foster carers should receive so much money for doing so little.

According to Hungarian traditions, children are placed without considering their special needs and former lives. No special attention is paid to placing them close to where they lived before so that they will have easy access to a familiar school, friends, parents, relatives, and so on. No attention is paid to former difficulties, abuse or other factors. When a foster placement breaks down, the foster carer is nearly always blamed, and sometimes the child, but never those professionals who made the decisions, placed the child or supervised the carers.

Schools, kindergartens and neighbours are not always supportive, and they can make the foster carers' and the children's lives even harder. Since there is no tradition of voluntary work or self-help groups in Hungary, many foster carers are very isolated, and do not know how to ask for help or how to support each other.

Major trends

As noted above, the Child Protection Bill which is due to come before parliament, aims to strengthen foster care and give it priority. Under this legislation, prevention and family preservation would be the preferred options, followed by adoption, then foster care, with institutional care as the last resort. There would be emphasis on permanency planning, more appropriate supervision, regular review of placements, and family rehabilitation programmes.

Non-governmental organizations, Churches and other bodies would be encouraged to run foster care services and training courses, but licensing would be obligatory. In 1997, there are plans to introduce a national training curriculum, which will be compulsory for all present foster carers under the age of 55 and everyone wishing to become a foster carer. It would be of benefit if Hungary had a much more specialized care system, reflecting the diverse needs of its children.

Role of national foster care association

There are several associations for foster carers, but there is no national foster care association.

Educom was established in 1987. It organizes excursions for foster families, gathers clothes and generally helps its members to help each other.

Fészek ('Nest') was established by foster carers and supervisors in Pesht County, near Budapest, to demonstrate partnership and co-operation for children and families. It holds regular meetings and training courses, and tries to influence policymakers and administrators by expressing its opinions about local and national policies concerning foster care.

The International Association for Children's Safety Foundation, Professional Foster Care Group was established in 1992 to provide foster care services, training and supervision for professional foster carers in Fejér County. It is the only non-governmental body to receive an annual guaranteed allowance from the state to run a foster care service.

Contacts: Béla Bene, Educom, 1022 Bimbó út 4, Hungary *Telephone*: (+36) 1-115-6148. Katalin Remete, Fészek, H-2030 Érd, Mályva utca 3, Hungary *Telephone*: (+36) 23-375-843. Dr Antónia Vilusz, International Association for Children's Safety Foundation, Professional Foster Care Group, H-1066, Teréz körút 24, Hungary *Telephone*: (+36) 1-269-5359.

Research

In Hungary, there has been little research on child welfare or child protection, and especially on foster care.

In 1987, Dr Judit Csáki and Vera Hazai undertook some research in the National Institute for Pedagogy on traditional foster carers. They sent questionnaires to all 20 Institutes for Child and Youth Protection to gather the relevant data. As well as hard data on decisionmaking with regard to placements, they were interested in more qualitative data on how potential foster carers were attracted, and what the general opinions were concerning foster care.

In 1995, in the course of a project aimed at developing the national foster care training curriculum, the author and colleagues sent 5,500 questionnaires to the 20 county institutions and asked them to distribute the questionnaires to all foster carers through their supervisors. As well as basic questions about their main problems, the questionnaire asked about their needs, former training, meetings, membership of associations, and their requests for vocational training, help, financial aid, and so on. The results of this research are still being documented.

Bibliography

Aczél, Á. and Somorjai, I. (1996) 'Kutatási beszámoló a nevelőszülők helyzetéről' (Report on foster parents), unpublished.

Bartos, K. and Zsámbéki, E. (1994) 'Sikertelen kihelyezések' (Failed placements), *Csálad, Gyermek, Ifjúság*, Vol. 2, pp.4–11.

Csáki, J. and Hazai, V. (1987) 'A hagyományos nevelőszülői hálózat néhány jellemzője Magyarországon' (Some features of the traditional foster care network in Hungary), *Gyermek és Ifjúságvédelem*, Vol. 3, pp.55–63.

Csorna, K. (1929) *A szociális gyermekvédelem rendszere* (The system of social child welfare), Budapest: Eggenberger.

Hanák, K. (1983) *Társadalom és gyermekvédelem* (Society and child protection), Budapest: Akadémiai.

Herczog, M. (1995) *A nevelőszülő helye és szerepe a gyermekvédelemben* (The role and place of the foster parent in the child welfare system), Budapest: Esély.

Szana, S. (1909) *Telepfelügyelői tanfolyam a budapesti állami menhelyen* (Training for supervisors at the Budapest State Asylum), Budapest: Gyermekvédelmi Lap.

10 India

R.R. Singh

Jurisdiction

India comprises 2.4 per cent of the world's land area and 16 per cent of its population. The population of the country was 846.3 million in 1991, and 900 million in 1994. Children aged under 15 years constitute 350 million (nearly 38 per cent) of the total population. India is a multi-lingual and multi-religious country. There are 25 states and seven union territories. Hindi is the official language. During 1992, the central government was organized into 36 ministries and eight departments. Matters pertaining to children and young people, among others, are dealt with by the Ministry of Human Resource Development (Departments of Women's and Children's Development, Health and Family Welfare, Youth and Sports, Education and Culture) and the Ministry of Welfare. With the establishment of local governments in the states, the process of devolution of power is under way.

In the field of welfare, legislation against untouchability, hostels for the children of scheduled tribes, integrated child development services, early childhood education, and special programmes for girls, the disabled and street children are some of the most important social initiatives. Under the directive of the Supreme Court of India, a Central Adoption Resource Agency (CARA) has been established to regulate in-country and inter-country adoption. It should be noted in connection with this that every year, over a million infants in India become 'throw-away babies' soon after birth, due to social and economic pressures on the parents. It is estimated that only a quarter of these find parental love through adoption (*The Pioneer*, 23 April 1995).

According to UNICEF (1995), the balance sheet of India on child development is rather mixed. Two million infants die each year from various avoidable causes and only 64 per cent of children reach class 5 in primary school. Estimates on the number of child workers range from 14 million to 42 million. The declining ratio of girls to boys in the 0–6 age range reflects the unequal treatment meted out to girls in comparison to boys. There are nearly 1.4 million 'missing girls' (those who died as foetuses, or due to infanticide or maltreatment) in eight states.

The 1991 Human Development Index (Chebbi, 1995) of the country shows marked regional disparities in terms of life expectancy, growth of population, infant mortality, literacy and per capita income. For example, the state of Kerala recorded the lowest infant mortality rate of 17 per 1,000 live births, and Orissa the highest, at 123 per 1,000. Whereas the literacy rate in Kerala was 90.6 per cent, it was only 38.8 per cent in Rajasthan. Bihar had the lowest per capita income at 2,539 rupees ($US72.5) and Punjab the highest at 8,281 rupees ($US236.6). In 1995, Bihar's per capita income was still the lowest at 3,650 rupees ($US104), and the per capita income of Punjab was 12,319 rupees ($US352), second only to Delhi at 14,714 rupees ($US420). The average per capita income for the country as a whole was 6,929 rupees ($US198) (*The Economic Times*, 23 April 1995). There is no agreement among scholars as to the extent of poverty in India. According to a conservative estimate, it is around 30 per cent. It is against this background that child welfare programmes, including foster care, should be examined.

History and origins

Foster care is known to have been practised in India since ancient times. Even Lord Krishna was brought up by foster parents. Children also used to be sent to *gurus* (teachers) to be educated. They lived with these teachers (in the *ashrams* on *gurukulas*) until their education was completed. *Gurus* acted as parent substitutes for them. Fostering the children of relatives or friends has always been quite common in all communities. Since time immemorial, work homes, free homes and boarding homes have also been in vogue (Chowdhary, 1988). After the Indian Constitution was adopted, its special provisions regarding children came into force. Commitment to child welfare in India thus reflects a synthesis between the continuation of traditional practices and the provisions of modern personal laws, penal laws and laws relating to criminal proceedings, where the responsibilities of the older members of the family towards children are spelt out.

Tracing the history of institutional services for children in India – both secular and denominational – Bose (1980) has listed the Ramkrishna Mission (founded in 1897), the Society for the Protection of Children in India (founded in 1898) and the All India Seva Samiti (founded in 1914) in the secular category. With respect to denominational institutions, the list includes St Joseph's Orphanage (founded in 1854), Little Sisters of the Poor (founded in 1882), the All India Shia Orphanage (founded in 1972) and the Dosabai Kotwai Orphanage (founded in 1913).

In Delhi, a pilot scheme was started in 1963 under the Children's Act (1960). The Act made a provision in subsection 1 of section 16 for the placement of children with 'fit persons' (Cheema, 1968). The superintendent of the foster care agency was responsible for taking appropriate action in the matter. Rules under the scheme cover such aspects as the age of the child, the age of the foster parents, their income, the number of their natural children, the consent of the child's parents if not deceased, the consent of the spouse, maintenance charges to those parents whose income is between 150 rupees and 500 rupees (between $US4 and $US14) per month, the availability of proper accommodation, sound health of the parents, and willingness to continue to foster until the child is 18 years of age.

The Constitution of India, under the chapter 'Directive Principles of State Policy' (Article 39) prohibits the abuse of children of tender age, and provides protection against exploitation as well as moral and material abandonment. Article 24 of the Constitution stipulates that no child below the age of 14 years shall be employed to work in any factory or mine or be engaged in any other hazardous employment. Article 45 provides for free and compulsory education for all children until they reach the age of 14 years.

Adoption is included in Entry 5 of the Concurrent List of Schedule 7 of the Constitution. This entry could be read together with Entry 20 on Social and Economic Planning, Family Planning and Population Control under the same schedule. In 1974, India formulated a National Policy for Children. In November 1990, the government endorsed all the 27 survival and development goals for the year 2000 agreed upon at the World Summit for Children. It also ratified the United Nations Convention on the Rights of the Child in 1992 and drew up a National Plan of Action: a Commitment to the Child-Juvenile Justice Act was passed in 1986, which replaced the Central Children's Act (1960). (Children Acts have been in force in Madras, Bengal and Bombay since the 1920s.)

The Child Welfare Wing of the Social Defence Bureau of the Ministry of Welfare deals with the problems of orphaned, delinquent and neglected children. As mentioned above, CARA was established to process cases of children requiring adoption. In India, there is no uniform law on adoption. Efforts to enact such a law have been made several times, but they have not met with success so far. Political consensus on such a sensitive issue in a pluralistic society has yet to evolve.

However, in order to streamline the process of adoption and also to safeguard children entering foster care, the government has recently decided to enter into bilateral agreements with other countries for the regulation of inter-country adoption of Indian children (*The Statesman*, 1 January 1996).

With respect to in-country adoption or guardianship, Hindus can adopt a child under the Hindu Adoption and Maintenance Act (1956). Muslims, Christians and Parsis can accept a child under their guardianship either by having recourse to the provisions of the Guardians and Wards Act (1890) or according to their own custom. As far as residential institutions are concerned, the Women's and Children's Institutions (Licensing) Act (1956) and the Orphanages and other Charitable Homes (Supervision and Control) Act (1960) are important. Among the legislative efforts in the nineteenth century, the Apprentices Act (1850) and the Reformatory Schools Act (1876) deserve mention.

In 1947, the Indian Conference of Social Work took up the question of substitute family care for the first time, but no progress was made on this issue. In 1961, the state of Punjab started a scheme for foster care. In Delhi, a pilot scheme began in 1963, and the Central Social Welfare Board (CSWB), an autonomous body funded by the central government, initiated a programme in 1964.

The CSWB assisted voluntary organizations at the rate of 50 rupees per child at that time. However, only three voluntary organizations became involved with this programme. These were: the Guild of Service (Madras) in 1964, the Family Service Centre (Bombay) in 1965 and the Maharasthra State Women's Council in 1966 (Modak, 1976). The Department of Social Welfare, Maharasthra, introduced a scheme of non-institutional services for homeless and destitute children in 1973–74 which was called a 'foster care scheme'. This scheme provided for the placement of orphan, destitute and homeless children in families, family homes and children's villages on a grant aid basis. Under this scheme, only 24 children had been placed with 20 families up to 1983–84.

In the voluntary sector, the SOS Children's Villages started in India in 1964. Subsequently, some of the state governments also established Cottage Homes for Children after the SOS pattern. With a view to expanding non-institutional services, the Ministry of Welfare launched a centrally sponsored scheme for the welfare of children in need of care and protection in 1979–80. This scheme was modified in 1984–85. Under this scheme, grant aid is provided by the central government to voluntary organizations for the care of children. Here, it would be appropriate to quote Naidu's 1986 study of children's institutions in Maharasthra, where 80 per cent of children were found to be malnourished at the time of admission.

Various estimates are available regarding the magnitude of the problem of children in need of care. Pathak and Saxena put the number of orphan children in India at 38.06 million in 1971, out of which the number of maternal, paternal and complete orphans was 19.24 million, 1.80 million and 1.92 million respectively. This amounts to 16.53 per cent of the total child population. On the basis of estimates made by Pathak and Saxena,

Khandekar has calculated that the number of total orphans in 1981 was 37,592,200, with 15,036,900 of these destitute. Pathak and Saxena have also provided later estimates (National Institute of Public Co-operation and Child Development, 1990) for the total number of orphans in India: their later figure is 30 million, with 12 million or 40 per cent destitute. Out of this number, only 110,000 destitute children had been provided with institutional care by 1983, and 9,289 destitute and orphan children were adopted between 1990 and 1993 (Government of India, 1994). One can thus surmise the plight of the rest who need care and protection.

With respect to the welfare of working children, the central government formulated a national policy on child labour in 1987. The Family Courts Act, which was passed in 1984, has yet to come into operation all over the country as an effective mechanism for child care in certain cases. In Delhi, the establishment of Family Courts has been suspended due to opposition by the local Bar Council and a strike by lawyers.

Administration and organization

Considerable confusion persisted until the late 1970s regarding the meaning of the terms 'adoption', 'foster care', 'sponsorship' and 'institutional care' in India. This is due to the fact that a child may be temporarily accepted into an institution before being offered for fostering or adoption, or the child in foster care may subsequently be adopted, restored to his or her own parents, or even re-admitted to the institution. Similarly, a sponsored child may stay with his or her own parents, foster parents or in an SOS-type cottage home before rehabilitation or final adoption. Thus, in dealing with the question of the guardianship of a minor – as is also the case in other family matters – three distinct legal systems prevail in India: Hindu Law, Muslim Law and the Guardian and Wards Act (1890). Guardians of minors may be natural, testamentary or appointed by a court. The court's paramount concern is the welfare of the child. The Hindu Minority and Guardianship Act (1956) has upheld the superior right of the father over a minor until he or she reaches 18 years of age. The prior right of the mother is recognized only in connection with the custody of a child below the age of 5. In the case of an illegitimate child, the mother has a better claim than the putative father (Government of India, Publication Division, 1994). In a judgment delivered on 6 February 1984, the Supreme Court ruled that all possibilities should be exhausted for in-country adoption before a child was offered for adoption abroad, and even in the latter case, preference should be given to Indians living abroad. The judgment also stipulated that a child care agency should not act merely as an adoption agency, and its report on the child should include the following information: original parents, present environment, health status, physical, intellectual and emotional development, and the assessment of a social worker.

The scheme for the care and protection of children includes both institutional and non-institutional services (Bose, 1980). During 1979–80, the scheme was applied to 40,407 children, and the expenditure incurred with respect to them was 33,727 million rupees (approximately $US1 million); while the scheme covered 9,665 children in 1974–75, its coverage in 1991–92 increased to 50,029 children, with a budget provision of 8.85 million rupees (National Institute of Public Co-operation and Child Development, 1994). At the end of 1991, 970 voluntary organizations were involved, and the number of children had reached 48,739. This scheme is being implemented through voluntary organizations, with 90 per cent grant aid from the central and state governments on a matching basis. There were 76 recognized adoption agencies in various states in 1992–94 (Ministry of Welfare, 1994–95). The placement of children in foster care is normally restricted to children younger than 6, although it can be extended up to the age of 12. In exceptional cases, children aged 12 years can be kept in foster placement for a further period of two years. The total cost is generally limited to 76.5 rupees ($US2) per child per month. The evaluation reports on this scheme (Bose, 1980) have recommended its continuation, expansion and consolidation.

Puthenkalam's 1969 study of 444 Catholic orphanages in India also showed that only 10 per cent of the children were orphans. Thus the orphanages had really become special boarding houses for poor children. Public foster care is being provided through cottage homes run on the SOS pattern by the state governments and the union territories. In this connection, special reference must be made to the Family Helper Programme of the Christian Children's Fund, which is assisting 80,000 children and their families through community-based intervention (Dave, 1993; Christian Children's Fund, 1991) in partnership with several institutions: 51 small, grassroots, non-governmental organizations (NGOs), 30 schools and 4 residential care institutions. One can only wonder how many of these children would have been eligible to receive foster care in the absence of such a preventive, developmental programme.

Who is placed in foster care?

Foster care is a temporary service for children who are at risk because their families are in crisis. The assumption is that the child will return to his or her own home when the crisis has passed. Although a sponsored child living with relatives may be included in the foster care category, children living in cottage homes or in the SOS Children's Villages will not be included.

However, all such children, fostered or otherwise, are placed through a Child (Juvenile) Welfare Board.

The need for foster care arises in the following situations: temporary or long-term crisis in the family (for example, death, desertion, separation or divorce); both parents working; abandonment of an illegitimate or unwanted child; loss of the child on the wayside; the child's physical or mental handicap; chronic illness or emotional maladjustment of the child; child abuse or neglect; affliction of the parents with leprosy or AIDS; prostitution on the part of parents or their incarceration; destitution; deprivation; orphanhood; hospitalization, homelessness or unemployment on the part of the parents; parental inability to provide care, protection or training, and children with special needs.

The criteria for the selection of foster families were evolved by an international body of NGOs – Children of the World 1995 – and include the following factors: motivation of parents to accept an unrelated child; cheerful disposition, especially with respect to the prospective foster mother; absence of severe health problems (tuberculosis or AIDS); observance of normal standards of hygiene; permanent postal address; possession of a ration card; freedom from drug addiction, alcoholism or immoral activity; permanency of job and regular source of income; settled place of abode; awareness of child's needs, and willingness to take an orientation course. Selection of families who do not require an allowance and are willing to meet the minimum needs of the child has been considered important in order to prevent commercialization (Bose, 1980).

With respect to the different categories of children in foster care, data on dependent children, behaviourally disordered children, homeless children, delinquents, developmentally disabled children, and mentally ill children are not available separately. Children who are victims of earthquake or riot have been placed in foster care, but large numbers of them have also been placed in institutions or cottage homes. Foster family care can therefore be regarded as an adjunct rather than an alternative to institutional care. Although this problem is largely societal, it is also due to the fact that the staff of social welfare organizations are more comfortable with institutional programmes. Thus, by and large, children in foster care in India may be regarded as dependent or destitute: a finding that could be inferred from the data from regional studies (Bose, 1980).

The data show that orphans in foster care comprise only 4.7–15 per cent of the total. As mentioned earlier, the number of children in need of care and protection, both in institutions and in foster care, was 50,029 in 1991–92. The scheme for the care and protection of children discussed previously appears most popular in two states, Tamilnadu and Karanataka, in that order: 179 agencies in Tamilnadu and 141 agencies in Karanataka received grants in 1991 for 10,743 and 5,565 children respectively. In contrast, there are 140,000 children in about 1,000 children's homes. During 1992, the number of children adopted outside the country was 3,469, while 3,304 were adopted inside the country (National Institute of Public Co-operation and Development, 1994). Of 450 children placed in foster care in Delhi, 19 were reported dead (Lalitha, 1977). Fifty-eight foster parents out of a total of 60 reported that their foster children were well-adjusted, although 45 of these parents did not know the difference between adoption and foster care (Lalitha, 1977).

Care providers

An evaluation of the Delhi scheme (Evaluation Cell, Delhi Administration, 1980) was conducted in the wake of growing concern about the exploitation of children as domestic servants. This study covered 583 foster parents, whose socio-economic characteristics varied widely. Out of a sample of 409 foster parents, the majority (65.7 per cent) lived in Delhi. Over 50 per cent of the foster children were 1 year old or less. In the majority of cases, the children's parentage was unknown. These children were brought to the agency by the Missionary of Charity, Nursing Homes or Hospitals. Some children were even picked up from the roadside. Of 370 foster families, 33 were illiterate, and the majority were in the low-income group: 51.4 per cent earned between 150 and 500 rupees per month. Further questions to a sample of 66 parents revealed that 56 found their lives more cheerful and purposeful as a result of taking in the child, while only six were unhappy and regretted accepting the child. On average, foster parents spent between 48 and 421 rupees on their foster children per month, but only 26 per cent of them were claiming Maintenance Allowance. It was surprising to note that only four Muslim families (1 per cent) had offered their services as foster carers.

Apte (1976) has drawn attention to the danger of collusion between biological and foster parents so that they can share the amount of grant aid for the child. Apto has further observed that children of less than 6 years of age are more suitable for foster care than older children, and maladjusted children or children with handicaps who require special treatment are unsuitable.

The evaluation report of the Maharasthra Pilot Project in Foster Care, which commenced in 1969, showed that 128 children had been placed with foster parents over six years (Apte, 1976). These children were referred by orphanages, foundling homes, family welfare agencies, families and individuals. The scheme provided for a probationary period and follow-up. Since it was difficult to obtain foster parents, most of the agencies depended upon relatives of the parents. Instances of parents developing a dislike for foster parents were also reported. Approximately 63 per cent of the children in foster care were in the 0–6-year age group. The decision to place children in day foster care was taken in 1972. Thirty-two children were in day care, compared to 94 in full-time care. Only two cases of children with behaviour problems were reported, and these children were placed in day care. Out of 128 foster parents, 34 were related to the father, and 38 to the mother. Twenty-seven foster parents were neighbours, 9 were acquaintances and 13 were strangers. The relationship of the others to the natural parents was not known.

If one compares the Maharasthra study results (Apte, 1976) with the report that only 1.1 per cent of the foster parents in Delhi were Muslims, the Maharasthra results are more encouraging. Twenty-eight per cent of the foster parents in this study (of a total of 126) were Muslims. In 79 cases (approximately 62 per cent), both spouses were living together, and in 36 cases, mothers were alone. In one case, a father was single, and in four cases, the foster parents were unmarried. Although the per capita income of foster parents was more than that of natural parents, both belonged to the low-income groups.

Financial support

Financial support to foster carers (both foster parents and NGOs) is provided by the central and state governments on a matching basis. The Central Social Welfare Board also gives grants to agencies for children in need. The revised scheme of foster care in Maharasthra suggests that UNICEF is also providing assistance in this area. Starting at 30 rupees (less than $US1) per child per month in Delhi in the early 1960s, financial support has been increased to 75 rupees per month generally. In Maharasthra in 1995, it was 300 rupees (about $US9). Whereas voluntary organizations receive a grant of 300 rupees per child per month, foster parents receive only 250 rupees of this. The remaining 50 rupees is retained by the voluntary organization concerned as a service charge. In order to fulfil the conditions of the grant, voluntary organizations are supposed to provide facilities to a minimum of 30–40 children at a time. Most of these organizations are engaged in welfare work, and foster care is only a part of their responsibilities.

Major problems

The multi-generational and multi-lateral nature of the 'Indian extended family and kinship network provides sufficient psycho-social and economic support to deal with the kind of situations which might otherwise give rise to the need for foster care. It is no wonder then that the concept of foster care in

India has yet to become widely accepted. While adoption was understood clearly as a formal type of care, foster care was assumed to be a social obligation. Cases are known where relatives virtually stormed the site of a disaster which left a child as the only survivor, and took up the responsibility of care alone or in rotation without removing the child from the scene. This is the intrinsic strength of Indian society, and it still manifests itself through foster parents, who are mostly relatives or friends. Given the influence of globalization and rapid social change, this asset needs to be protected.

As far as foster care as a formal service is concerned, there are many problems: lack of conceptual clarity; inexperienced staff; poor supervision and follow-up; a low ceiling on the grant per child during a period of inflation; a greater demand for new-born children; gender preference in a patriarchal society; considerations of caste and religion; foster care as *de facto* adoption; unawareness on the part of parents of the difference between foster care and adoption; maintenance of confidentiality in the case of intended adoption; interference by biological parents; probable connivance between low-income natural parents and foster parents related to them in order to share the grant provided for the child; absence of back-up services and the necessary legislation and licensing; birth of the foster parents' own child and the consequent changes in the family's priorities; the foster child as a harbinger of ill omen; non-appearance of foster parents before the Juvenile (Child) Welfare Board on a given date after accepting the child; non-submission of periodic reports on the child; absence of an attached foundling unit in voluntary organizations and their dependence on local families; uneven development of foster care services in the states and variations in the standards of services; discrimination in foster care as a result of varying rates of payment by funding agencies or donors; preference for partial foster care; economic considerations in the selection of children; inadequate assessment of the capability of the prospective foster family; delays in the release of grants; poor utilization or diversion of the grant; the concern of NGOs to maintain a minimum number of children in order to qualify for the grant, and also poor public education regarding the secularization of foster care. One can see from this long list of problems that foster care, though a much needed service, has a long way to go in India, and it needs to develop flexibility, responsiveness and innovation in order to respond adequately to the needs of children in a multi-cultural society.

Major trends

As a result of the prevailing confusion between adoption and foster care, and also because of sponsorship and sponsored foster care, a drift into permanence is very likely to occur. Moreover, the state governments tend to swing into action during periods of disaster, and the best alternative that suggests itself to them is that of cottage homes, which constitute a form of institutionalization. Adoption within the country through foster care by relatives is another trend in the wake of ethnic conflicts or riots. In quite a few cases, foster care is an informal mutual arrangement, and the same applies to *de facto* adoption, subject to its legalization in due course. There also appears to be a preference for guardianship and partial foster care (day or night care) rather than full foster care.

Role of national foster care association

To date, no national association concerned exclusively with foster care has emerged in India. NGOs which were already working in the field of social welfare, or women's or children's welfare (including in-country and inter-country adoption agencies) have taken the responsibility for foster care as well. Notable among them are: the Guild of Service (Madras), the Indian Association for the Promotion of Adoption (Bombay), the Maharasthra State Women's Council (Bombay), the Indian Council of Social Welfare (Bombay), the Indian Council of Child Welfare (New Delhi) and the Voluntary Co-ordination Agency for Adoption (Bombay). The Ministry of Welfare, Government of India, publishes a list of institutions which it assists in its annual report.

Research

Perusal of bibliographies in the field of Indian foster care research does not give an encouraging picture. While there are studies on institutionalized children, the impact of institutionalization on children, the sponsorship programme, the family helper project and adoption, much research is still required in the area of foster care. The *Indian Journal of Social Work* reports on conferences or seminars organized by the Indian Council of Social Welfare (Bombay), formerly known as the Indian Conference of Social Work, and by the Indian Council of Child Welfare. In addition, a mimeographed *Compendium of Reading Materials* published in 1990 by the National Institute of Public Co-operation and Child Development contains a few articles on foster care and non-institutional services for destitute and non-destitute children. In other words, foster care is subsumed under non-institutional or child welfare services.

However, two evaluation reports of the foster care scheme in Delhi and one in Bombay deserve mention. These are: Apte (1976) and Lalitha (1977), and Evaluation Cell, Delhi Administration (1980). The first two are mimeographed reports, and the third, though published, is poor in presentation. Apte's study also contains illustrations which show the process of foster care. None of these studies, however, could be called major research studies.

Therefore, there are many priority areas of research which deserve attention, from the proper gathering of baseline information to the development of tools for measuring impact through longitudinal or retrospective studies, as well as process studies or well-designed case studies. The studies which suggest themselves are: profiles of foster families, children, and families which relinquish their children; comparison of the psycho-social development of foster parents' own children and foster children; the differential impact of institutional care and foster care on children; the impact on children of foster care, sponsored foster care and their variants; multiple foster parenting and its effect on children; determinants of success in foster care; the rehabilitation or social life of fostered children; partnership between biological and foster parents in child care; partnerships between NGOs and foster parents; links between (or transition within) different phases of social parenting (sponsorship, institutionalization, foster care, adoption and reinstitutionalization); societal response to or preference for different forms of foster care; conflicts between siblings in foster or adoptive families; breakdown in foster care and adoption; modes of conflict resolution or problem-solving in foster care; social thresholds of coping among biological and foster parents; exploitation or abuse of children in foster care; social deviance among foster children; the comparative costs and benefits of foster and institutional care; the process of disclosure of parentage; differential patterns of adjustment of abandoned, abused, sick and runaway children in social care; psycho-social deprivation among foster children; gatekeeping by voluntary organizations; indigenous forms of foster care; the impact of assisted reproductive technology on the acceptance of children in foster family care, and social work inputs in substitute family care. These priority areas also require policy and practice interventions.

Bibliography

Apte, M. (1976) *Foster Care: A Non-Institutional Child Care Service* (mimeograph), Bombay, Tata Institute of Social Sciences, pp.38–41 and 56–62.

Bose, A.B. (1980) 'Welfare of children in need of care and protection', in *Profile of Child in India: Policies and Programme*, New Delhi: Ministry of Welfare, pp.144–65.

Chebbi, V.K. (1995) 'Rating people's development', *The Economic Times*, 6 October.

Cheema, J. (1968) 'Attitude of Government Employees Towards Foster Family Care', Delhi School of Social Work, project report for MA degree.

Chowdhary, D.P. (1988) *Inter-Country Adoption*, New Delhi: Indian Council of Child Welfare, pp.26 and 31.

Christian Children's Fund (1991) *National Office Plan 1991–96*, New Delhi: CCF, p.6.

Dave, N. (1993) 'Family Helper Programme: A Community-Based Family Intervention', New Delhi Christian Children's Fund, unpublished paper.

Evaluation Cell, Delhi Administration (1980) *Evaluation Report on Foster Care Service in Delhi*, Delhi: Planning Department, pp.i, 2–3, 6–7, 10–11, and 13–14.

Government of India (1994) *INDI: 1994*, New Delhi: Publication Division pp.7–29, 41–59, 84, 202–7, 220–7, 260, 480, 671, 673, 715 and 726.

Jacob, H. (1995) 'A whole new world', *The Pioneer*, 23 April.

Jacob, K.K. (1977) *Evaluation of the Centrally Sponsored Scheme for Destitute Children in Rajasthan* (mimeograph), Udaipur: Udaipur School of Social Work.

Jain, S.P. (1979) *Child and Law*, New Delhi: Indian Law Institute, p.43.

Lalitha, N.V. (1977) *Foster Care Service in Delhi: A Study* (mimeograph), New Delhi: National Institute of Public Co-operation and Child Development.

Ministry of Welfare (1994–95) *Annual Report 1994-95*, New Delhi: Ministry of Welfare, pp.99–100 and 219–21.

Ministry of Welfare (1980) *Profile of Child in India: Policies and Programmes*, New Delhi: Ministry of Welfare.

Modak, U. (1976) 'Foster family care: An Indian perspective', *Indian Journal of Social Work*, Vol. 37, No.2, pp.141ff.

Naidu, U. (1986) *Causes of Deprivation of Family Care of Institutionalized Children*, Bombay: Tata Institute of Social Sciences.

National Institute of Public Co-operation and Child Development (1990) *Compendium of Reading Material on Institutional and Non-institutional Services for Children* (mimeograph), New Delhi: NIPCCD.

National Institute of Public Co-operation and Child Development (1994) *Child in India: A Statistical Profile*, New Delhi: NIPCCD, pp.116, 117, 272–5 and 287.

Puthenkalam, J. (1969) 'Catholic orphanages in India', *Social Action*, Vol. 19, No.2, p.153.

Srinvasan, K.D., Saxena, P.C. and Kanitkar, T. (eds) (1970) *Demographic and Socio-economic Aspects of Child in India*, Bombay: Himalaya Publishing House, pp.523–37 and 655.

Tolfree, D. (1995) *Residential Care for Children and Alternative Approaches to Care in Developing Countries*, London: Save the Children, pp.13 and 29.

UNICEF (1995) *The Progress of Indian States: 1995*, New Delhi: UNICEF, pp.2–5, 23–4 and 27.

11 Ireland

Robbie Gilligan

Jurisdiction

Ireland is an island situated at the westernmost point of Europe, west of the island of Britain. This chapter deals with the state of foster care in the Republic of Ireland, which comprises 26 of the 32 counties of Ireland. The other six counties in the north remain under British rule following the partition of the country in 1922. The republic covers 70,000 square kilometres. Its population of 3.5 million is relatively homogenous in ethnic, religious and cultural terms. The annual income per capita in 1994 (based on GDP) was 75 per cent of the European Union average (Eurostat, 1996). Irish welfare provision is reasonably well established, and has many of the expected features of the international welfare state. Its development tends to be constrained by economic rather than political imperatives: restraints on welfare provision tend to derive from relative lack of money, rather than lack of will based on ideological resistance.

Responsibility for services for children and their families spreads across five government departments (See Table 11.1). Foster care is part of the brief of the Department of Health at a central and strategic level, and of the eight regional health boards at a day-to-day and operational level. The use of foster care for children and young people is confined to those being served on welfare grounds: it is not part of the response offered by the juvenile justice system.

History and origins

Foster care has an interesting history in Ireland. In earlier versions, its use was often associated with political as much as with welfare purposes. In the native (Gaelic) Brehon Law system, fostering was used as a means of forging

135

**Table 11.1   Distribution of child–related responsibilities
across central government departments**

Health	Child protection Social work services in child care Foster family care Residential child care services (for non–offenders) Family support services Adoption
Education	Schools Special residential schools (for offenders) Pilot preschool programmes
Social Welfare	Income maintenance/support schemes Anti–poverty initiatives Community information services Support to voluntary sector for community development
Justice	Probation and welfare service Juvenile Courts Day and prevention programmes Probation hostels
Environment	Public sector housing provision Grant aid to voluntary sector housing providers Responsibility for ensuring facilities for homeless persons aged over 18

links – and defusing any potential conflict – between the family placing and the family receiving the child, for whom placement was seen as a developmental opportunity (Kelly, 1988). In the English law which succeeded the Irish law as colonial power took hold, fostering was used as a means of transmitting values sympathetic to the new regime (Powell, 1982–83). The roots of the modern system can be traced to the Irish Poor Law Amendment Act 1862. Significant recent landmarks in development have included a new version of the regulations in 1983, and the new system of regulations of 1995, which for the first time gave formal recognition to placement with relatives, as distinct from foster care, which is seen as placement with non-relatives. Table 11.2 sets out a chronology of developments in the evolution of foster care (formerly referred to as 'boarding out') from 1862 to date.

**Table 11.2   Chronology of major legal and policy developments
in the evolution of foster care**

1862 Irish Poor Law Amendment Act – this is considered the starting point of
the modern system of foster care. It allowed children under 5 (under 8
where the child's health required it) to be placed with families instead of
the dreaded workhouse, which was the contemporary public response
to child and family poverty. Gradually, the maximum age was edged
upwards.

1897 Infant Life Protection Act – this granted powers to appoint female
inspectors who were to visit, and if necessary remove, children placed
in families.

1927 The Report of the Commission on the Relief of the Sick and Destitute
Poor favoured the 'continuation and extension' of the use of boarding
out (foster care).

1954 Boarding Out Regulations, based on provisions of the Health Act (1953),
began the gradual modernization of the service.

1970 Health Act – this led to the establishment of eight regional health boards,
which took over responsibilities for foster care. The committee on
Residential Care included proposals for the improvement of foster care
provision in its recommendations.

1972 Health Boards began to appoint professional social workers, whose
duties included the assumption of responsibility for the operation of the
foster care service.

1977 The Fostering Resource Group was established within the Eastern
Health Board – the largest – the first such specialist recruitment/support
team in the republic.

1982 Founding of the Irish Foster Care Association.

1983 New Boarding Out Regulations.

1991 Child Care Act – this provided for the streamlining of the legal basis of
foster care and gave legal recognition to the placement of children with
relatives.

1993 The Irish Foster Care Association hosted the Eighth International Foster
Care Organization World Conference.

1995 New regulations enacted for the placement of children in foster care and
for the placement of children with relatives under the Child Care Act
(1991) – these marked the formal introduction of this form of placement.

Administration and organization

The management of the foster care service is the responsibility of the eight Regional Health Boards as part of their functions under the Child Care Act (1991). This involves them in the recruitment and support of foster carers, the placement of foster children, the management of contact with natural families, and the review of placements. In the Irish system, there has been no role for voluntary agencies in foster care, although the new regulations (1995) now offer health boards the possibility of commissioning voluntary bodies to undertake the assessment of foster carers on their behalf. While foster care has long been the placement of choice in policy and professional terms, a recent official strategic review of health service development considered that, despite a long-established policy preference for its use, the fostering service was 'still under-developed' (Commission on Health Funding 1989, p.357). An impetus to further development may flow from the Child Care Act (1991) and the associated regulations covering the placement of children with relatives or foster carers which came into force in late 1995 (Department of Health 1995b; 1995c).

Regulations under the Child Care Act (1991) covering the placement of children with foster carers or with relatives

Care Plan

Before placing a child in foster care or with relatives, health boards are required to prepare a care plan which must deal, among other things, with:

1   the aims and objectives of the placement;
2   the support to be provided by the health board for the child, the caregivers concerned and, where appropriate, the parents of the child;
3   the arrangements for access to the child by a parent, relative or other named person, subject to any order concerning access by a court;
4   the arrangements for the review of the plan.

Where it is not possible to prepare the plan in advance, preparation must be completed 'as soon as practicable' thereafter. In preparing a plan, the board must consult the responsible caregiver, and 'insofar as is practicable the child and every person who in law is a guardian of the child'. The board must inform the responsible caregiver, and 'insofar as is practicable the child and every person who in law is a guardian of the child' of the 'particulars' of the plan.

Visits to children placed with foster carers/relatives

Health boards are required to ensure that children placed are visited as often as necessary: not less than once every three months in the first two years of placement, and not less than once every six months thereafter.

Reviews

Boards must ensure that an 'authorized person' reviews the case of each child in care and the care plan required under the regulations as often as necessary. The first review must be held within two months of placement. Thereafter, reviews must occur not less than once every six months in the case of a child in care for less than two years, and not less than once a year otherwise. It is not required that a review be held in the form of a meeting.

In reviewing a case, a board must 'have regard to':

- any views furnished by the child, the parents of the child, the responsible caregiver, and any other person whom the board has consulted in relation to the review;
- a report of a visit to the child;
- the latest available school report on the child (where relevant);
- any other information considered relevant.

Relevant people (as for care plans) are to be informed of the outcome of the review, and a note is to be entered on the case record. A person with a *bona fide* interest in the child may request a special review, and the board must agree to this unless it believes it unnecessary. In such a case, it must give its reasons in writing.

There appears to be no explicit requirement that a child be consulted before a review, although if a child should happen to furnish views, they must be considered. On the other hand, there is a clear statement in relation to 'promotion of welfare', that boards must, within constitutional requirements, observe (a) the paramountcy principle concerning the welfare of children, and (b) give 'due consideration, having regard to his or her age and understanding, to the wishes of the child'.

Who is placed in foster care?

According to the latest available data (1992), there are 3,090 children and young people (or 2.7 per 1,000 aged under 18 years) in the care of the eight Regional Health Boards (Department of Health, 1995a). About three out of four (73.9 per cent) of these children and young people are in foster care, a proportion which has been steadily rising over the past decade. As recently as 1983, only half of the children in care were fostered (Gilligan, 1993). Possible explanations for this upward trend in the use of foster care include the closure of a number of traditional residential children's homes, which foster care is then called upon to replace, and the steady effort of the health boards and their social workers to recruit more foster carers. The reliance on foster care may also be linked to aspects of adoption policy. It has been noted that there are legal and cultural impediments to the widespread use of adoption for the permanent placement of children against parental wishes (O'Halloran, 1994).

The available evidence suggests that children are admitted to care at a younger age than previously, and younger children may be more likely to be in foster care (O'Higgins, 1993).

Care providers

On the basis of information kindly supplied by the health boards, it is possible to estimate that there are approximately 1,839 sets of foster carers (which represents 2.24 foster care households per 1,000 households of more than one person nationally). The health boards indicate that in 1994, they recruited a total of 255 new sets of foster carers. It is not possible to say how these broke down between 'traditional model' carers and 'new' carers. Table 11.3 shows

Table 11.3   Comparison of existing and newly-approved foster families by health board

Health board (% of national population)	No. of existing foster families (% of national total)	No. of foster families newly approved in 1994 (% of national recruitment)
Eastern (35.3%)	604 (32.8%)	44 (17.2%)
Midlands (5.8%)	149 (8.1%)	24 (9.4%)
Mid Western (8.8%)	228 (12.4%)	33 (12.9%)
North Eastern (8.5%)	198 (10.8%)	34 (13.3%)
North Western (5.9%)	96 (5.2%)	11 (4.3%)
Southern (15.1%)	243 (13.2%)	26 (10.2%)
South Eastern (10.9%)	185 (10.1%)	73 (28.6%)
Western (9.7%)	136 (7.4%)	6 (2.4%)
National	1,839	255

the number of existing foster families and the number newly approved in 1994 for each of the regional health boards.

Some evidence on the experience of foster carers is discussed under 'Research' below.

Financial support

The level of basic allowances is set nationally, and is generally subject to annual review. The picture has been complicated in recent years by the emergence of carer schemes where a considerably higher rate is payable. In addition to the basic allowance, there are also items of essential expenditure for which foster carers may seek reimbursement (for example, purchase of essential items not otherwise supplied, and school, medical or travelling expenses, etc.). Also, boards have discretion in making payments as regular supplements to the basic allowance in recognition of the special demands or circumstances of a particular placement.

During 1995, the Irish Foster Care Association (1995b) made a submission to the health boards and the central government Department of Health calling for a substantial increase in the basic allowance. There is certainly evidence that the relative value of the allowance has fallen since the early 1980s (see Table 11.4).

Table 11.4   Trends in relative value of fostering allowance 1982–96

	1982	*1989*	*1996*
Weekly fostering allowance rate	28.50	35.50	44.20*
Average weekly industrial earnings	126.69	205.86	267.52
Allowance as % of average earnings	22.5%	17.2%	16.5%

Sources: Department of Health; Central Statistics Office; Gilligan (1990).

* This rate applied with effect from 5 May 1995. An allowance of £IR54.80 (approximately $US76.7) is payable in respect of a young person aged 16 or over, which represents 20.5 per cent of average industrial earnings.

Major problems

A number of issues can be identified which seem likely to take on greater importance in future.

Inadequacy of support

The need to initiate or develop further respite care, training and support groups for foster carers has been identified (O'Sullivan and Pinkerton, 1994, pp.99–100) and has been acknowledged by at least one of the health boards (Mid Western Health Board, 1993, p.100). Concerns about support are also mentioned by carers in Gilligan (1996b). In addition, as already mentioned, the Irish Foster Care Association (1995b) has recently made a submission to the relevant authorities seeking increases in allowances to reflect what they see as the real economic cost to carers of fostering.

Problems of recruitment

There seems to be increasing difficulty in recruitment, especially for long-term placements (Eastern Health Board, 1995, p.83). The reasons for this are undoubtedly complex, but it is essential that the question is examined fully from a policy perspective.

Disruption

There is strong anecdotal evidence of increasingly challenging behaviour among the children placed, and of a growing risk of disruption in placements. Unfortunately, without proper analysis of agency records or research, it is not possible to be more definitive on this point at this stage.

Major trends

A number of trends may be discerned, both in the demands made on foster care and in the organization of foster care provision. On the latter point, there is a discernible trend towards specialist schemes/initiatives targeting the needs of specific groups: seeking emergency or other placements for adolescents; for Traveller (native Irish Gypsy) children with Traveller families, or for inner-city children in inner-city families. There is also a growing appreciation of the potential of placements with relatives (Eastern Health Board, 1995, p.81). This trend is driven partly by the shortage of alternative viable placements in residential or foster care.

There is growing recognition of the implications of providing for a population of children who may have experienced abuse. Gradually, guidance material for foster carers is emerging which reflects the increasing frequency of histories of abuse – sexual and otherwise – among children placed. A recent leaflet, *Keeping Foster Placements Safe*, from the Irish Foster Care Association (1995a) refers, among other things, to the possibility of allegations of abuse against foster carers, and the trauma they may provoke. In its recently-published *Child Protection Guidelines*, the North Eastern Health Board (1994, p.48) includes specific guidance to foster carers on how to respond to concerns about abuse involving any child in care.

There is some evidence of a greater appreciation of the importance of direct work with the child to assist him or her to recover from the trauma of events leading up to and involved in separation from the family of origin. In one county, the social work service responded to problems of placement breakdown by establishing a treatment team, whose brief was to work intensively with the 30 per cent of the children in care (all fostered) who needed extra help. It was reasoned that failure to provide this assistance would lead to a continuing pattern of breakdown. In her description of this work, Gogarty (1995) highlights the ongoing significance for children in care of the loss of their own families. The work of Gallagher (1995) in the same county also suggests that a great deal of attention is now being paid to facilitating contact between children in care and their natural families. While her study area may not be totally representative and may be particularly attentive to this issue, it is likely that this question is receiving more practical attention, driven by two factors – new professional understanding, and legal pressures derived from the expectations of the Child Care Act (1991) and of recent Superior Court judgments.

The future poses many challenges for foster care in Ireland: recruiting and supporting carers represents a considerable challenge for the agencies; coping with and responding to the children's needs will be a great challenge for the carers. Both agencies and carers will have much to do to meet the needs of foster children for meaningful links with their natural families. Much will also have to be done to introduce purposeful planning into the system, whether at the level of the individual case or of the system at local, regional and national levels. In addition, more research is undoubtedly required.

Finally, what will the system look like in ten or twenty years? Crystal ball-gazing is hazardous, but I would not be surprised to find a greater role for specialist carers and for relatives, and a reduced role for 'traditional model' foster families. What seems certain, however, is that in Ireland, as elsewhere, more thought will have to be given to an effective 'technology of support' for foster carers – whether traditional, specialist or related to the child (Gilligan, 1995).

Role of national foster care association

The Irish Foster Care Association has 800 members in 17 branches. Founded in 1981, the association draws its members from the ranks of carers, social workers and others sympathetic to the needs of children in care. Its activities include the provision of information and support to members, the publication of a quarterly newsletter and books and leaflets from time to time, contact with agencies and government bodies on matters concerning fostering, and publicity and training activities which promote foster care – including videos and seminars. A highlight in the short history of the association was its successful hosting of the Eighth International Foster Care Organization's International Conference in Dublin in July 1993. An edited version of the proceedings has been published by the Irish Foster Care Association (McTeigue, 1995).

Contact: Ms Pat Whelan, 60 Grangewood, Rathfarnham, Dublin 16, Ireland
Telephone and Fax: (+353) 1-494-4229.

Research

Unfortunately, there is a very limited body of research on the fostering experience, whether from the perspective of the child, the carer, the carers' children, the social worker, or the child's biological parents or other relatives. This problem is compounded by the very limited nature of official statistics about the operation of the fostering system.

Official national statistics on children in care in Ireland tend to be scant and slow in appearing. As has been observed elsewhere, there is a great need to enhance their quality and immediacy (Gilligan, 1996a). Specific suggestions for improvement include the provision of separate information on the characteristics of children in foster care, as opposed to those in all other forms of care (O'Sullivan and Pinkerton, 1994, p.106), and the generation of information about decisionmaking constraints and processes underlying the fostering service (O'Connor, 1987, p.78).

Academic or research literature on foster care in Ireland is fairly scarce, which has been deplored by O'Connor (1992) and O'Sullivan and Pinkerton (1994). O'Higgins and Boyle have undertaken analysis of data on children in care at the national level and in one region. This work has yielded certain information about the use of foster care. In their analysis of 1982 national data, they found foster care to be much more common among younger children (under age 7) and among those in voluntary placements (O'Higgins and Boyle, 1988). In O'Higgins's analysis of 1989 data on one health board region, she found a greater tendency to foster care among (a) admissions of children under 7 years of age, and (b) among all children in care under 15 years of age (O'Higgins, 1993).

On the more specific question of the extent of contact between children in foster care and their biological families, Gallagher (1995) completed a month-long study of access contacts between children in foster care in one county and their parents or relatives. Of the 79 children in the study (representing, as it happens, all children in care in that county at the time of the study), only 17 (21.5 per cent) had no contact with a family member over the study period. Thus virtually 4 out of every 5 children in care in the study county had contact with their family of some kind during the month in question. The social workers involved rated these contacts as a positive experience for the child in 74 per cent of instances, and a mixed experience in a further 18 per cent. Only 8 per cent of these contacts were considered a negative experience for the child.

Gilligan (1996b) reports on findings from a postal survey of foster carers in one Irish health board region. There was a total of 73 respondents, representing a response rate of 54.4 per cent. While the non-response rate poses difficulties, the findings are still of interest, given the paucity of research on the carer's perspective in the Irish context. A majority of the respondents seemed broadly contented in their role, although different minorities had varying concerns. These groups had problems with the level of administrative and professional support available to them, with the prospect of being parted from the child, and in the relationship with the child's biological parents. In terms of motivation to foster, altruism seemed to rank highly. From a range of choices, a large majority of respondents selected one of two answers considered to reflect altruistic motivation: 'I wanted to help under-privileged children' or 'I knew of a child who needed a home.' Seventy-seven per cent of foster mothers and 81.6 per cent of foster fathers selected these categories, compared to 47 per cent and 53 per cent respectively in Rowe et al.'s (1984) study, on which the categories used in Gilligan's (1996b) study were based. Possible explanations for the higher rate in Ireland might include the strongly rural character of this Irish sample and the relatively high degree of religious adherence still evident in Irish rural communities (McGréil, 1991).

Bibliography

Commission on Health Funding (1989) *Report of the Commission on Health Funding*, Dublin: Stationery Office.

Commission on the Relief of the Sick and Destitute Poor (1927) *Report*, Dublin: Stationery Office.

Department of Health (1995a) *Survey of Children in the Care of Health Boards in 1992*, Vol. 1., Dublin: DoH.

Department of Health (1995b) *Child Care (Placement of Children in Foster Care) Regulations 1995*, Dublin: DoH.

Department of Health (1995c) *Child Care (Placement of Children with Relatives) Regulations 1995*, Dublin: DoH.

Eastern Health Board (1995) *Review of Adequacy of Child Care and Family Support Services in 1994*, Dublin: Eastern Health Board.

Eurostat (1996) *Facts Through Figures 1996: A Statistical Portrait of the European Union*, Luxemburg/Brussels: Statistical Office of the European Communities.

Gallagher, S. (1995) 'Parents, families and access to children in care: The implications of the Child Care Act 1991', in Ferguson , H. and Kenny, P. (eds) *On Behalf of the Child: Professional Perspectives on the Child Care Act 1991*, Dublin: A. and A. Farmar, pp.121–41.

Gilligan, R. (1990) *Foster Care for Children in Ireland – Issues and Challenges for the 1990s*, Dublin: University of Dublin, Trinity College, Department of Social Studies, Occasional Paper No. 2, 36 pp.

Gilligan, R. (1993) 'Ireland', in Colton, M. and Hellinckx, W. (eds) *Child Care in the EC: A Country-specific Guide to Foster and Residential Care*, Aldershot: Arena, pp.118–38.

Gilligan, R. (1995) 'Making a success of fostering – what we want for the children, what we need for the adults', in McTeigue, D. (ed.) *A Journey Through Fostering: Proceedings of the Eighth International Conference of the International Foster Care Organization, Dublin, July 1993*, Dublin: Irish Foster Care Association, pp.3–22.

Gilligan, R. (1996a) 'Irish child care services in the 1990s: The Child Care Act 1991 and other developments', in Hill, M. and Aldgate, J. (eds) *Child Welfare Services: Developments in Law, Policy, Practice and Research*, London: Jessica Kingsley pp.56–75.

Gilligan, R. (1996b) 'The foster carer experience in Ireland – findings from a postal survey', *Child-Care, Health and Development*, Vol. 22, No. 2, pp.85–98.

Gogarty, H. (1995) 'The implications of the Child Care Act 1991 for working with children in care', in Ferguson, H. and Kenny, P. (eds) *On Behalf of the Child: Professional Perspectives on the Child Care Act 1991*, Dublin: A. and A. Farmar, pp.105–20.

Irish Foster Care Association (1995a) *Keeping Foster Placements Safe*, Dublin: IFCA.

Irish Foster Care Association (1995b) *Allowances* (mimeograph), Dublin: IFCA.

Kelly, F. (1988) *A Guide to Early Irish Law*, Dublin: Dublin Institute for Advanced Studies.

McGréil, M. (1991) *Religious Practice and Attitudes in Ireland – Report of a Survey of Religious Attitudes and Practice and Related Issues in the Republic of Ireland 1988–89*, Maynooth, County Kildare: Survey and Research Unit, Department of Social Studies, St Patrick's College.

McTeigue, D. (ed.) (1995) *A Journey Through Fostering*, Dublin: Irish Foster Care Association.

Mid Western Health Board (1993) *Review of Child Care and Family Support Services*, Limerick: Mid Western Health Board.

North Eastern Health Board (1994) *Child Protection Guidelines North Eastern Health Board*, Kells: North Eastern Health Board.

O'Connor, P. (1992) 'Child care policy: A provocative analysis and research agenda', *Administration.*, Vol. 40, No. 3, pp.200–19.

O'Connor, S. (1987) 'Community care services: An overview, Part 2', *National Economic and Social Council Community Care Services: An Overview*, Dublin: National Economic and Social Council.

O'Halloran, K. (1994) *Adoption in the Two Jurisdictions of Ireland – A Comparative Study*, Aldershot: Avebury.

O'Higgins, K. (1993) *Family Problems – Substitute Care: Children and Their Families*, Dublin: Economic and Social Research Institute.

O'Higgins, K. and Boyle, M. (1988) *State Care – Some Children's Alternative: An Analysis of the Data from the Returns to the Department of Health, Child Care Division 1982*, Dublin: Economic and Social Research Institute.

O'Sullivan, E. and Pinkerton, J. (1994) *Focus on Children: Blueprint for Action*, Dublin and Belfast: Focus On Children.

Powell, F. (1982–83) 'Social policy in early modern Ireland', *Social Studies – Irish Journal of Sociology*, Vol. 7, No.1, pp.56–66.

Rowe, J., Cain, H., Hundleby, M. and Keane, A. (1984) *Long Term Foster Care*, London: Batsford.

12 Israel

Zmira Laufer

Jurisdiction

Israel is a small country, bordered on one side by the Mediterranean Sea, with a population of 5,327 million people. The lifestyle is Western and predominantly modelled on the United States in its consumer trends, dress and culture (Shamgar-Handelman, 1986). The population is composed of Jews (81 per cent) and non-Jews (19 per cent), who include Muslims (14 per cent), Christians (3 per cent) or Druze and others (2 per cent). Ninety-two per cent of Israel's residents live in urban centres, and most of them are employed in the service sector (70 per cent). Only 24 per cent work in industry (Central Bureau of Statistics, 1994).

Israelis benefit from a large system of advanced, universal social services which have been made part of its national laws, such as national health insurance, social insurance, child allowance, old age benefits, unemployment insurance and guaranteed income.

In comparison with other Western countries, the characteristics of Israel's households are somewhat extraordinary. In 1994, out of 1,404 households surveyed, 54 per cent were raising children under the age of 17, and the majority (90 per cent) of these were two-parent households. Sixty-nine per cent of these households had more than one child. Israeli Jewish families had an average of 3.2 children. It should be noted that among the 6 per cent of the overall number of families in Israel who were under the care of welfare agencies (this figure included most of the families who had children in placements), the average number of children per family rose to 4.1. Among families with six or more children, the percentage of families under care also increased, to 16 per cent (Katz et al., 1994).

The Israeli divorce rate is also relatively low in comparison with other Western countries (3.8 per 1,000), as is the relative proportion of one-parent households. Divorcees form the largest group of one-parent households (50 per cent), followed by widows. Only 9 per cent of one-parent households are headed by unmarried mothers (Central Bureau of Statistics, 1994).

Based on the above data and surveys which were conducted on the subject of the family in Israel, it can be said that from the standpoint of values, Israeli society is a 'family society' (Perets and Katz, 1981; 1990) in which children are highly valued, not only by their families but also by the community, and that children's welfare is considered the responsibility of Israeli society as a whole (Shamgar-Handelman, 1990).

History and origins

Instances of foster care can be found in many biblical stories. Moses was unwittingly placed in the foster care of his biological mother by his foster mother, Pharaoh's daughter, and Queen Esther was raised by her uncle, Mordecai, as his foster daughter. Until the nineteenth century, foster care was still seen as the most valuable and humanitarian option for children at risk when orphanages and other organized establishments for refugee children were being developed in the Middle East.

The roots of modern foster care in Israel were laid in the 1920s, when public bodies began to get involved. In contrast to the past, when placement was mainly a private family matter based on personal contracts drawn up between family members, at this point, civil authorities and voluntary organizations took upon themselves more and more responsibility for it. Later in the century, the Israeli government began protecting and safeguarding the rights of children through such laws as the Compulsory Education Law (1949), the Age of Consent Law, the Prohibition of Child and Youth Labour Law (1953), the Amendment to the Law of Evidence – Child Protection (1955), the Special Education Act and the Prevention of Abuse of Minors and Helpless Children (1989). The principles underpinning these laws are:

1 Legal decisions concerning a child should give priority to the child's best interests.
2 All children are equal before the law. The law does not differentiate between male or female children, children born in or out of wedlock, or biological or adopted children.

This reflected a wider acceptance of public responsibility for the welfare of children in Israeli society in general, and for children at risk in particular, and was based on the Israeli ideological concept expressed in the Geneva Declaration on Children's Rights (1924 and 1959) and in the United Nations Convention on the Rights of the Child, ratified by Israel in 1991.

Before examining foster care in Israel in depth, it should be emphasized that its central features in the modern era are, first, the use of foster care as a long-term placement option, and second, that supply does not meet demand. This state of affairs has been a source of great worry and unease for the past thirty years for all those involved in child welfare. It is evident that the present situation is the result of *ad hoc* programmes being implemented sporadically, so that a single, efficient system has not been allowed to develop, and co-operation could not evolve between the different foster care services and projects, such as fund-raising programmes, recruitment, training and supervisory programmes, follow-up, and ongoing treatment projects aimed at integrating foster families, placed children and their biological families (Laufer, 1979; Benbenisti and Oyserman, 1991). Today, several innovative programmes are being introduced into Israeli practice which seem to herald the dawn of a new era in which foster care will progress in both qualitative and quantitative terms.

Administration and organization

Legal position

The field of foster care has yet to be recognized legally, and Israel has yet to enact a foster care law. In contrast, adopted children and their adoptive families are covered by the Adoption Law (1981), and children placed in authorized residential settings are protected under the Residence Supervision Law (1995).

The few legal arrangements which exist concerning foster care are partial at best, and embedded in different laws. They are primarily to be found in the Welfare Code of the Ministry of Labour and Welfare, and as such, constitute a set of internal instructions without legal validity (Morag, 1990).

For example, a child placed in foster care privately by his or her family is protected legally under the Residence Supervision Law (paragraph 8) and the Penal Code (paragraph 535). According to the Penal Code, a parent or legal guardian of a minor who transfers that minor to the care of someone other than the child's parent, uncle, aunt, grandparent or legal guardian, without the consent of the welfare authorities, is breaking the law. It should be emphasized that the law is not strictly enforced, and there are numerous private foster care and adoption arrangements which are not authorized by welfare authorities.

Since 1945, various attempts have been made to set up committees to examine and make recommendations about legislation governing foster care. Some of the subjects studied have been: supervision and training of foster families; the status of foster families in treatment and legal decisions concerning the children; defining the authority of biological and foster parents; arrangements for private adoption; adoption by foster families; children's rights at the conclusion of foster care, and the treatment contract with the foster family. As a result of intensive activities on the part of various organizations, public pressure and pressure brought to bear by the mass media, the Committee on Foster Care at the Ministry of Labour and Social Affairs should succeed in promoting the legislation.

Structure and budget

The Ministry of Labour and Welfare's Central Authority maintains a network of foster families. A review of the way it operates shows that, in practice, it employs three principal models of foster care concurrently, plus a new family group care 'cluster' model.

The first model may be called 'inclusive'. The worker treating the family, usually under the auspices of the local welfare agencies, generally recruits, selects and trains the foster family. He or she is also responsible for follow-up and deciding whether to continue or discontinue the process. This model customarily recruits families from the child's own community to act as foster families.

The second model may be labelled 'integrated', and is commonly implemented in large communities or cities, where the Department of Welfare Services maintains a Child and Youth Division which would be responsible for:

- counselling services for persons directly under the care of welfare agencies in cases of children at risk who continue to live at home;
- directing the committees making decisions to authorize the removal of children from their biological parents' home;
- follow-up and training of foster families.

These professional activities are combined with continuation of support for the child's family, to be given by an agency worker in the family's area of residence. This combined model also exists for children who are placed in residential settings.

The third model, the most common, can be termed 'centralized', where the Ministry of Labour and Welfare, through its area offices, offers foster care services which supply foster families, training and follow-up. The majority of welfare agencies in Israel take advantage of these services. This model has also been implemented by the Ministry of Education, which is the second largest supplier of foster families.

Today, choosing which of these models to implement is based on the personal views of the different professionals, and the theoretical knowledge and practical experience of the practitioners. Despite having recognized the importance of empirical research and a statement of aims, the services have not successfully implemented the comparative study of the models which was meant to assist them in defining policy and directing resource allocation.

The family group care 'cluster' model

This is a relatively recent development in the Israeli group care system. This model is structured around a group of 4–20 extended foster families living in several apartments or houses located in a single neighbourhood and belonging to the placement agency. Each family cares for up to 12 children, aged 6–14, in addition to their biological children. Some services are provided centrally: for example, laundry, the main meal and cleaning. Mothers receive a full salary for their work in the home, and may not take on any other job. Fathers receive a partial salary to cover the afternoon hours devoted to the children. In addition, every complex has an administrator, a social worker, a psychologist and a child and youth care worker; these are often part-time positions, depending on the size of the complex. Most clusters are set up in small, urban or semi-urban communities. The population of these areas is seldom more than 25,000.

The model attempts to combine the positive and well-documented advantages of both residential group care and traditional foster care. Some features of the latter are individualization; the warmth and protective nature of family-based, caring environments; more options for absorbing siblings when necessary; the opportunity for support from a peer group facing the same experiences (such as separation from parents); more consistent and accessible professional follow-up and guidance, and reduced trauma when a family leaves the programme (because the family may leave, but the children remain in the same setting, the same community and among the same peer group).

Two points should be made here. First, the drop-out rate for families participating in the cluster model is high, and second, in practice, the model raises the following question: are there different outcomes between the three most frequently used placement models (inclusive, integrated and centralized) on the one hand, and clusters on the other? Doubts have been raised as to whether untrained families are capable of coping with their complex role (Laufer, 1996).

Who is placed in foster care?

For historical and cultural reasons, child placement in foster and residential care carries little stigma, and enjoys wide public and professional support

(Sharon, 1986). Compared to other countries, Israel had, and still has, the highest number per capita of placed children (Jaffe, 1983; Sharon, 1986; Ben-Arie, 1993). Nevertheless, the trend towards family empowerment and the development of services within the community designed to reduce the need for child placement has also gained prominence in Israel. This trend has significantly reduced the number of children of those who have held Israeli citizenship for some time (as opposed to new immigrants) in residential care, but has not affected the number of children in placements.

In 1972, for example, almost 20 per cent of the total population of children aged 13–17 were in residential care compared to England, where only 3 per cent of children under the age of 18 were placed. However, by 1992, only 11 per cent of children aged 13–17 in Israel were in residential care (Ben-Arie, 1993; Central Bureau of Statistics, 1994).

The large waves of immigration from the CIS and Ethiopia to Israel in the past few years have produced a sharp rise in the number of children in residential care. Generally, adolescents from the CIS tend to be placed in residential care, while younger Ethiopian children tend to be placed in such settings. The rationale for this is the belief that living in such environments is the most efficient way to integrate immigrants into the new culture. This premise, it should be noted, has been a subject for argument since the 1950s, because of the differences it creates between the child and his or her family, and due to its contribution to the undermining of parental status in the new society. At present, there are no statistics describing the rise in the number of children in residential settings. Likewise, there have been no studies on the number of placed children of new immigrants from the latest waves of immigration which have increased Israel's Jewish population by 12 per cent. Therefore, the following section is a description of the practice of placement among Jewish Israelis, excluding these latest arrivals. In addition, it does not include a description of the practice among non-Jewish populations, in which the placement options are limited, and whose children constitute 2 per cent of those in registered placement settings.

Care providers

It is important to note that placement in a foster family in Israel has changed from being simply one alternative to being the treatment of choice. Today, about 1,600 foster families, under public supervision, raise approximately 3,600 children. These families live in all parts of the country – in urban, rural and kibbutz settings.

The Ministry of Labour and Welfare supervises about 1,450 families with around 2,600 children (including mentally challenged children). The Ministry of Education supervises some 70 kibbutz families with 130 children, and 80 families in seven family group care clusters with about 1,000 children (Ben-Arie, 1993).

There are also an unknown number of placements in foster homes run privately by families or institutions not supervised or managed by public authorities, in spite of the Residence Supervision Law (1965), which obliges anyone having custody of a child who is not a close family member to report the fact to the authorities within seven days. It is important to stress that due to the lack of foster families, the statistics presented here do not reflect the demand for this type of treatment.

Financial support

At present, with a few exceptions, resources for foster families are allocated within the budgets of the social services departments. These budgets are funded by local authorities and the Ministry of Labour and Welfare. Additional resources contributed by other bodies (government or private) are almost never utilized. Biological parents share in the expenses of child support, according to their income. However, since most of these parents live below the poverty line, their contribution is minimal, to say the least.

Payment to foster families is centralized. The majority of these families are paid by either the Ministry of Labour and Welfare or the Ministry of Education, whereas local authorities process the families' accounts or inquiries. This division often leads to conflict, due to communication problems and other bureaucratic difficulties.

Foster families in Israel are not considered agency employees, but work as 'self-employed' subcontractors to the agencies. (The only exceptions are the families participating in the cluster model discussed above.) This status exempts the welfare agencies from paying social benefits to these families, such as social insurance, health insurance or pensions.

Families who care for foster children not diagnosed as mentally or physically disabled receive a monthly salary of 1,500 new shekels. This sum does not include the costs of extra education (for example, private tutors, supplementary lessons or summer camp) or other expenses (for example, spectacles, psychotherapy or clothing). The payment is broken down as follows: 42 per cent for food, 11 per cent for education and cultural activities, 21 per cent for miscellaneous expenses and 26 per cent for compensation to the family. Families who are caring for children with special needs receive a supplement of between 11 and 19 per cent of the salary. A supplement is also paid for caring for younger children aged between birth and 6 years. For purposes of comparison, it should be noted that the average Israeli wage earner in 1993 was paid 3,353 new shekels (approximately $US1,140) per month (Central Bureau of Statistics, 1994). On the one hand, this may be seen as a positive indication of the country's investment in foster children. Yet on the other hand, it would appear that the standard of living of many foster families is higher than the average Israeli wage earner, even though so many of these families continually protest at the low level of payments, which they feel do not cover the actual costs of caring for the child. To date, no data have been collected about the socio-economic situation of Israeli foster families, although such data would enable the authorities to make appropriate changes.

In addition, it should be emphasized that more resources are budgeted for services for children living outside their natural homes (for example, for dental treatment, and supplementary lessons) than for children at risk who continue to live at home. This fact is a source of great unease for professionals working to strengthen these families and reduce the need to place children outside their natural homes.

Major problems

Recruitment and training

As mentioned earlier, demand for carers far outstrips supply. This situation has arisen because there is no efficient mechanism designed to recruit suitable families, while at the same time, the drop-out rate among foster families is very high. Recruitment of new families by the Ministry of Labour and Welfare or local services is generally sporadic, and is conducted through advertisements in the mass media. However, it is important to emphasize that many of the families who apply are not responding to the advertisements, but apply because they have had earlier contact with foster care through family members or neighbours.

Why are so few families willing to care for foster children? This can be explained by interrelated changes in Israeli society. The nuclear family in Israel is changing: families are smaller, with fewer children, the divorce rate is rising, as is the number of single-parent families. There has been a rise in the cost of living per person per family, and a rise in mobility. Changes in women's employment styles have also had an influence: more women are working outside the home, and increasing numbers of women are concentrating on developing their own careers, so there are more dual-career families.

In addition to the lack of foster families, there is the necessity of coping with the high drop-out rate, which forces children to move from family to family, and means that there are fewer suitable placement alternatives. This situation has prompted two groups into action. Practitioners have made great efforts to develop training programmes and screening tools for families, while researchers have focused on analysing the foster family's internal and external characteristics. These efforts are also intended to help build a profile of the 'suitable foster family' in order to minimize the drop-out rate.

An additional reason for the high drop-out rate is related to the preparation of prospective families for foster parenthood in practice. Theoreticians and practitioners are agreed that foster care requires the operation of a parental process more complex and demanding more skill and knowledge than ordinary parenting. Professionals across the board view foster parenthood as a profession that requires formal training, and they agree that a significant number of the families who drop out do so because they are unsuited and ill equipped for the role.

Even though these views are accepted by almost all those who work in the field, a review of the practices of the services which place children in foster care reveals a severe lack of training programmes, both for the first stage (preparation for their role as foster parents) and for the next stage (performing that role). Very frequently, children are placed with foster parents who have had no prior training.

Until recently, a minority of services ran sporadic programmes designed to screen and prepare candidates for the job. The emphasis in these programmes was mainly on providing a basic orientation. The programmes were essentially standardized, and did not focus on the unique features of individual families. Today, there has been a renewed effort and investment of resources by the Ministry of Labour and Welfare in promoting foster care training through three-month courses which integrate a screening process and a basic training programme for new recruits, through development of programmes for families already functioning as foster families and through programmes for social workers, to train them to be group leaders for these families. To ensure that these programmes are incorporated into an overall programme and do not suffer the fate of earlier endeavours, participation in a recruitment and training course must be made mandatory, as well as a part of social workers' study programmes. Indeed, from 1996, all new foster families will have to participate in such a course before or at the time they take up their positions. In addition, it should be noted that attempts are also being made to encourage researchers to conduct evaluation studies of all stages of the decisionmaking process, and to assist in systematizing the processes and establishing the programmes.

At present, there is no obligation for foster families operating under the auspices of the Ministry of Education to take the course. However, families are being strongly encouraged to participate in continuing education courses, and resources have been allocated to assist them in this.

Major trends

The abiding preoccupation in the field of foster care in Israel is the unending argument over which is preferable – foster care or residential care. The past thirty years have not seen any basic changes in the way the service is supplied by the public sector. Amendments to the foster care system come in waves. These usually begin with advertisements, attempts to strengthen training programmes, improvement in financial conditions, training and appeals, or the beginning of research. These waves are followed by a lull in all the activities until the next wave. It is important to stress that those who promote these renewed activities are always deeply involved with the subject – sometimes practitioners and sometimes policymakers who believe strongly in the issue, who feel a professional obligation or who have a sense of mission. The burnout rate among these protagonists explains the lulls between campaigns.

The majority of professionals (paediatricians, psychiatrists, social workers, psychologists and others) fantasize about the idealized foster family with unique qualities which will be able to stimulate positive changes and encourage development on the part of the child and his or her biological parents. In reality, the picture of the ideal foster family has not been fully defined. It is open to individual interpretation. There is a lack of in-depth, high-quality empirical research examining the stages of foster care which would either support and verify expectations as realistic or refute them. This is also true in the case of the cluster model described above.

Today, we appear to be witnessing the beginning of a professionalization process to revolutionize the system and bring about permanent, positive changes. This process is being spurred on by the combination of four factors which are unlike any which have been at work up until now. The cluster model, which is being used more and more frequently, provides these forces with added impetus.

The first factor results from the system looking to its own best interests, to guarantee that it continues to exist. In the past, if a foster family dropped out, apart from the wasted investment in a training programme (if one existed), there were no other public economic repercussions. In contrast, the cluster model requires a large investment of public funds, for which welfare officials must account. Alongside these policymakers, the professional bureaucrats running the model will see it as in their own best interests for the model to succeed, because their jobs are contingent on its success.

The second factor is found in the area of employment. The cluster model allows more certainty and planning for a longer duration of employment. Employees receive a monthly salary, which includes the usual social benefits.

The third factor is the group of parents which is created in each cluster and which can become a pressure group.

The fourth factor, which is unfortunately the most limited, is the result of 'mass distress'. Breaking up a family care group cluster has repercussions for a large group of children, their families, the foster families and their children.

To sum up, the evolution of welfare provision in Israel from an altruistic to a professional service has generally ignored foster care. The very age of this tradition (going back to biblical times, as noted earlier) may have made it difficult to view it as anything but an altruistic service. This, in turn, may have served as a disincentive to make it a professional service: it was always enough to have good intentions.

Today, there is general consensus that children at risk need, beyond a roof over their heads and a warm home, the parental care of specially trained people. Working with the forces of change described above, foster care in Israel is now being transformed into a profession, and may well be on its way to becoming a realistic career option. Such a process is immensely important, since its success should ensure a constant and consistent supply of carers, ready and able to meet market demands.

Bibliography

Ben-Arie, A. (1993) *Children in Israel: Statistics Yearbook* (in Hebrew), Jerusalem: Joint Distribution Committee.

Benbenisti, R. and Oyserman, D. (1991 'A clinical information system for foster care services in Israel', *Society and Welfare*, Vol. 11, pp.148–55 (in Hebrew).

Central Bureau of Statistics (1994) *Statistical abstracts of Israel*, Jerusalem: Hamakor Press.

Jaffe, E. (1983) *Israelis in Institutions: Studies in Child Placement, Practice and Policy*, New York: Gordon and Breach Science Publishers.

Katz, R., Sharlin, S. and Lavee, Y. (1994) 'Families in distress in Israel: Socio-demographic characteristics and implications for family policy', *Society and Welfare*, Vol. 14, pp.235–48 (in Hebrew).

Laufer, Z. (1979) 'Proposal for recruiting foster families', *Society and Welfare*, Vol. 2, pp.401–6 (in Hebrew).

Laufer, Z. (1990) 'The question of foster care partnership'. In Glook, N. (ed.) *Placement of Children in Family Foster Care*, pp.29–31 (in Hebrew).

Laufer, Z. (1996) 'The family group care "cluster": Hopes and risk', *Community Alternatives*, Vol. 8, pp.43–51.

Morag, T. (1990) 'The need for a foster care law', in Glock, N. (ed.) *Placement of Children in Family Foster Care*, Proceedings of the National Conference on Foster Care, pp.19–23 (in Hebrew).

Perets, Y. and Katz, R. (1981) 'Stability and centrality: The nuclear family in modern Israel', *Social Forces*, Vol. 59, pp.687-704.

Perets, Y. and Katz, R. (1990) 'The family in Israel: Change and continuity', in Bar-Yosef, R. and Shamgar-Handelman, L. (eds) *Families in Israel*, Jerusalem: Akademon (in Hebrew).

Shamgar-Handelman, L. (1986) 'The place of children in household division of labour: Unpaid work in the family setting', *Israel Social Science Research*, Vol. 36, pp.1–66.

Shamgar-Handelman, L. (1990) 'Childhood as a social phenomenon: Israel national report', *Eurosocial*, Vol. 36, pp.1–66.

Sharon, N. (1986) 'A policy analysis of issues in residential care for children and youth in Israel: Past, present, future', *Child and Youth Services*, Vol. 7, pp.111–22.

13 Italy

Tiziano Vecchiato

Jurisdiction

Situated in southern Europe, Italy has a surface area of 301,312 square kilometres. After the Second World War, there was a period of industrial growth during which the Republic was established. This led to the development of state social and health services. However, the economic crisis of recent years has resulted in a restructuring of the welfare system and has stimulated the growth of voluntary services and private initiatives.

As of 1 January 1991, Italy had a population of 57,746,163 of which 12,849,533 were aged 0–18. The distribution within this age group is given in Table 13.1. There are 20,305,000 families in Italy, of which 15,726,000 are couples with children. According to the National Report on Poverty, 1993, presented in July 1994, families in poor living conditions represent 10.7 per cent of all families, corresponding to 6,462,000 persons. There are more than 1 million poor children under 13 years of age: 1 child out of every 7. Their families are considered poor because their consumption per capita is lower

Table 13.1 Age distribution of children and young people, 1 January 1991

Age	Totals
0–4	2,829,355
5–9	3,019,669
10–14	3,535,739
15–18	3,464,790
0–18	12,849,553

Source: Census (1991).

than 50 per cent of the average. On average, a two-person family in Italy could spend 1,110,000 lire ($US694) each month in 1993.

History and origins

In the nineteenth century, before the unification of the small Italian states, vulnerable children were already being fostered out. The Maternity and Child Welfare Organization Act (R.D. 24 December 1934, No. 2,316) provided placements with families not just for vulnerable children, but also for children who could not receive adequate care from their parents because of psychological or material neglect. Also, the Civil Law of 1942 (Articles 403 and 404) provided similar measures: placements in foster care were provided to allow guardianship or in cases where the parents were separated. The law that set up the Juvenile Court (Royal Decree 20 July 1934, No. 1,404) also provided foster care for minors with problematic behaviour and minors placed in the custody of social services.

Moreover, Article 155 of the Civil Law provided foster family care in cases where the parents were separated and it was impossible for one parent to look after the child. Law 898 of 1 January 1970 also provides for foster care placement in cases of divorce and cases where it is impossible for a parent to look after the child. Articles 330 and 333 of the Civil Law provide for foster care placement over extended periods when the relationship between the natural parents and the child is so meaningful that the breaking of family ties is inadvisable even though temporary placement of the child away from home is necessary.

Law 184 of 4 May 1983 on adoption and foster care reinforces this reluctance to break family ties, and regulates foster care with the aims of helping the family regain its functions and promoting the return home of the child. In particular, the law asserts that every child has the right to grow up and be educated in his or her own family (Article 1). Minors who are not living in an adequate family context may be looked after by a substitute family, possibly by a family with children, by a single person (Article 2) or in a family-type community home where the aim is the support and education of the child (Article 2).

Administration and organization

Interventions and services for children and families are the responsibility of the central government. Individual regions have two major tasks: (1) establishing regional laws that serve to implement the national laws; (2) producing regional rules and procedures regarding service functioning, operating standards, allocation of funds, and control of the activities carried out by the various services.

Local authorities and social and health care departments established by the regions directly manage services for children and families through psycho-social and economic assistance and support, or other kinds of interventions. These interventions range from family therapy to home care, and from small community homes to institutional care. Local services and the Ministry of Justice Services for Minors intervene in collaboration when the case concerns the Juvenile Court or the justice system in general. In particular, interventions by local services concern the following:

- social and health factors, including preventive and therapeutic services aimed at the psychological, developmental and social dimensions of health, and diagnostic and rehabilitative services regarding the protection of the health of children and adolescents;
- socio-educational factors, aimed at promoting the health and overall development of children, families and individuals within their own environments;
- social care factors, which contrast with marginalization and poverty, with particular reference to protection, information and sensitization in collaboration with different services, Juvenile Courts and organized volunteers.

Foster family care is provided by local services subject to the consent of the parents or guardians, and also the consent of minors older than 12 years of age, or sometimes even younger. The Juvenile Court magistrate makes a decree whereby the foster care provision may be implemented. The Juvenile Court intervenes in those cases where the parents or the person who has the legal power to look after the child do not consent to foster family care (Law 184, Article 4). A decade of experience following Law 184 led to suggested improvements which are still being considered through the parliamentary process. In particular, such improvements aim to:

- distinguish between short-term foster care, where the family is considered capable of overcoming temporary difficulties, and longer-term or permanent foster care, where it is impossible for the family to overcome the difficulties in the short term, but where conditions are not such as to warrant planning for adoption;
- with respect to short-term foster care, abolish the need for the Juvenile Court magistrate to make a decree in cases where parents have given their consent; instead, a judicial provision would apply only when foster care results from separation or divorce, parents refuse their

consent or request judicial intervention, or there are civil provisions connected with a legal inquiry in which the minor is charged;

- stipulate that magistrates making a judicial decision about foster care, whether short- or long-term, must seek the collaboration of social services;
- specify the foster carer's duties and powers more completely in order to facilitate both the child's first stay in foster care and the relationships between social services and the natural family.

Judicial measures

In general, there are two kinds of foster care In Italy: foster care with the consent of the natural family, and foster care decreed by the Juvenile Court when the natural family is opposed to the foster care placement and does not give its consent.

The authorities will normally aim for foster care with the consent of the family, in order to avoid the conflict and trauma resulting from a forced separation. Foster care placements to which the natural families consent are provided by the local authorities or other bodies (the town council or social and health care department) in accordance with regional laws. After deliberation, the responsible authority decides whether the child should be placed with a family, a single person, or in a community home; it also regulates the length of stay and the amount of money to be given to the carers, and entrusts local services with the task of monitoring the progress of the child and the natural family in collaboration with other services.

A number of tasks must be undertaken before the decision can be made. The consent of the natural family and a commitment from the prospective foster parents must be obtained, and the opinions of the minor must be solicited if he or she is older than 12 years, or younger in some cases. The Juvenile Court magistrate then makes the decision in accordance with the law, ensures that nothing has been neglected, that the laws concerning adoption have not been violated, and that the length of stay in foster care has been determined. The length of stay can be extended through another decision made by the magistrate. He or she must be informed periodically about how the foster care placement is working out.

When the natural family does not give its consent to foster care, the Juvenile Court intervenes and makes its own provision for foster care, after having heard the views of the natural family and the minor. On this basis, the court evaluates the proposal for foster care prepared and submitted by the local authorities, and the town council or the social and health care department is entrusted with the task of finding an appropriate family to foster the child. Such an evaluation determines the length of stay in foster care, and may include other provisions. After identifying and receiving a commitment from the foster parent, the local authority implements the Foster Care Order, fixing the amount of financial support and determining what other services will be provided. Local authorities keep the Juvenile Court informed about the progress of the child in foster care. Usually, local services follow internal rules, derived from regional standards, and prepare a foster care plan, as described below.

The foster care plan

In Italy, the foster care system is very complex, because the national law has been interpreted in a variety of ways by the regions, according to differences in political affiliation and different regulations assigning responsibility for foster care either to town councils or to social and health care departments. Foster parent associations often exercise an important role, and their presence and activities have varying effects upon local authorities.

The directives to town councils and social and health care departments regarding the structure and operation of the foster family care service issued by the Tuscany Region (directive to local authorities and social and health care departments, 25 July 1994, No. 348) represent a current and well-articulated example that has influenced practice in certain regions which have invested many resources in childhood problems and foster care.

Such directives result from a demand for local co-ordination of foster care in terms of the selection of foster families, their training, and the counselling of professionals engaged in the foster care plan. Operationally, the directives include the establishment of a Foster Care Centre (*centro affidi*) which has wider terms of reference than the limited area of responsibility of the town council, and which promotes and manages support activities to local social services. The Foster Care Centre simply co-ordinates existing resources: it ensures that each project is carried out in accordance with the directives and priorities laid down by regional plans and programmes.

The Foster Care Centre has a variety of functions: it finds potential foster families through advertising initiatives, it runs groups to examine problems carefully and sensitize participants to foster care issues, and it promotes positive relationships with volunteer organizations devoted to the protection of minors. Other functions include the evaluation and selection of families, and the investigation of allegations regarding minors who are in difficulty or who are temporarily lacking the family conditions necessary for their growth. These activities take place in collaboration with local services, and the best solution is chosen. Subsequently, two other tasks must be accomplished: the matching between minor and foster carer, and the establishment of a treatment plan on which the foster care contract will be based.

Other functions of the Foster Care Centre include reviews of the treatment plan and planning the stages of reunification, in collaboration with local services. Furthermore, the centre provides advice and support to local services and foster parents' groups. It promotes the application of public and community resources to foster care issues, facilitates the implementation of treatment plans, evaluates the experiences of families and professionals, and collects information in order to develop a database and an information management system at the local and regional level.

Interventions are structured around the main problems that services have to cope with: analysis and evaluation of the requirements of people who wish to become foster carers; providing training and support to foster carers; careful examination of the minor's personality and relations with the natural family; evaluation and matching; formulation of plans and contracts; assessments of the implementation of the plan and the final evaluation, and operating standards and measuring instruments.

The contract with the family is seen as a necessary and positive measure to facilitate collaboration between social services and the family, as it determines the respective commitments and responsibilities of each party. Generally speaking, such contracts must provide for: general and specific goals, to be accomplished by the various parties according to their responsibilities; the planned length of stay; a programme specifying interventions and the people who will receive them; restrictive clauses established between the parties or by the magistrate; the commitments of the natural family; the commitments of the foster family; the commitment of the local authority and services, with special reference to financial aid; the commitment of individual professionals involved in the implementation of the plan, and the methods and timescale of assessments.

Who is placed in foster care?

Foster family care developed as a response to various areas of difficulty. The first area concerns very young children who are placed away from their families because of severe emotional deprivation or as a result of abuse and violence. In these cases, foster family care can be viewed as 'first aid': a means of caring for the child while longer-term solutions are being sought.

More than half of the children placed in foster care, including all types of foster care placements, are aged 6–12 years old. Fifteen per cent are aged from birth to 5 years, and 38 per cent are aged between 13 and 18. Data also show two important aspects: most foster care placements last for more than three years, and there is a low percentage of reunifications. If the 'conclusion' of a foster care placement is categorized as reunification or its failure, less than half of the foster care placements in which there is a known conclusion end with reunification with the natural family.

New areas of concern are developing: for example, disabled minors. Foster families are given specific training to help them cope with the problems of these children, and are supported by foster parent associations in accordance with the self-help model. Another area of concern is children with severe diseases, such as AIDS, but a major current development is foster care for pre-adolescents and adolescents with disturbed behaviour and psychological and emotional problems. In such cases, a range of community-based services has been developed in addition to foster family care. Minors who are in foster care or community homes as a result of delinquent behaviour are often subject to orders from the Juvenile Court. In addition, the high influx of migrant families from outside the European Union is placing greater emphasis on the problems of intervention with the abandoned children of migrants. When it is impossible to find a foster family of the same ethnic origin, the foster family is required to have a good knowledge of the child's culture and ethnic background.

Foster family care can be implemented in several ways: it can be used for part of the day or week, when parents cannot guarantee that they will always be able to be with their children, or it can be used for a short or long pre-determined period, when parents have to leave home, for example to go into hospital. In these cases, the children are looked after by families whom they already know. The most common situation in which long-term foster care is provided is when the natural family is facing serious problems and a speedy return home for the child will not be possible. In such cases, local community services provide ongoing support to the natural family to prepare the ground for successful reunification; however, because problems often persist, foster care can be long-term, sometimes continuing until the child is 18 years of age.

Care providers

Foster care services may be provided by organizations dealing specifically with foster care: such organizations mostly exist only in large urban areas. Alternatively, in smaller centres, services may be provided by generalist organizations, where staff, or sometimes only a single social worker, deal with all manner of situations, including foster care.

On a national level, there are few data regarding foster care. One source of data is a survey on foster family care in Italy, 1988–89, carried out by an inter-regional technical work group for minors: a consultative and supportive body which facilitates co-ordination between social services councillors. A report presented at the Committee for Justice of the Chamber of Deputies (1992) shows the number of foster care placements to be 8,762. The data show a cultural and social change, in which the trend is for families to become more involved in social solidarity and social policy at the local level. With respect to geographical distribution, it may be noted that in the north of Italy, 55 per cent of children are placed in foster care, whereas in the south, 26 per cent are placed in foster care.

With respect to different types of foster care placement, placements with relatives (43.7 per cent) are more common than placement with non-relatives (34.4 per cent) or placement in community homes (15.5 per cent). However, there is a geographical difference: foster care with non-relatives or in community homes is predominant in the north of Italy, while in central and southern Italy, placement with relatives predominates.

Financial support

The national law does not define conditions and modes of payment for the economic support of foster families. Regional laws cover this area, and also regulate different forms of third-party insurance in favour of foster parents. In addition, the magistrate can order some allowances and other economic contributions to be paid to the foster parents on a temporary basis, depending on the length of the child's stay (Article 80, Law 184). If the foster parents work, one parent may take a leave of absence from work for the first three months after the child has come into the family, provided that the child is less than 6 years old: the parent will be compensated for this leave of absence. As is the case with natural children, the foster parent may also stay away from work when the foster child is ill, provided that the child is less than 3 years old, on production of a doctor's certificate. In the case of long-term foster care, the minor needs to be registered as a member of the foster parents' family.

In 1994, financial aid ranged from a minimum of 500,000 lire (about $US315) per month to a maximum of 750,000 lire (about $US470) in the case of foster carers who were not related to the child, while in the case of relatives, the level of financial aid was lower. In some cases, additional support may be given to cover special expenses: for example, health care costs which the family could not afford itself.

Major problems

During the last decade, interest in foster care in Italy has become more widespread and more consolidated, partly due to systematic sensitization activities undertaken by associations involved in foster care. These associations often work from a Christian value base, and in the next few years, there will be major developments in foster care within this area of social commitment.

Under the influence of these groups, local authorities have organized to deal systematically and coherently with minors' needs. Problems are related to a need for more flexibility, a need for social service interventions to become more child-focused, and a need to involve the foster family in the intervention plan in a more systematic way and with reference to different types of problems. The main failing, still characterizing several interventions, concerns reunification with the natural family and inadequate support to the child and parents during the first stage of reunification. Lack of investment in this phase often leads to failures and new separations.

The literature and methodological considerations seem to concentrate on those cases in which it is appropriate to place the minor away from the natural family: to look at ways in which to receive the minor into another family or an adequate residential home. There is no systematic body of work on methodologies appropriate for managing the stages of removal, reunification and facilitating the return home.

This implies that reunifications are often managed in a fragmentary and intuitive way, and consequently run a high risk of failure. Often, the return home is seen as a goal rather than as a motivation for a concrete work programme whose timescale and outcomes can be evaluated. This is due in part to the fact that current legislation provides a commitment to successful reunification in principle, but neither the regions nor the local authorities have provided adequate resources to implement reunification in reality.

In some contexts, the return home is not seen as a new stage requiring support activity, but as an obligation imposed by the judicial authority through the revocation of previous measures; such conditions make it difficult for professionals to provide support, accepting that reunification may break down or that their reunification plan may not work. Sometimes, this situation leads to a decrease in activities related to reunification, because organizations are aware of the difficulties that lie ahead: professionals receive little training in this area, there are too few support groups for foster families undergoing reunification, and there is an inability to help the natural family face and overcome its problems. Researchers and professionals are trying to clarify the meaning of the 'family-type community home', which the law suggests is a type of foster care different from foster family placements.

In particular, even if there is no national law on social services, the regions should define precisely how to regulate foster care on the basis of different possible scenarios: pre-adoption foster care, removal without reunification, temporary foster care, self-help support to the minor, and volunteering organized by groups of families.

A further problem area, for which services are still unprepared, is the increasing rate of separations and divorces, which often place parents in conflict and have an adverse effect on children. Professionals are required to mediate such conflicts, and if necessary, to manage the separation of the child from one of the parents while maintaining links with both of them. In some respects, this is a new mode of foster care, similar to traditional foster care in its psycho-social impact and its emotional and interpersonal relapses. A child with separated parents has two families which are incompatible and do not allow the child to 'return home', as might be the case if the child's two families were the foster family and the natural family.

Major trends

This section concentrates on foster care issues on the local and regional levels. In the region of Tuscany, a significant period in the development of foster care occurred around the end of the 1960s and the beginning of the 1970s. The law on special adoption (5 June 1967, no. 431), the debate on total institutions, and the beginning of the experience of social and health *consorzi* (linked groups of institutions) accelerated the search for alternative solutions to complement the traditional solutions of adoption, small community homes and foster family care.

Consider the province of Florence as an example: in 1968, there were 67 institutions housing 5,490 children: by 1973, this number had fallen to 49, housing 1,392 children. In 1993, the whole region contained 88 community homes, with 672 children, an average of 7.6 children per home, with an age distribution as shown in Table 13.2.

Table 13.2   Age distribution in community homes in the province of Florence, 1993

Age	No.	%
0–1	19	2.83
1–5	51	2.59
6–11	128	19.05
12–14	117	17.41
15–18	221	32.89
18+	129	19.19
not known	7	1.04
Total	672	

Table 13.3 indicates which organizations sent the minors to the community homes.

Table 13.3   Identity of organizations which sent minors to community homes, 1993

Organization	No.	%
Local social services	289	43.01
Local social services following judicial instructions	193	28.72
Ministry of Justice Services for Minors	41	6.10
Family	86	12.80
Private institutions	32	4.76
Local social services in collaboration with the Ministry of Justice Services for Minors	6	0.89
Unknown	25	3.72
Total	672	

The main reasons for foster family care are: loss of a parent (through death, imprisonment or other causes); and incapacity of one of the parents, or both, in facing material and emotional problems because of alcoholism, mental illness, an irregular lifestyle, drug addiction, separation, family disintegration or abuse. About two-thirds of foster care placements are made with the parents' consent.

Torino, the regional seat of government of Piemonte, represents a reference model for many other Italian towns. In 1976 and thereafter, the town council enacted several measures which systematically regulated foster care by defining tasks and responsibilities related to the promotion of foster care, the selection and training of families, support during the care episode, and the recovery of the natural family. Furthermore, in 1976, financial support for the foster family was provided at a level of 150,000 lire (about $US93) per month.

Several other measures followed with respect to children being fostered by relatives (1980) and the provision of additional financial support for foster carers looking after totally disabled children (1985). In 1986, another provision addressed the issue of daytime service, setting a level of financial support for foster carers equal to 70 per cent of the rate provided for residential foster care. In 1990, the possibility of foster care in a community home was extended to those who, having reached the age of 18, could not return to their families. In 1990, financial support for a foster family was about 640,000 lire ($US400) per month.

From 1976 to 1993, 2,732 foster care placements were made in Torino: 1,937 with non-relatives and 795 with relatives. In relation to future planning, Torino arranged a fostering project for 1995 with the aim of giving priority to the development of daytime foster and residential care which would have the consent of the parents. There are a number of reasons for providing such care: to provide help to natural families; to sensitize the whole population with regard to foster care issues; to find new foster carers; to educate people so that they understand the problems faced by families and children in trouble; to guarantee a homogeneous and appropriate evaluation of people available to take minors in care; to guarantee an information or training course to all families or single people interested in foster family care; to guarantee uniformity in the selection of foster carers and to provide an opportunity to all interested persons to be considered for selection; to guarantee support groups for foster families; to prepare new rules for social care services; to train professionals, either by encouraging them to reflect upon their work or by bringing in experts; to guarantee family-based interventions for young children or minors who experience long stays in hospital or in residential care, and to gather data in a more systematic way on children who have been removed from their families, on the identification of minors in need of care, and on the utilization of resources by the different social services operating in the area.

Similar ways of operating exist in seven social and health care departments of the region of Umbria (in central Italy), which agreed to the so-called *Progetto Affidi* ('Foster Project') of the Province of Perugia. This project provides the framework for a multi-disciplinary group whose aims are: to collaborate with different professionals over the preparation of a foster care programme; to identify institutions and organizations in the area which might wish to become involved; to inform them and sensitize them to issues; eventually, to organize meetings with volunteers and the office for the protection of minors; to urge the necessity of de-institutionalizing all minors presently living in residential care, while collaborating with various services to change existing structures; to support professionals during the evaluation of cases; to establish contacts both with the group that evaluates families and the data bank through which matches between families and minors are made; to support services through the different stages of matching; to evaluate the development and implementation of foster care and the development of programmes based on the natural family, and to evaluate the termination process of foster care and the reunification programme.

Even in the absence of a homogeneous national context, some data may be presented for various regions: three in the north of Italy (Lombardia, Veneto and Piemonte) and one in the south (Puglia). Tables 13.4 and 13.5 present these data for the north and south respectively.

In the south of Italy, the situation is more complex. In the province of Napoli, the first foster family care experiences go back to the beginning of 1980, coinciding with the development of a cultural sensitivity that led to the approval of Law 184. However, it is necessary to consider the distinctive

Table 13.4   Data for Veneto, Lombardi and Piemonte

Regions (up to 31/12/93)	Foster care to non-relatives	Foster care to relatives	No. of institutions	Minors in institutions	No. of community homes	Minors in community homes
Veneto	422	409	27	698	110	559
Lombardia	900	1,100	68	1,014	153	1,158
Piemonte	499*	553*	68	701	82	402

* This data applies up to 31/12/92.

Table 13.5   Data for Puglia

Puglia	Foster care placements by mutual consent	Foster care placements by judicial order	Total
1988	12	40	52
1989	16	102	118
1990	27+1*	117	144+1*
1991	38+10*	178+48*	216+58*

* This data pertains to minors from Albania.
Source: Latorre (1994).

173

features of the region (Campania), where a community-type model similar to foster family care has been facilitated by the high number of very large families among the population. In these families, it is usual to leave the child to be brought up by relatives or a family friend, while still maintaining links with the natural parents.

At present, the region is preparing new rules for the foster family care service. It will provide for the development of a foster care service at community and provincial levels, run by one or more social workers, a psychologist and/or a child psychiatrist. Such a service should promote foster care, find and train foster parents, set a level of financial support for foster carers, and above all, prepare a social and educational plan for each case.

However, it is important to note that over the whole region, the situation is diverse, and many towns still ignore the existence of 'alternatives' to institutionalizing minors. Generally, in the south of Italy, foster family care is more difficult to develop for a variety of reasons. First, natural families mistrust foster family care and view it as stigmatizing, in that it demonstrates their inadequacy as caregivers. For this reason, natural families prefer to place children in an institution. In addition, local governments appear to have a chronic inability to develop the kinds of social services which exist in the large towns and provincial seats. A further reason can be found in the greater social similarities between foster and natural families in the north of Italy: this means that socio-economic changes for the fostered minor will be smaller. If this were not the case, natural parents might be afraid that their child would grow to prefer the more comfortable conditions of the foster family's life.

Other difficulties lie in the fact that it is very hard to promote acceptance of foster care among the general population, and there is a scarcity of foster carers, except for those groups of families which are very committed to social solidarity, based on Catholicism.

Role of national foster care associations

National Association of Adoptive and Foster Families (ANFAA–Associazione Italiana Famiglie Adottive e Affidatarie)

ANFAA was started in 1962. Its membership includes all Italian adoptive and foster parents who wish to join. It promotes the development of foster care, trains families, and is active in the whole arena of provision for minors. It is based in Turin but is influential throughout the whole of Italy.

Papa Giovanni XXIII Association

The Association is based in Rimini. It runs community homes for minors and for physically disabled adults. It also co-ordinates groups of families who are available to foster.

Association for the Promotion of Minors' Right to a Family

This organization co-ordinates the activities of more than forty Italian associations (including the two noted above) which deal with foster care adoption and the protection of children. It is based in Lucca at the National Centre for Voluntary Organizations.

Contacts: ANFAA, Via Artisti 36, 10124 Torino, Italy *Telephone*: (+39) 11-8122327 *Fax*: (+39) 11-8122595. Association Papa Giovanni XXII, Viale Tiberio 6, 47037 Rimini Forlì, Italy *Telephone*: (+39) 541-55025. Association for the Promotion of Minors' Right to a Family, c/o Centro Nazionale per il Volontariato, Via Catalina 158, 55100 Lucca, Italy *Telephone*: (+39) 583-419500 *Fax*: (+39) 583-419501.

Bibliography

AAVV (1985) *Dal ricovero all'affidamento: cambia una legge o una mentalità*, Padua: Fondazione E. Zancan.

AAVV (1987) *L'adozione e l'affidamento: problemi e prospettive*, Rome: AAI.

AAVV (1993) 'L'affido a dieci anni dalla legge 184', in *Famiglia Oggi*, n. 3/93, Milan.

AAVV (1994) 'L'affidamento familiare nella legge e nella prassi', in *Minori giustizia*, n. 1/94, Milan: Angeli.

Amione, F. (1990), *Gli affidamenti familiari a Torino. Catamnesi sulla esperienza di un decennio*, City of Turin Torino.

Busnelli, E. and Vecchiato, T., (eds) (1986) 'Bisogni e risposte per l'età evolutiva', *Servizi sociali*, n. 4/86, Padua: Fondazione E. Zancan.

Busnelli, E. and Vecchiato, T. (1991) *La promozione del benessere psicofisico in età evolutiva*, Rome: Ministry of Health Central Studies.

Carugati, F., Emiliani, F. and Palmonari, A. (1975) *Il possibile esperimento*, Rome: AAI.

Cirillo, S. (1986) *Famiglie in crisi e affido familiare*, Rome: La Nuova Italia.

Dell'Antonio, A. (1992) *Avere due famiglie*, Milan: Unicopli.

De Rienzo, E., Saccoccio, C. and Tonizzo, F. (1994) *Una famiglia in più. Esperienze di affidamento*, Turin: UTET.

Iafrate, R. (1989) 'L'affido familiare come intreccio di rappresentazioni', in *Il Bambino incompiuto*, n. 3/89, Milan: Unicopli.

Ichino Pellizzi, F. (ed.) (1983) *L'affido familiare*, Milan: Angeli.

Latorre, C.M. et al. (1994) 'Indagine sull'applicazione della legge 4/5/1983 n. 184 in provincia di Bari', *Il Bambino incompiuto*, n. 1, Milan: Unicopli.

Macario, G. (ed.) (1992) *Comunità per minori e progetto educativo*, Florence: Region of Tuscany.

Maurizio, R. and Peirone, M. (1984) *Minori, comunità e dintorni*, Turin: EGA.
Ministry of the Interior (1980) *Adozione, affidamento familiare, comunità alloggio*, Rome: DGSC.
Moro, A.C. (1991) *Il bambino è un cittadino*, Milan: Mursia.
Palmonari. A. (ed.) (1991) *Comunità di convivenza e crescita della persona*, Bologna: Patron.
Province of Perugia (1993) *Minori in difficoltà e affido familiare*, Perugia.
Region of Tuscany (1989) *Le comunità di tipo familiare per l'accoglimento dei minori*, Florence: Regional Council of Tuscany.
Vecchiato, T. (1986) 'La comunità alloggio: un modello polivalente di intervento sociale', in *Il Bambino incompiuto*, n. 3/86, Milan: Unicopli.
Vecchiato, T. (1993) '*Culture di* servizio per l'età evolutiva: esperienze residenziali, comunitarie e di accoglienza familiare', in *Il Bambino incompiuto*, n. 2/93, Milan: Unicopli.
Vernò, F. (ed.) (1989) *Minori: un impegno per la comunità locale*, Padua: Fondazione E. Zancan.

14 Japan

Sadao Atsumi

History and origins

The history of foster care in Japan can be traced back to the eleventh century. At this time, it was common for the Royal Family and aristocrats to entrust their children to their acquaintances to be nursed and brought up. Later, this custom spread to the common people.

It was in 1907 that foster family care began to be promoted as a system. The movement was started chiefly by religious leaders and volunteers, who advocated that foster family care was better than collective care.

The foster parent system under the Child Welfare Law (1948)

When the Second World War ended in 1945, there were a large number of orphans and children in need of protection. However, most of the institutions and homes to take care of them had been reduced to ashes. It was extremely difficult to reconstruct families and to meet the immediate requirements of children.

It is desirable that children in need of protection be brought up in a family atmosphere. This was the prevailing opinion when the Child Welfare Law was enacted in 1948, and thus the foster parent system came into existence as a public system. This system was expected to play an important role in the promotion of child welfare services, together with institutional care.

On 4 October 1948, the Vice-Minister of Health and Welfare made an announcement regarding foster care, in which he clarified the contents of the foster care system. In commemoration of the Vice-Minister's announcement, October has been designated 'Foster Parent Month', and 4 October 'Foster Parent Day'. Ever since the announcement, a nationwide campaign supporting the foster parent system has been conducted in October every year.

The precepts of the Child Welfare Law are :

1 'Foster parents mean such persons as have been deemed competent by the Governor of the Prefecture and who wish to bring up a child who has no guardian or whose supervision by his guardian is deemed inadequate.'
2 A foster parent in whose care a child is placed by the governor of the prefecture must bring up the child according to the law. On the other hand, 'expenses required for delegation of custody shall be disbursed by Prefectures', and 'the National Treasury shall bear half of the expenses disbursed by local public bodies'. In addition, the governors of the prefecture disburse foster parent allowance.

Major trends

Table 14.1 shows the change in the number of foster parents and the number of children placed per year since 1949. The trend towards a lower number of foster children is mainly due to the fact that the number of orphans and children who need such care has decreased. Additional reasons stem from the concentration of the Japanese population in urban centres, and changes in the family structure, housing situation and lifestyle. At the same time, changes in people's way of thinking and the contemporary orientation towards a nuclear family lifestyle have also had an effect.

Table 14.1   Change in the number of foster parents and the number of children placed per year, 1949–94

	Registered foster parents (A)	Actual foster parents (B)	No. of children placed	Ratio (B)/(A) %
October 1949	4,153	2,909	3,278	70.1
December 1955	16,200	8,282	9,111	51.1
December 1960	19,022	7,751	8,737	40.7
December 1965	18,230	6,090	6,909	33.4
December 1970	13,621	3,705	4,729	27.9
December 1975	10,230	3,225	3,851	31.5
December 1980	8,933	2,646	3,188	29.6
December 1985	8,659	2,627	3,322	30.3
December 1990	7,841	2,472	2,669	31.5
September 1994	8,176	2,179	2,624	26.7

Improvement in government payments

When the foster care system came into being in 1948, the households to which foster children were entrusted were provided with the foster parent allowance and expenses necessary for child rearing.

In step with the advance in the government's social welfare programmes, various improvements have been introduced to promote the foster parent system. Foster parents are now supplied with money for living and school expenses and those expenses related to helping foster children find employment. The amount of support has been increased on an annual basis.

Since 1973, expenses for foster children entering senior high school have been covered. Moreover, living expenses are also provided for high school students aged over 18. Since 1979, expenses for holding special events during the summer or on some other occasion have also been disbursed.

The foster parent allowance, which had been 500 yen ($US4.5) per child per month was raised to 1,000 yen ($US9) in 1972, 4,000 yen ($US36) in 1975, 8,000 yen ($US72) in 1980 and 20,000 yen ($US182) in 1993. Table 14.2 shows the government payments for foster care per child in 1993.

Other trends are:

- Revision of the Income Tax Law – in 1967, with the partial revision of the Income Tax Law, children who were placed in foster care became dependent family members, as stipulated in the law, and foster parent families became entitled to the corresponding concessions with respect to Income Tax.
- Subsidy to National Foster Parent Association – since 1973, an annual subsidy from the national budget has been granted to the National Foster Parent Association for the development of the foster care system.
- Beginning of the short-term foster parent system – the number of children who are temporarily in need of care because of disaster or the illness of their parents is growing. In order to meet increased demands for short-term child care, a temporary fostering system was set up in 1974.

Revision of the foster care system

In order to take into consideration changes in social conditions in Japan, the revision of the civil law, and so on, the foster care system was revised on 1 January 1988.

The aim of the revision was the further development of the foster care system for children in need. The revised foster care system emphasizes that

Table 14.2   Government payments for foster care per child, fiscal year 1993

Allowance	Frequency of payment	Amount (yen)
Cost of living	Monthly	
General (6–18)		45,350
Infants (0–5)		45,720
School expenses	Monthly	
Primary school		1,970
Junior high		3,890
School trips	Annually	
6th year (primary)		17,200
3rd year (junior)		47,000
Expenditure at school entry	Annually	
Primary		36,900
Junior high		42,800
Year-end allowance		4,850
Expenditure at job entry		42,000
Funeral expenses		106,500
Medical expenses		Full amount
School lunches		Full amount
Heating costs (winter)	Monthly	1,200–6,480
Vocational training		Full amount
Special upbringing allowance (expenses for high school)	Monthly	
Public school		20,740
Private school		30,690
At school entry		47,600

Expenses of summer events/special occasions		3,000
Preparation costs when placed in care		31,500
Foster parent allowance	Monthly	20,000

foster parents should be recruited from among ordinary people, and trained to become excellent foster parents.

The major points in the revision are as follows:

1 Utilization of private organizations – private organizations such as the National Foster Parent Association, persons recognized by law in relation to social welfare, and other non-profit organizations are to be utilized for the promotion, publicity and guidance of the foster care system.
2 Revision of the investigation of foster parent applicants – the number of factors to be considered in the investigation has been reduced. For example, such considerations as religion, social standing, general reputation in the local community, distance from a school and conditions in the school have been deleted.
3 Revision of the standards for the approval of foster parents – unnecessary conditions were deleted, for example:

   – that mothers fostering infants should have breastfed children;
   – that foster parents should not have children of their own who are the same age as the foster children.

4 Approval of one-parent families – single parents may be approved as foster parents, provided they are qualified to care for and bring up children.
5 Re-appraisal of foster parents – once registered, a re-appraisal of foster parents is to be conducted at intervals of five years, or more frequently.
6 Expansion of the type of foster children referred – children who are physically disturbed, disabled or mentally retarded are to be assigned to qualified foster parents with the requisite knowledge and experience.
7 Approval of dual placement – dual placement in foster care and a day care institution is approved in the case of children who need to commute to the institution to receive training and guidance.
8 Training for foster parents – training and workshops for foster parents are to be financed by the national government.

Who is placed in foster care?

The following data are taken from a survey conducted by the Children and Families Bureau, Ministry of Health and Welfare (1995). The survey is dated 1 December 1992, and the data were collected by the Children and Families Bureau in co-operation with the Minister's Secretariat, Statistics and Information Department.

The purpose of the survey was to obtain basic data to promote the welfare of children in need of protection through an understanding of (1) the characteristics and condition of children placed with foster parents mainly because of an inadequate home environment, and (2) the characteristics and condition of their foster parents in accordance with the provisions of the Child Welfare Law. The findings of the survey are given below.

Characteristics of foster children

Age of foster children

Table 14.3 shows the age distribution of foster children as of 1 December 1992. The total number of children in Tables 14.3–14.7 was 2,678, a decrease compared to the 3,284 reported in the previous survey of 1 October 1987. The average age of foster children was 9.6 years, a small decrease over the previous figure of 9.7.

Ages of children at placement

Table 14.4 shows that the largest number of children were placed at the age of 2, and 74.6 per cent were placed with foster parents when they were aged 6 or less, compared to 71.4 per cent in the 1987 survey.

Placement period of foster children

The placement period was most commonly less than one year. The average placement period was 5.2 years, marginally longer than that reported in the 1987 survey (5.1 years). Table 14.5 shows the number of foster children by placement period.

Placement routes of foster children

Major placement routes for foster children were: from their natural parents, 26.4 per cent (31.7 per cent in the 1987 survey); from an infant home, 38.3 per cent (32.5 per cent in the previous survey), and from a children's home, 26.4

Table 14.3   Age distribution of foster children, 1 December 1992

Age	No. of foster children	%
0	57	2.1
1	119	4.4
2	174	6.5
3	185	6.9
4	165	6.2
5	145	5.4
6	118	4.4
7	131	4.9
8	123	4.6
9	134	5.0
10	156	5.8
11	139	5.2
12	177	6.6
13	148	5.5
14	159	5.9
15	176	6.6
16	134	5.0
17	142	5.3
18+	95	3.5
Boys	1,418	52.9
Girls	1,260	47.1

per cent (26.0 per cent in the 1987 survey). Table 14.6 shows the number of foster children by placement route.

School grade of foster children

In the 1992 sample, 34.4 per cent of the foster children were in preschool (31.9 per cent in the 1987 survey). Table 14.7 shows the number of foster children by school grade.

Physical condition of foster children

Table 14.8 shows the number of foster children with physical impairments.

Table 14.4   **Age of children at placement, 1 December 1992**

Age	No. of foster children	%
0	295	11.0
1	347	13.0
2	583	21.8
3	389	14.5
4	227	8.5
5	156	5.8
6	177	6.6
7	88	3.3
8	88	3.3
9	69	2.6
10	49	1.8
11	41	1.5
12	47	1.8
13	28	1.0
14	30	1.1
15	30	1.1
16	16	0.6
17	15	0.6

Table 14.5   **Number of foster children by placement period,
1 December 1992**

Period	No. of foster children	%
Less than 1 year	545	20.4
1–2 years	334	12.5
2–3 years	240	9.0
3–4 years	179	6.7
4–5 years	174	6.5
5–6 years	154	5.8
6–7 years	146	5.5
7–8 years	171	6.4
8–9 years	151	5.6
9–10 years	131	4.9
10–11 years	104	3.9
11–12 years	106	4.0
12 years +	241	9.0

Table 14.6   Number of foster children by placement route,
1 December 1992

Route	No. of foster children	Percentage
From natural parents	706	26.4
From infant home	1,027	38.3
From children's home	708	26.4
From another institution	44	1.6
From another foster home	86	3.2
Other	107	4.0

Table 14.7   Number of foster children by school grade, 1 December 1992

Grade	No. of foster children	%
Preschool	920	34.4
1st–3rd grade primary school	396	14.8
4th–6th grade primary school	448	16.7
Lower secondary school	492	18.4
Upper secondary school		
Public	267	10.0
Private	104	3.9
Other	51	1.9

Health of foster children

At the time the 1992 survey was conducted, 11.9 per cent of foster children were found to be in a 'sickly condition', compared to 12.2 per cent in the 1987 survey. Table 14.9 shows the number of foster children with various ailments.

Areas demanding foster parents' attention

A majority of foster parents (58.4 per cent) said that it was necessary for them to pay particular attention to certain aspects of the foster child's development. Table 14.10 shows the areas involved.

Table 14.8   Physical impairments of foster children, 1 December 1992

Type of impairment	No. of foster children	%
Weak constitution	32	1.2
Crippled	17	0.6
Sight & auditory impairments	26	1.0
Speech impairments	11	0.4
Weak-minded	36	1.3
Epilepsy	8	0.3
Other	43	1.6
Total with impairments	162	6.0

Table 14.9   Foster children in a 'sickly condition', 1 December 1992

Type of ailment	No. of foster children	%
Cramp	15	0.6
Diarrhoea	14	0.5
Feverish	36	1.3
Colds	122	4.6
Other	198	7.4
Total with ailments	318	11.9

Study, art and sports

The 1992 survey paid particular attention to foster children's activities in the areas of study, arts and sports. Table 14.11 shows the proportion of foster children who received guidance with respect to study at home, and who participated in art and sport at home and school respectively.

School attainment

The level of attainment at school achieved by the majority of foster children (73.9 per cent) was 'average'. Table 14.12 presents findings in this area in more detail.

Table 14.10   Focus of foster parents' attention, 1 December 1992

Focus of attention	No. of foster children	%
Child's peace of mind	518	19.3
Relationships with friends	316	11.8
Relationships with families	201	7.5
Interest in study	390	14.6
Discipline	583	21.8
Social awareness	180	6.7
Total requiring special attention	1,564	58.4

Table 14.11   Foster children's activities, 1 December 1992

Activity	No. of foster children	%
Home		
Study	527	19.7
Art	453	16.9
Sport	391	14.6
School		
Art	263	15.4
Sport	648	38.0

Table 14.12   Foster children's attainments in schoolwork, 1 December 1992

Level	No. of foster children	%
Excellent	154	9.0
Average	1,261	73.9
Below average	281	16.5
Unknown	11	0.6

The natural home environment of children in placement

The 1992 survey examined factors relating to the natural homes of children in placement. Such factors included: reasons for coming into care; the status of the children's natural parents; the proportion of children with natural and step-parents; the guardians or protectors of children whose natural parents were dead or missing; the children's relationships with their natural families, and the future prospects of foster children with regard to reunification or a different placement. Tables 14.13–14.18 present the survey's findings in these areas.

Reasons for protective care

The major reasons for children coming into care were found to be: refusal of voluntary care by parents, 21.2 per cent; missing parents, 17.5 per cent; divorce of parents, 9 per cent, and the status of the child as a 'foundling', 7.8 per cent. Table 14.13 presents the reasons for protective care in further detail.

Table 14.13   Reasons for protective care, 1 December 1992

Reason	No. of foster children	%
Death of father or mother	123	4.6
Missing father or mother	468	17.5
Divorce	241	9.0
Parental discord	39	1.5
Incarceration of parent	57	2.1
Hospitalization of parent	156	5.8
Working parents	143	5.3
Mental disorder of parent	140	5.2
Neglect	120	4.5
Abuse or overwork	50	1.9
Foundling	210	7.8
Parent refused voluntary care	568	21.2
Financial reasons	81	3.0
Too many other children	34	1.3
Other	248	9.3

Natural parents of children in placement

As Table 14.14 shows, the proportion of foster children with one or both of their natural parents still alive when placed in foster care was 69.8 per cent, a smaller proportion than children placed in institutions. As Table 14.15 shows, of those 1,869 foster children with one or both parents still alive, the majority (54.6 per cent) had only their natural mother.

Table 14.14 Natural parents of foster children, 1 December 1992

Parental status	No. of foster children	%
Alive	1,869	69.8
Dead	462	17.3
Missing	344	12.8
Unknown	3	0.1

Table 14.15 Identity of foster children's natural parents, 1 December 1992

Parent(s)	No. of foster children	%
Natural father	354	18.9
Natural mother	1,021	54.6
Father and stepmother	34	1.8
Mother and stepfather	59	3.2
Step-parents	7	0.4
Stepfather	10	0.5
Stepmother	9	0.5
Unknown	1	0.1
Total	1,869	

Protectors of foster children with parents dead or missing

As Table 14.16 shows, the most common carers for the 806 foster children whose natural parents were dead or missing were grandparents.

Relationships of foster children with their natural families

As Table 14.17 indicates, 84.4 per cent of all 2,678 foster children were out of touch with their natural families. This finding illustrates the difficulties presented in trying to place children back home.

**Table 14.16   Those caring for foster children with no parents,
1 December 1992**

Carer(s)	No. of foster children	%
Natural grandparents	179	22.2
Step grandparents	3	0.4
Brothers or sisters	15	1.9
Brothers or sisters-in-law	2	0.2
Uncle and aunt	44	5.5
Uncle and aunt-in-law	7	0.9
Foster parents	20	2.5
Others	229	28.4
No one	148	18.4
Not clear	153	19.0
Unknown	6	0.7
Total	806	

**Table 14.17   Relationships of foster children with their natural families,
1 December 1992**

Degree of contact	No. of foster children	%
In touch		
Temporary return	120	4.5
Meeting	129	4.8
Phone or letter	155	5.8
Out of touch	2,261	84.4
Unknown	13	0.5

Future prospects of foster children

Table 14.18 presents the likely future placements of the 2,678 foster children surveyed in 1992.

Table 14.18 Prospects of foster children, 1 December 1992

Prospects	No. of foster children	%
Return to carers	125	4.7
Return to other relatives	4	0.1
Remain with foster parents	1,474	55.0
Adoption by foster parents	947	35.4
Other	128	4.7

Care providers

The 1992 survey examined foster parents and their situation with respect to the following factors: the reason for wishing to foster; the number of years for which foster parents had been registered; the number of foster children per foster home; the age of the foster parents; their occupation; their annual income, and the type of house they lived in. Tables 14.19–14.24 present these findings in more detail.

As of 1 December 1992, the total number of foster homes in Japan was 2,194, a decrease of 448 households (17 per cent) over the 2,642 households reported in the 1987 survey.

Reasons for wishing to foster

As Table 14.19 shows, the most prevalent reason for wishing to foster was the desire to bring up a child (33.5 per cent, compared to 32.5 per cent in the 1987 survey). The reason next most frequently expressed was the desire to adopt a child (31.9 per cent, compared to 31.6 per cent in the 1987 survey).

Registration period

As Table 14.20 shows, 39.8 per cent of foster homes had been registered for less than five years, compared to 40.4 per cent in the 1987 survey. However, 14.2 per cent of foster homes had been registered for over 15 years, compared to 10.6 per cent in the 1987 survey.

Table 14.19   Reasons for wishing to foster, 1 December 1992

Reason	No. of foster homes	%
Interested in child welfare	438	20.0
Sympathy towards children	273	12.4
Desire to bring up a child	735	33.5
Desire to adopt a child	699	31.9
Other	49	2.2

Table 14.20   Registration period of foster home, 1 December 1992

Period	No. of foster homes	%
Less than 5 years	873	39.8
5–9 years	559	25.5
10–14 years	446	20.3
15 years +	312	14.2
Unknown	4	0.2

Number of foster children per foster home

As Table 14.21 shows, the majority of foster homes cared for one child (61.0 per cent, compared to 79.3 per cent in the 1987 survey). Homes with two foster children accounted for 32.2 per cent, compared to 15.6 per cent in the 1987 survey.

Table 14.21   Number of foster children per home, 1 December 1992

No. of children	No. of foster homes	%
1 child	1,338	61.0
2 children	510	23.2
3 children	201	9.2
4 children +	142	6.5
Unknown	3	0.1

Age of foster parents

As Table 14.22 shows, the largest age group for foster parents was 40–49 years old: 44.3 per cent of all foster fathers surveyed fell into this category (compared to 40.4 per cent in the 1987 survey), as did 46.3 per cent of foster mothers (compared to 40.6 in the 1987 survey). There was also an increase in the proportion of foster parents in their fifties (31.4 per cent, compared to 30.1 per cent for foster fathers, and 26.3 per cent, compared to 24.0 per cent for foster mothers in the 1987 survey), but a decrease in the proportion of foster parents in their thirties (10.8 per cent, compared to 16.9 per cent for foster fathers, and 18.7 per cent, compared to 27.0 per cent for mothers in the 1987 survey). In other words, the data suggest a trend for foster parents to belong to the older age groups.

Table 14.22   Age of foster parents, 1 December 1992

Age groups	Foster fathers No.	%	Foster mothers No.	%
Less than 30	2	0.1	13	0.6
30–39	236	10.8	410	18.7
40–49	972	44.3	1016	46.3
50–59	689	31.4	576	26.3
60 +	233	10.6	158	7.2
Unknown	62	2.8	21	0.9
Total	2,194		2,194	

Occupation of foster parents

As Table 14.23 shows, the largest category in terms of occupation of foster parents was 'technician' (20.5 per cent), followed by 'office work' and 'administrative work' (12.1 per cent and 10.6 per cent respectively).

Annual income of foster homes

Compared with the annual income of ordinary homes, 6,288,000 yen ($US57,164), the annual income of foster homes is slightly larger at 6,899,000 yen ($US62,718). (The figure for ordinary homes is based on the National Life Basic Investigation in 1991.)

Table 14.23   Occupation of foster parents, 1 December 1992

Occupation	No. of foster homes	%
Social welfare	56	2.6
Religion	125	5.7
Teacher	76	3.5
Technician	450	20.5
Administrative work	232	10.6
Office work	266	12.1
Sales	188	8.6
Agriculture or fishery	200	9.1
Labour	210	9.6
Service	127	5.8
Other	264	12.0

Type of residence of foster parents

As Table 14.24 shows, the majority of foster families (80.4 per cent) owned and lived in a detached home.

Table 14.24   Type of residence of foster parents, 1 December 1992

Type of home	No. of foster homes	%
Owned		
Detached	1,763	80.4
Condominium	91	4.1
Public condominium	40	1.8
Public corporation house	33	1.5
Company home	56	2.6
Rented		
Detached	90	4.1
Condominium	91	4.1
Lodging	2	0.1
Other	11	0.5
Unknown	17	0.8

Role of national foster care association

Brief history

In October 1954, the National Foster Parent Association (NFPA) was founded as a voluntary, nationwide organization of foster parents. In July 1966, the NFPA was recognized by the national government as a corporate 'juridical person', composed of prefectural foster parent associations. In March 1971, the NFPA was reorganized into the present National Foster Parent Association (Japan) as a juridical foundation.

The NFPA is no longer merely a liaison body between member associations and foster parents. Although it continues to play this role, it now also plays a leading role in the promotion of foster care in Japan.

Major activities

The NFPA conducts various activities in line with the spirit of the Child Welfare Law. These activities have the following aims: to promote the welfare of children who are in need of foster care; to acquaint people with the foster care system, and to seek membership among those who are interested in fostering. The NFPA also undertakes research on foster care, gives guidance to foster children and foster parents, and holds consultations. Its major activities are:

- A general assembly is held in October every year.
- The NFPA journal, *Foster Parents' Reports* is published on a quarterly basis. In addition, two books are published every year.
- Recruitment campaigns for foster parents are conducted.
- Training courses are provided to foster parents.
- Information on the foster parent system is made available.
- Posters are displayed during Foster Parents' Month.
- Research is undertaken into foster care services.

Recommendations to the government

At its general assembly, the NFPA adopts resolutions calling on the government (Minister of Health and Welfare) to take action to improve the foster parent system.

The recommendation to the government adopted at the 38th General Assembly was as follows:

1   to fully subsidize a nationwide drive for promotion of the foster parent system;
2   to staff the Child Guidance Centres of the prefectural government with specialists in foster care;
3   to reconsider expenditures required for foster care in light of actual conditions;
4   to raise allowances for foster parents;
5   to take measures to establish a new foster care system for mentally retarded and physically handicapped children;
6   to revise the foster parent-related provisions of the Child Welfare Law to extend the upper limit on a foster child's age to 20 from the present 18.

Bibliography

Children and Families Bureau, Ministry of Health and Welfare (1995) *Survey Concerning the Actual Condition of Foster Children as of December 1, 1992*, Tokyo: National Foster Parent Association.

15 Netherlands

Tjalling Zandberg

Introduction

In this chapter, attention is focused on the various forms of foster care in the Netherlands. After outlining the position of foster care within the youth care and youth protection system, some general characteristics will be discussed. With the help of the so-called 'functional approach', which has recently been introduced into the Netherlands, the various forms of foster care will subsequently be placed into a framework which takes into account the length of placement, the age of the child concerned, the organization involved, the intensity of the care provided and the methods employed. For each type of care discussed, references to the literature are provided, so that the interested reader may find a more detailed account of the method and/or results of the study. The chapter concludes with a description of some recent developments which will strongly influence the future and quality of foster care.

Demography

In the Netherlands in 1993, there were 4,024,643 minors out of a total population of over 14 million. In 1985, the age of majority was lowered from 21 to 18. As a result, the number of minors entitled to benefit from youth care and youth protection services has dropped considerably (in 1975, there were 4,853,066 minors aged under 21). The population of the Netherlands is expected to reach about 18.8 million people by the year 2010, but the proportion of juveniles is expected to drop from 30.9 per cent to 23.8 per cent, giving a total of 4,474,400.

In 1993, the total approved capacity of residential facilities for young people with psycho-social problems under the jurisdiction of the Health

197

Department was 8,251 places; there were 703 places under the Justice Department, and 150 places under the Department of Education and Sciences. In 1995, the total capacity of residential care for minors with psycho-social problems was estimated at 9,100 places. A total of 3,450 places are approved for semi-residential youth care, or the work form of day care, entirely financed by the Ministry of Health, Welfare and Sport.

In 1993, there were 9,165 foster care places, of which voluntary foster care accounted for 4,235 and judicial foster care 4,930. Voluntary foster care falls under the jurisdiction of the Ministry of Health, Welfare and Sport, while judicial foster care falls under the jurisdiction of the Ministry of Justice (*Rijksplan Jeugdhulpverlening*, 1995).

Within the Dutch youth care system, the following types of care occur: preventive and ambulant care, day care, day and night care (all kinds of homes) and foster care. In the first two types, both young people and their parents are being helped while the family remains intact. The last two types involve out-of-home placement.

Care workers rightly feel that everything possible must be done to prevent out-of-home placement. This view is based on the widely accepted notion that problems in child rearing can seldom be explained solely by problems within the child, but are also caused by difficulties in the parents themselves and in their environment. This view is discussed by Rink (1992), who identifies related variables in child rearing: the child, the parent, the type of situation in which the parents find themselves, and the wider context of that situation. As a fictitious example of interrelated variables, consider the situation of an overactive child who finds it hard to focus his attention. The child's mother has recently entered into divorce proceedings, and is still struggling with the father over how much contact the child will have with each parent. In addition, due to financial problems, she is obliged to move. Moreover, her parents and ex-in-laws are constantly bothering her with unwanted advice. This example demonstrates that the objective of caregiving can generally be characterized as the resolution or reduction of the problems within the total child rearing situation.

An important indicator in deciding whether to opt for an out-of-home placement is the extent to which the individual family members can be influenced. If parents, in spite of intensive help, remain unable to cope with their problems or continue to neglect or abuse their children, an out-of-home placement is indicated.

In the Netherlands, over 50 per cent of children placed out of home are placed with foster families, and there are foster care places for about 10,000 young people. A foster family placement is considered an excellent solution, since it is widely acknowledged that a family context, as opposed to children's homes, allows a number of important basic principles of child rearing to be achieved: the child's living situation is well structured, there is personal attention and affection, and there is more continuity of relationships (Tilanus, 1994; Zandberg, 1988).

About half the placements with foster families result from a judicial decision (e.g. a supervision order). If the parents, considering the circumstances, agree that the child should be fostered, there will be fewer problems for everyone involved with the placement. Problems arising from placement may include disagreement over the optimal amount of contact between the child and the natural parent, guilt feelings on the part of the child, and failure to keep appointments.

The source of many foster care placements is the judicial system. The majority of those placed have traditionally been so-called 'custody youths'. Since 1970 the number of 'custody youths' has declined sharply, whereas the number of young people under supervision has grown (Werkgroep Pleegzorg, 1991).

The remaining placements are made on a voluntary basis. Following an initial increase in the number of voluntary placements (in 1986, there were 4,350 placements of this type), there has been a decline in the number over the past few years (in 1993, there were only about 3,000). Voluntary placements are usually shorter-term than the placements resulting from a judicial decision. Moreover, relatively few children aged 12 years or less are voluntarily placed with foster families (Tilanus, 1992).

General characteristics of foster care

Before identifying the various types of care within the field of foster care, it might be helpful to look at those characteristics which apply to all forms of foster care in the Netherlands.

First, the foster carers who are directly concerned with the day-to-day rearing of the children are all volunteers – they do not hold a paid position within an organization, but are raising a foster child in their family for a short or long period on a voluntary basis while receiving only minor compensation. This volunteer status sometimes presents difficulties for the foster parents as it can mean that they are not considered equal partners within the care service. For example, a decision may be made to have the child return to his or her natural parents, even though the foster parents are convinced that this is very unwise.

Another characteristic of all types of foster care is the temporary nature of the placement. The length of stay may vary from a few days in an emergency foster home to several years in a foster family where the child has settled well. The placement of a child in a foster family is thus quite different from settling a child permanently with substitute parents who take on the full responsibility for raising the child and officially have parental control over the child. In this latter case, the parents are adoptive parents, not foster parents.

In addition, all foster family placements are characterized by the fact that the child is placed with a family through the mediation of a recognized authority. There are ambulant aid organizations which have acquired the authority to place children on the basis of knowledge, expertise and experience. The majority of judicial placements are made through family guardian agencies, and to a lesser extent through the Councils for Child Protection. There are a number of organizations which deal with voluntary placements.

Two distinct functions within foster care may be identified: direct care carried out by volunteers or foster parents, and pedagogical care, undertaken by professionals attached to whatever service is responsible for guiding the foster family (*Eindrapport Harmonisatie van Normen*, 1992). However, it should be noted that pedagogical aid is somewhat incidental: the foster child, the natural parents and the foster parents are supervised by a professional, usually a social worker, in some cases for a week at most.

Foster care is considerably cheaper than residential care, since foster care employs volunteers who receive only meagre compensation for their effort. In 1994, a place in a foster family cost $US7,000 per year, whereas a place in an institution cost on average $US35,000 per year (*Plan Jeugdhulpverlening*, 1995).

Forms of foster care

Using the functional approach, the various types of foster care can be categorized into a number of clusters. In the past, categorization has often been based on the different facilities used, but categorization on the basis of function has the advantage that concrete activities can be used as a starting point. These activities or functions pertain to the entire youth care service, and an additional advantage of the functional approach is that the types of care offered within that service can become more flexible. For example, different forms of care, such as preventive/ambulant care, day care, foster care, and day and night care fulfil many of the same functions, and the organizational or administrative barriers which separate them can easily be removed. A direct result of removing these barriers has been the development of multi-functional organizations for youth care over the last few years. Another advantage of the functional approach is the fact that a direct link can be made between cost and future achievement. In the future, a foster care service will often be part of a multi-functional organization. Based on functions, foster care will consist of the following 'aid variants' (an aid variant comprises a number of functions):

- For day and night foster care, a basic variant and two intensive variants can be identified. The basic variant consists of two functions: permanent residence and care (24 hours a day) and incidental pedagogical aid for a few hours a week. Where there are more severe problems concerning the foster child, more pedagogical aid – a greater intensity of aid – will be necessary. This intensity is manifested in more intensive (multi-disciplinary) supervision of the foster parents and natural parents, and a greater degree of (professional) expertise on the part of the foster parents.

● With respect to foster day care, a basic variant and an intensive variant can be identified. The basic variant comprises partial residence and care for a number of hours a day and incidental pedagogical aid for a few hours a week. If more serious problems should arise concerning the foster day care child, more intensive care must be provided. This increased intensity is manifested in further multi-disciplinary guidance for the foster day care parents and natural parents, and/or a greater degree of professional expertise on the part of the foster day care parents.

On the basis of functional categorization applied in matrix form, the following current types of foster care can be placed in the four care variants shown in Figure 15.1.

Foster day and night care		
	Basic	**Intensive**
	● weekend family	● family programmes
	● vacation family	● family homes
	● short-stay family	● therapeutic family care
	● crisis intervention	● Intensive Foster Care Project
	● foster family	● coaching-plus
	● boarding foster family	
Foster day care	● recognized care variant is not (yet) known	● foster day care

Figure 15.1   Foster care variant matrix

The remainder of this section presents a description of each care variant of the various forms of foster care. Recent research results will be included, where available.

Basic variant for day and night foster care

Weekend and/or vacation family

According to Tilanus (1992), this type of foster placement is often provided for children residing in institutions who have no home to go to for the weekend or for holidays. A placement with this kind of family is also used if it is desirable for the child to be removed from his or her own family for a short time to enable the family to calm down. In both situations, the child's place of residence before and after the short stay remains unchanged: in the institution or with his or her own natural family. Institutions, foster family agencies (organizations aimed at recruiting and selecting foster families) and ambulant aid organizations all make use of families which are willing to provide this form of care. Sometimes, these families are recruited through advertisements to find a carer for a specific child. Such families are often not able or willing to care for a foster child on a permanent basis.

Short-stay family

This type of placement is used when a child can no longer stay in the family or in the residential home, because some crisis has occurred and the child immediately needs another place to stay. Since the child's future is uncertain, more permanent arrangements are looked into while the child is with the short-stay family. As the term suggests, these placements are of limited duration. Usually, a place is requested for a period of three months, with the possibility of a brief extension (Tilanus, 1992). The placement may be prolonged, for example, when a vacancy will definitely become available in the most suitable residential home at a future date.

Crisis intervention

This predominantly occurs in voluntary youth care and is widely used for young people who have run away from home (or sometimes residential home) as a result of acute problems and who apply to the organizations mentioned above for immediate aid and a place to stay. The maximum time for which the young person is allowed to stay is six weeks. In recent years, there has been a growing demand for this form of care, since it is considered to be a good alternative to the short residential stay. According to Mateman and Wouda (1990), crisis intervention can be characterized as follows: providing 'first aid' and a place to stay (finding a suitable family); identifying and coping with the problem (finding out what is really the matter and what must be done to prevent more problems); social-societal care (for example, arranging social security benefits and housing); psychodynamic aid, and family intervention. These characteristics make it clear that, during the period of crisis intervention, there are high expectations of the client, the short-stay family and professionals.

Foster family

In foster families, minors are raised and cared for by one or more adults because of serious problems between the young person and one or both of his or her parents. Apart from the general characteristics mentioned earlier in this chapter, there are no clear-cut definitions of foster families. Besides considerable variation in the duration of the placement, mentioned earlier, there is also a variation in the severity of the problems. Sometimes, there is little wrong with the child and a great deal wrong with the parents, or vice versa. In either case, there are indications that help is needed, and that placement in a foster family is an appropriate way of providing that help. If, at the time of placement, it is ascertained that it will be impossible for the child to return home, the foster family and agency staff should adopt a different perspective than would be the case if reunification of the child with the natural family was anticipated. Nevertheless, all foster family placements strive to achieve one of the following goals (Werkgroep Pleegzorg, 1991):

- determination of whether the child can be expected to go home in due course, or whether a short stay with this foster family should be followed by a prolonged stay in another care facility or foster home;
- determination of the type of child who would best fit into this foster family.

With respect to responsibility for the young person, there is an essential difference between the voluntary and judicial frameworks. In the first case, the parents are formally and legally the commissioners who request help for their child; in the second case, the commissioners are the (family) guardian agency or the Council for Child Protection.

Placing children with members of the family requires a different approach on the part of the foster parents and supervisors.

Research (Van Ooyen-Houben, 1991) shows that the problems concerning children in the 0–11 age range prove to be more severe in residential care than in foster care. In the case of foster children, the group of judicial placements resulting from a child protection measure shows the most problematic family background (Van der Ploeg, 1993). Van Reeuwijk and Berben (1988) suggest that the following are the most important problems with respect to foster children: recalcitrancy, running away, relationship problems, dependency, depression and loneliness. The most important problems in the home situation were found to be: relationship problems between parent and child, parental pedagogical incompetence, relationship problems between the parents, emotional problems of the parents, abuse, addiction problems, affective neglect, incest, delinquency and prostitution. In addition, it appears from their study that many foster children have prior experience of being in care: 58 per cent had been placed out of home previously, two-thirds of the foster children and their families had previously received ambulant care, 24 per cent came from an earlier foster family placement and 10 per cent came from a residential home.

Boarding foster family

This type of foster family is intended for older youths who are able to function independently to a reasonable extent, but for whom a stable background to fall back on remains desirable. A placement with a boarding foster family often serves as a preparatory phase for independent living.

Intensive variants of foster day care and night care

Family programmes

Family programmes are intended for young children who have been placed out of the home (the emphasis is on children aged 0–6) whose future prospects are unknown. This means that it is unclear whether the child can return to his or her own parents, or what the most appropriate placement will be in the event that it is impossible for the child to return home (Van der Zanden and Buffing, 1991). The decisive factor for an out-of-home placement, apart from problems with the children themselves, usually concerns the family situation and/or problems with the natural parents. One characteristic of the family programme is that instead of a group or residential home, use is made of the so-called 'programme families', who receive the same compensation as foster families. The responsibility for administering care through the family programmes is thus in the hands of the residential organizations for youth care. The parents receive guidance from the ambulant organization which is also responsible for the placement. The maximum duration of the placement is usually about six months, after which time a decision about the most appropriate future placement must be made.

It appears from research (Van der Zanden and Buffing, 1991) that the target group of the family programmes consists of children who have severe psycho-social problems, which are sometimes more serious than those of the average residential population. The importance of a multi-disciplinary approach is emphasized, family programme parents have access to assistance 24 hours a day (which they find important), and they can fall back on the residential home in case of emergency. The way to comply with these conditions is to be connected to a residential facility. In addition, research shows that according to the parents involved, the children profit from a placement in a project family; they become more spontaneous and make more contact with others; they behave more calmly; they are less aggressive and less anxious, and moreover, they tend to show less developmental retardation. Based on the generally positive results, the study concludes with the recommendation to set up similar programmes in every district.

Family homes

In contrast with the family programmes, family homes (Van Lieshout, 1984; 1988; Meijs, 1984) have a longer history. The first family home was introduced in 1971. A family home takes in a larger number of young people (usually four), and the parents receive compensation for their work in addition to the normal allowance for housekeeping. They have to sign a contract for several years and then move from their own home to the family home (with or without their own children).

Before young people are placed in a family home, it will have been determined that they can no longer live in their natural homes. The aim of the placement is preparation for self-support. Sometimes, the family home is used as a stepping stone to a foster family placement. Most young people come from a therapeutic home, and the family home then serves as the last phase of their treatment programme. Family homes also form part of a residential care facility. Consequently, those involved can call on assistance from staff from the multi-disciplinary team, who are constantly available.

Therapeutic Family Care (TFC)

TFC is the best-known form of intensive foster care. It also has the longest record: the first programme began in 1957. This type of care is directed at children and young people for whom severe forms of emotional and/or pedagogical neglect, and sometimes physical abuse, necessitate an out-of-home placement (Tilanus, 1992). The most important indicator should be the early onset of developmental disorders.

The literature (Hart de Ruyter et al., 1968; Graafsma, 1979; Sanders-Woudstra, 1979) makes it clear that TFC is intended for children and their parents who, during the child's early years, have experienced a poor or deficient parent–child relationship. The ensuing severe behavioural problems (Hart de Ruyter speaks of 'psychopathiform behaviour') in the child cannot be dealt with in a normal foster family. In order to facilitate normal development, it is necessary to place the child in a specialized foster family. This specialization is manifested through a strict selection of candidate families and intensive coaching (sometimes several times a week during placement). TFC programme staff, in consultation with the foster parents, draw up a treatment programme which is evaluated regularly. Several years of treatment may be required. An important aspect of the treatment is additional psychotherapy for the child. This is directed at working through the conflicts of the past and also the conflicts involved in growing into the foster family (Graafsma, 1979).

In the Netherlands, there are seven regional organizations for TFC, with a total capacity of about 350 places (Werkgreop Pleegzorg, 1991). A multi-disciplinary team is attached to the TFC programme, including a social worker, a child psychiatrist, an orthopedagogue and a child psychologist. Some organizations have an 'Intensive Care Unit': this is a group home where children are being prepared for a foster family placement, but it also functions as a crisis centre should the situation in the foster family be urgent.

Intensive Foster Care Project

In the Netherlands, attention on a small scale is paid to foster care for the mentally disabled. Within this group, children with psychiatric and/or behavioural difficulties were found to be particularly problematic, and residential placements failed to yield the desired results. It was found that 'family rearing could possibly contribute to revitalizing a stagnating development, so that behavioural problems could be affected in a positive way, and as a result, social skills and self-support could increase and societal adaptation, socialization and integration could be stimulated' (Prins et al., 1992, p.1). In view of the level of difficulty and the high risk of failure involved in placing mentally disabled children with severe behavioural problems in foster families, the Intensive Foster Care Project was initiated (Brants and Van Gennep, 1992). With respect to organization and structuring of treatment, the project strongly resembles TFC although the methods employed in the project are adapted to the specific target group. The Intensive Foster Care Project also works with selected foster families which are intensively guided by a multi-disciplinary team. The study that is linked to the project (Prins et al., 1992) has yielded an elaborate description of the methods, and it has established that the methods are both successful and feasible. According to the researchers, there is every reason to integrate this form of care into general health care for the physically disabled.

Coaching-plus

Coaching-plus is an intensive form of foster care for young people aged 15–17 who cannot fit into a normal foster family because of behavioural problems (Berger, 1993). The programme has been developed by the Paedological Institute of the Free University in Amsterdam. It is one of the practical elaborations of the 'task-skill model' (Slot, 1988). This model is based on learning theory, and the basic principle is that behavioural problems in young people are due to limited abilities and social skills. These limitations lead to increasing retardation and behavioural problems. The coaches (foster parents) teach the young people skills in situations as they occur in daily life. This spontaneous learning is designed step by step (from simple to more complicated skills; from little to greater independence and responsibility). Selected coaches receive prior training which prepares them for the coaching role. During treatment, the young people are intensively guided by their own trained coach with the assistance of a supervisor. The methods used by coaches and supervisors are described in two manuals (Berger, 1992a; 1992b). Apart from the usual compensation for foster families, the coaches or foster parents also receive a small additional recompense for their efforts. The programmatic nature of this kind of treatment is revealed in its limited duration: six to nine months. The relevant research (Berger, 1993) shows, among other things, that the recruitment and selection of 'coaching' foster parents is not a simple matter, that the treatment has yielded hopeful results, and that the programme is better incorporated into a residential organization than into an ambulant organization. The study concludes with a positive finding: the methods employed in Coaching-plus have much to offer foster care, and can also be utilized in foster care programmes that are less intensive.

Foster day care

Foster day care can best be described as the placement of a child in an ordinary family for part of the day. This placement is considered necessary when the family situation has stagnated. The selected and trained foster day care families fulfil the role of 'supplementary parents'. They are intensively guided by associates involved in the programme, who guide the natural parents as well. This new variant within foster care developed from a three-year experiment directed at children and their parents, who could apply for day care although placement of the child in a group care setting was not, or was no longer, indicated. The target group consists of children aged 4–12 who cannot be treated in a group care setting but are committed to day care treatment in foster families for a longer timespan than usual. At present, the programmes are linked to six day care centres. The relevant study (Strijker and Zandberg, 1994a) shows that foster day care families are characterized by a higher than average positive home climate, lucid communication and strong, positive discipline. The children's stay in this type of family reduces problematic behaviour, according to their mothers. Moreover, the foster day care family appears to present clear exemplary modelling for the natural family, which will improve the family structure and decrease interpersonal conflicts. Interesting findings include not only the predominantly positive developmental results and an elaborate description of the methods, but also the design of a probability model whose use can offer an indication of what living climate is best suited to a particular request for care in a foster family (Strijker and Zandberg, 1994b).

Major trends

One of the main issues in foster care in the Netherlands is that it has not yet adopted a clear position within youth care and youth protection. The main reason was, and still is, the large number of ambulant organizations involved in the practice of foster care. Since the introduction of the Youth Care Act in 1992, foster care has received legal recognition as a separate service. This recognition has brought about a drastic decline in the number of services which request fostering placements. On the one hand, this decline can be explained by mergers, and on the other by a conscious reduction in the number of services placing children in voluntary youth care through regulation of recognition. There is a widely-held view that the Netherlands should strive for a single service within the care area (Werkgroep Pleegzorg, 1991). This development is fully under way, and has the great advantage that scattered knowledge and skills can be brought together in one facility. An important point is the organizational separation between placement and care stipulated in the Act. Briefly summarized, this distinction boils down to the principle that one body is responsible for placement, and the other body then takes over and provides care.

In the final report by the foster care working group (Werkgroep Pleegzorg, 1991), foster parents are seen as partners in the care service. This means that foster parents are entitled to make decisions, and that foster parents should be guided in a co-operative manner. This view has been adopted by the authorities and will strengthen the foster parents' position. In this way, a long-cherished wish of the Dutch Association of Foster Families will be fulfilled (Nederlandse Vereniging voor Pleegezinnen, 1990).

Bibliography

Berger, M.A. (1992a) *COACHING-plus, handleiding voor coachgezinnen*, Amsterdam/Duivendrecht: Paedologisch Instituut.

Berger, M.A. (1992b) *COACHING-plus, handboek voor coaching-plus begeleiders*, Amsterdam/Duivendrecht: Paedologisch Instituut.

Berger, M.A. (1993) *Het COACHING-plus project, opzet en ervaringen*, Amsterdam/Duivendrecht: Paedologisch Instituut.

Brants, L. and van Gennep, A. (1992) *50 jaar tegendraads*, Amsterdam: William Schrikker Stichting.

Eindrapport Harmonisatie van Normen (1992) The Hague: Ministerie van Welzijn, Volksgezondheid en Cultuur (WVC).

Graafsma, T. (1979) 'Psychotherapie met kinderen in de therapeutische gezinverpleging', in *Facetten van Jeugdberschming*, Utrecht: Werkverband Instellingen Jeugdhulpverlening Nederland (WIJN), pp.51–8.

Hart de Ruyter, T., Boeke, P. and Van Beugen, M. (1968) *Het moeilijk opvoedbare kind in het pleeggezin*, Assen: Van Gorcum.

Jong, N. de (1985) 'Beheersaspecten vsn de (jeugd)gezondheidszorg tegen de achtergrond van ziektekostenverzekering', in *Symposium medische kindertehuizen en jeugdgezondheidszorg, zorg of vak?*, Utrecht: Nationale Ziekenhuisraad (NZR).

Mateman, H. and Wouda, L. (1990) *Crisishulp in beeld*, Leiden: Centrum Onderzoek Jeugdhulpverlening (COJ).

Meijs, J.C.A.M. (1984) *Gezinshuizen van het Leger des Heils*, Hilversum.

Nederlandse Vereniging voor Pleeggezinnen (1990) *Pleegouders als gelijkwaardige partner in de jeugdhulpverlening*, Utrecht: Nederlandse Vereniging voor Pleeggezinnen.

Plan Jeugdhulpverlening (1995) Leeuwarden: Provincie Friesland.

Prins, J., Van den Dungen, E., Janssen, C. and Baartman, H. (1992) *Project Intensieve Pleegzorg*, Amsterdam: Sectie speciale pedagogiek, Vrije Universiteit.

Rijksplan Jeugdhulverlening (1995) The Hague: Ministerie van Volksgezondheid, Welzijn en Sport en Ministerie van Justitie.

Rink, J.E. (1992). 'Het SOG-Project: Orthopedagogische Thuishulp in het kader van een Justitiële Maatregel', in Rink, J.E. and Vos, R.C. (eds) *Justitiële en niet-justitiële thuishulp*, Leuven/Apeldoorn: Garant.

Rink, J.E. (1995) *Pedagogical Mismanagement and Orthopedagogy*, Leuven/Apeldoorn: Garant.

Sanders-Woudstra, J.A.R. (1979) 'Enkele gedachten over de therapeutische gezinsverpleging in Rotterdam en omstreken' in *Facetten van Jeugdbescherming*, Utrecht: Werkverband Instellingen Jeugdhulpverlening Nederland (WIJN), pp.48–50.

Slot, N.W. (1988) *Residentiële hulp voor jongeren met antisociaal gedrag*, Amsterdam/Lisse: Swets and Zeitlinger.

Strijker, J. and Zandberg, T. (1994a) *Dagpleegzorg: Eindrapport*, Groningen: Stichting Kinderstudies.

Strijker, J. and Zandberg, T. (1994b) 'Some pros and cons of foster day care', in Rink, J.E. et al. (eds) *The Limits of Orthopedagogy: Changing Perspectives (Part 2)*, Leuven/Apeldoorn: Garant, pp.75–86.

Tilanus, C.P.G. (1992) *Jeugdhulpverlening en de overheid*, Utrecht: Uitgeverij Sociaal Wetenschappelijk Pers (SWP).

Van Lieshout, J. (1984) *Gezinshuizen: Model en methodiek*, Amsterdam: Sociaalagogisch Centrum Het Burgerweeshuis.

Van Lieshout, J. (1988) *Jongeren Gezinsproject: Model en methodiek*, Amsterdam: Sociaalagogisch Centrum Het Burgerweeshuis.

Van Ooyen-Houben, M. (1991) 'De ontwikkeling van jonge kinderen na een uithuisplaatsing', Leiden: Rijksuniversiteit, dissertation.

Van der Ploeg, J.D. (1993) 'Pleegzorg', in Van der Ploeg, J.D. (ed.) *Orthopedagogische Werkvelden*, Leuven/Apeldoorn: Garant, pp.57–67.

Van Reeuwijk, P.M.C. and Berben, E.G.M.J. (1988) *Vrijwillige pleegzorg, een kwantitatieve analyse*, The Hague: Coordinatiecommissie Wetenschappelijk Onderzoek Kinderbescherming (CWOK).

Van der Zanden, A.P. and Buffing, F.A.L. (1991) *De gezinsprojecten: pleegzorg ineen residentieel kader*, Rijswijk: Ministerie van Welzijn, Volksgezondheid en Cultuur (WVC).

Werkgroep Pleegzorg (1991) *Voorzien in Pleegzorg*, Rijswijk/The Hague: Ministerie van Welzijn, Volksgezondheid en Cultuur/ Ministerie van Justitie.

Zandberg, T. (1988) *Kleinschaligheid in de residentiële jeugdhulpverlening*, Groningen: Stichting Kinderstudies.

16 Philippines

Maria Paz U. de Guzman

Jurisdiction

Being largely Roman Catholic, Filipino families adhere closely to the Church's stand in favour of the rhythm method of family planning, as opposed to the state policy of providing every opportunity to make the most appropriate choice with regard to family planning. For this reason, the Philippines has one of the highest birth rates among the developing countries, in which there are collectively estimated to be 120 million women who do not want to become pregnant but use no 'modern' method of family planning (Catley-Carlson, 1994).

The Philippines is a 'young' country, in the sense that 50 per cent of the population are presently aged 20 years or less. Of these, it is estimated that half live below the poverty level.

In his book, *The Philippines: Pearl of the Orient*, Ramon Roces y Pardo (1988) describes the Philippines in a nutshell:

> Situated along the western edge of the Pacific Ocean, or at latitudes 4° 23' and 21° 25'N and longitudes 116° and 126° 30'E, the Philippine archipelago assumes a roughly triangular configuration with the Batanes Islands in the north as the apex and Tawi-Tawi and Sarangani Islands of the south as the base. Y'ami, the northernmost island, is 241 kilometres south of Taiwan, while Saulog, the southernmost island, lies 48 kilometres east of Borneo.
>
> The archipelago has approximately 299,404 square kilometres in land area, although Luzon and Mindanao alone, the two largest islands, represent 65 per cent of the total land area. More than half of the total population of 60 million lives in these two islands, and only about one-tenth percent of the 7,107 islands is inhabited.
>
> The climate is tropical with three pronounced seasons: wet from June to October, cool and dry from November through February, hot and humid from March through May. Apart from the southwest and northeast monsoons, typhoons and

tropical storms account for 50 per cent of the rainfall. The eastern sections of the country, from Leyte to Batanes, feel the brunt of incoming typhoons.

Named after King Philip II of Spain, the Philippines has had a multi-coloured history. It is often said that Filipinos have 'split-level' personalities (Bulatao, 1965) because of this heritage. Contemporary Filipinos have somewhere in their past traces of either Chinese, Indian, Spanish American, or two or more of these genetic influences, which has led to 100-plus cultural and linguistic groups in the country. Social scientists describe Filipinos as adaptable, chameleon-like and pliant as the bamboo tree, because of their rich historical–cultural mix. Like the wide gastronomic range of their rich fiesta fare, Filipinos are at once hot and cold, spicy and bland, Western and Asian, Latin and Oriental. Another popular description of the Filipino is that often found in sociological papers: the Filipino today is a product of having been in the monastery or nunnery for nearly 400 years and then thrust into Hollywood for 50 years.

History and origins

Filipinos have always had a soft spot for the children of their less fortunate relatives. A tradition of looking after an orphaned godchild, a child of a sibling, a cousin or any member of the extended family, including those of one's house servants, is still practised. Apart from the notion of 'reciprocity', this tradition may have biblical underpinnings for the God-loving Filipinos. Hence, there are countless cases of informal foster care nationwide which are unregistered and therefore not licensed by the Department of Social Welfare and Development (DSWD).

Philippine Plan of Action for Children for the Year 2000 and Beyond

According to an official document (Council for the Welfare of Children, 1992) detailing the country's child welfare target objectives for the year 2000 and beyond, the Philippines hopes to reduce the number of institutionalized children by 80 per cent. It plans to do so by encouraging legal local adoptions, and by promoting foster care and other alternative parental care, such as guardianship and inter-country adoption.

Beginnings of foster care

Jocano (1980) mentions Act No. 2,671 of January 1980, which created the Government Orphanage, as emphasizing the importance of child welfare in social work. Before this, the Public Welfare Board, which was under the supervision of the Department of the Interior, co-ordinated the activities of various charities. In a paper delivered during the first National Congress on Adoption and Foster Care, Balanon (1992) dates the beginning of formal foster care in the Philippines to 1962, when the then Social Welfare Administration (SWA, now the DSWD) jointly sponsored a Foster Family Care Project with UNICEF.

Five years later, foster family care was given academic and practical importance in the study by Eufemio (1967). In 1983, the DSWD issued Administrative Order No. 63, which called for the nationwide implementation of foster care.

There are no government orphanages in the Philippines nowadays. Rather, there are child care facilities all over the Philippines, each known as a Reception and Study Centre for Children (RSCC), which are mandated to admit children, assess them and decide on the best possible permanent placement for them: reunion with the natural family, adoption, guardianship or foster care. Various non-governmental organizations (NGOs) which are licensed to operate as child welfare agencies also carry out similar tasks. However, because of the lack of foster families and the lack of funds specifically earmarked for foster care, RSCCs have become long-term residential care institutions for younger children.

The Child and Youth Welfare Code, as embodied in Presidential Decree 603, provides that all abandoned and neglected children are wards of the state under the principle of *parens patriae*. In this connection, Article 3 states that every child has the right to a wholesome family, and that the dependent and abandoned child shall be provided with the nearest substitute for a home.

More recently, as the 39th signatory to the United Nations Convention on the Rights of the Child and the World Declaration on the Survival, Protection and Development of Children, the Philippines formulated an inter-agency national plan of action for children, the *Philippine Plan of Action for Children for the Year 2000 and Beyond* (Council for the Welfare of Children, 1992). One of the five major areas of concern in this document is family and alternative parental care, which subsumes formal foster care.

Administration and organization

The Bureau of Child and Youth Welfare (BCYW) of the Department of Social Welfare and Development has direct control over all agencies delivering foster family care services to children and young people. The BCYW issues each agency a licence to operate, and then, after a certain period of operation, it issues a Certificate of Accreditation to those agencies whose services have been monitored, evaluated, reviewed and deemed to be up to standard. Supervision is generally carried out by the local BCYW office where the programme operates.

At present, six NGOs, one of which is affiliated to a religious organization, provide foster care services for a number of children and young people. These organizations are all based in Manila:

- the Kaisahang Buhay Foundation (KBF);
- the NORFIL Foundation;
- the Parenting Foundation of the Philippines (PFP);
- Creating Responsive Infants By Stimulation (CRIBS);
- Concordia Children's Services (CCS);
- Home of Joy (HOJ).

Through the various regional offices of the BCYW, the government operates foster care programmes in the following locations:

- Leyte and Samar, in co-operation with the PFP;
- Cebu, previously in co-operation with the KBF;
- Davao;
- Legazpi;
- Cagayan de Oro.

Approximately 75 per cent of the children fostered are aged 6 years or less. The other 25 per cent are older children with a history of having been abused, being given into prostitution, or with special needs resulting from mental retardation, cerebral palsy or correctable physical defects such as a cleft palate and hare lip, or those born to a mentally ill parent or a parent serving a prison sentence.

Who is placed in foster care?

In principle, all dependent and abandoned children and young people, whether mentally, behaviourally or physically handicapped, may be placed in foster care. At present, however, the majority of children served are those younger ones (aged 6 and under) who have relatively few special needs, although almost all are disadvantaged or neglected in more ways than one. The use of foster care in the Philippines as an alternative to institutional care is therefore very minimal indeed. This situation appears to be primarily due to lack of funding, and only peripherally due to a lack of professional will, in so far as the country's social workers and caregivers are all convinced of the efficacy of foster care. Perhaps a uniquely Philippine characteristic of foster care is the large group, possibly 40 per cent, of fostered children who are eligible for and awaiting more permanent placements.

In 1992, the Parenting Foundation of the Philippines, in co-operation with Child Hope and under the leadership of Teresita Silva, placed in foster care five young street children, aged 6–8 years. The PFP provided the foster homes and carried out the supervision and supportive monitoring of the foster homes, while Child Hope provided 50 per cent of the funding.

The PFP is currently carrying out a training programme with five selected foster families which each show the potential to become a 'reinforced foster family': a family which can provide effective foster care to delinquent and street children. The primary concern raised by this select group of families is the difficulty they perceive in instilling proper values because of the 'hardened' character of older street children. This fear may be unfounded, and it must definitely be overcome if a wider population of children is to be served in foster care.

Care providers

As mentioned above, most foster care providers fall under the auspices of private agencies (NGOs). Table 16.1 gives a breakdown of foster carers sponsored by various private sector organizations, employing statistics for 1994.

Table 16.1   Foster carers sponsored by private-sector organizations, 1994

Agency	No.	%
Kaisahang Buhay Foundation	141	44
Parenting Foundation	86	27
NORFIL	64	20
CRIBS	24	7
Concordia Children's Services	3	1
Home of Joy	3	1

Note: The data in this table were obtained from the respective organizations through personal phone calls. With respect to the public sector, which is missing from the table, the figure furnished by Mrs Thelsa Biolena for 1995 from the National Capital Region or Metro Manila is 21 licensed families for 13 children served. It should be noted that foster care comprises only a very small part of the government's child welfare programmes and services.

The DSWD's Bureau of Child and Youth Welfare lists the following requirements for licensing foster families:

1   professional home study, covering the following areas:
    - family composition
    - family dynamics and relationships
    - motivation to foster
    - home and physical surroundings;

2   police clearance;
3   Income Tax return, if any;
4   recent family photograph;
5   foster placement authority/contract.

In general, there are two types of foster care providers at present: regular and volunteer. Regular foster families receive financial support: reimbursement of all ordinary expenses incurred, but not exceeding $US40 per child per month, plus $US35 as an incentive. These figures reflect levels of payment provided by the Parenting Foundation of the Philippines Inc. to its regular foster families. Reports given at the annual consultative Congress on Foster Care indicate that other organizations provide similar amounts. Regular foster families are generally lower middle-income earners, and therefore all extraordinary expenses immediately become the agency's responsibility.

Volunteer foster families receive no support whatsoever, except for extraordinary expenses such as hospitalization and schooling. These families are generally well-off, and have a higher level of education. There are a few expatriates in this category.

A policy which seems peculiar to the Philippines is a provision stated in the foster care placement authority (FCPA) or contract which is issued for every child placed. Signed by the foster parents and the agency involved, the FCPA stipulates that the family may not adopt the child they foster. This has been an occasional area of dispute between the government regulating authorities on the one hand and the agencies and foster families on the other (Del Castillo, 1989; De Guzman, 1993). In a lucid article, Del Castillo (1987) surmises that the purpose of the DSWD's policy on foster care is to prevent 'child shopping'. This supposedly occurs when prospective adoptive parents initially apply to become foster parents and accept children into foster care, until they find a child they want to adopt.

Since no justification has been provided for the policy of forbidding adoption, conjecture is rife. The following are presumed to be the likely negative consequences if a foster family was allowed to adopt a child in its care:

- Child Welfare agencies could connive with interested parties to set up 'identified adoptions', where prospective adoptive parents identify or locate a child and arrange for the child's foster placement preparatory to adopting. This may be a form of child shopping, with the added advantage that the child is identified beforehand. It is highly debatable whether adoption via fostering (regardless of original intent) is detrimental to the child (Del Castillo, 1989) or whether there is anything immoral or illegal (as is the case in adoption through simulated birth) about adoption through fostering.
- Once foster parents adopt, they are no longer inclined to foster another child; or, even if they are still willing, having an adoptive child tends to leave little room for the placement of other children with the family. The fact that a foster family is lost to the agency can hardly be seen as a negative consequence when we remember that the programme exists to benefit the child, and not vice versa. A foster family which becomes an adoptive family should be viewed as a success, if only in terms of permanency, protection of legal rights, and protection of the cultural heritage of the child.

The need to understand the rationale behind this policy cannot be overemphasized. In the context of thousands of homeless children and an expressed official policy to increase the number of legal adoptions by Filipinos, it seems indefensible.

Licensing procedure

The first step in the licensing of foster families involves their participation in a foster care forum conducted by the licensed child welfare agency. The participants may have been invited or recommended by a foster family, a religious group or another social welfare agency. Sometimes, informal screening is undertaken prior to the forum, so that only those who are genuinely motivated are invited to attend. After attending the forum, those still interested are visited by a social worker attached to the child welfare agency, who interviews all family members. Finally, a home study is prepared and submitted to the DSWD for approval, with all required documents attached. When the approval is given, the family receives a licence, and a child may be placed.

Financial support

Foster carers receive, on average, $US75 per child per month. This does not include extraordinary expenses, such as medical, hospital and dental needs and schooling and immunizations, which are borne by the agency. At the moment, there are no standard payment schedules, and it is acknowledged by all foster care administrators that the average level of support provided is inadequate, since it is less than the official minimum daily wage of $US6 or the minimum monthly wage of $US150.

Major problems

With respect to foster care in the Philippines, the major problems in the child welfare system may be summarized as follows:

- Large numbers of children and young people need alternative parental care, whereas governmental and non-governmental resources are scarce.
- Very few families have heard of foster care.
- Those who are aware of foster care are reluctant to become foster carers for one or more of the following reasons:

    - the anticipated pain of separation;
    - the long stay in care, which makes separation more difficult;
    - potential carers feel that they may not be able to cope with a difficult child;
    - they fear a lack of support when problems arise;
    - it is difficult to maintain the enthusiasm and motivation of volunteer carers;
    - there is no law enabling the DSWD to allocate a sizeable portion of its budget for foster care;
    - there is a need for a law recognizing the value of foster care: e.g. a law providing tax breaks for fostering.

Major trends

At present, foster carers see themselves as providing a service of 'love': a religious or charitable act undertaken for love of children or as one's share in nation-building. Foster care administrators tend to take advantage of the fact that low pay reinforces the idea of a charitable act so that no cognitive dissonance is felt by those who wish to foster a child from charitable motives. Hence, potential foster parents are encouraged to offer their services through frequent reference to noble motives.

Foster carers in the Philippines are still a long way from becoming full-time or part-time paid workers. Foster care as a child welfare service still needs to be recognized nationally and politically as a valuable remedial or rehabilitative tool, or even as a therapeutic intervention to counteract the effects of early childhood disadvantages such as institutionalization, deprivation and neglect. It is possible that even among professionals, the preventive value of foster care is not fully appreciated.

Nevertheless, social welfare in the Philippines is still largely dependent on an intact family system, so it is even more important that families become involved in the provision of alternative parental care. Perhaps the DSWD service of providing support with a view to helping couples stay together and care for their young ought to be more widely implemented and given greater emphasis. To a certain extent, some NGOs are achieving this end by offering community-based assistance to families who are at risk.

Role of national foster care association

In December 1994, social workers and foster parents from several NGOs came together to provide each other with mutual support and to exchange experiences, ideas and plans regarding foster care. The meeting was well attended, and the need to form a nationwide network of foster carers was expressed.

At the moment, the KBF, NORFIL and the PFP each support their individual groups of foster families. Reaching out to all sectors involved in fostering and networking with other foster carers outside one's own agency are recognized as sure ways of learning and growing in the challenging and demanding task of caring for children and young people.

Contacts: Kaisahang Buhay Foundation (KBF), 58 Tenth Avenue, Cubao, Quezon City, Philippines *Telephone*: (+63) 912-1159 or 911-4180 *Fax*: (+63) 912-1161. NORFIL Foundation, 16 Mother Ignacia Street, cor. Roces Avenue, Quezon City, Philippines *Telephone*: (+63) 996-902 or 922-5119 *Fax*: (+63) 998-005. Parenting Foundation of the Philippines Inc., 17 Chapel Drive, Mintcor, West Service Road, SSH, Muntinlpa City, Philippines *Telephone*: (+63) 842-1560 *Fax*: (+63) 842-1560.

Research

No research studies have been undertaken on foster care in the Philippines since Eufemio's dissertation (1967). However, a few papers giving food for thought may be found among the following:

Proceedings of the First Congress of Adoption and Foster Care (1992) BCYW and ACCAP.

Proceedings of the Second Metro Manila Congress on Adoption and Alternative Parental Care (1994), BCYW and ACCAP.

Proceedings of the First Regional Forum on the Family and Alternative Parental Care (under the auspices of CWC and the National Task Force on the Family and Alternative Parental Care).

Proceedings of the First Asia-Pacific Regional Conference of the International Forum for Child Welfare 'Children and Family, Our Regional Challenges' (1995).

Bibliography

Balanon, L.G. (1992) 'Situation of Foster Care in the Philippines', unpublished.

Bulatao, Rev. J.C.S.J. (1966) *Techniques of Group Discussion*, Loyola Heights, Quezon City: Ateneo de Manila University Press.

Catley-Carlson, M. (1994) 'Commentary: The decisive decade on Family Planning', in *The Progress of Nations*, New York: UNICEF.

Council for the Welfare of Children (1992) *Philippine Plan of Action for Children for the Year 2000 and Beyond* .

De Guzman, M.P.U. (1993), 'Position Paper on the DSWD Policy on Foster Care', unpublished.

Del Castillo, L.T. (1989) 'A review of the legal provision and social services for dependent, abandoned and neglected children', *CSWCD Bulletin*, 5, April–December.

Eufemio, F.C. (1967) 'Foster Mothers of the Foster Family Care Programs: Their Responses on the PARI and their Role Performance', University of the Philippines, MA dissertation.

Jocano, F. L. (1980) *Social Work in the Philippines: A Historical Overview*, Quezon City: New Day Publishers.

Roces y Pardo, R. (1988) *The Philippines: Pearl of the Orient*, Manila: Filipinas Publishing.

17 Poland

Zofia Waleria Stelmaszuk and Wanda Klominek

Jurisdiction

Poland is a republic in Central Europe bordered by Germany, the Baltic Sea, the Kaliningrad oblast of Russia, Lithuania, Belarus, the Ukraine, the Czech Republic and Slovakia. It covers an area of 312,677 square kilometres (Glowny Urzad Statystyczny, 1996a, p.16) and its capital is Warsaw. For administrative purposes, the country is divided into 49 provinces.

There are 38,609,399 inhabitants, 61.8 per cent living in cities, and 38.2 per cent in rural areas (Glowny Urzad Statystyczny, 1996a, p.49). Nearly all of the population are ethnically Polish. Roman Catholicism is the dominant religion (91.2 per cent), while 1.4 per cent of the population are Russian Orthodox, 0.2 per cent 'Old' Catholic, 0.4 per cent Protestant, and the remainder belong to other faiths (Glowny Urzad Statystyczny, 1996a, pp.67–8). The age of majority is 18, and there are 10,644,803 individuals aged under 18 (Glowny Urzad Statystyczny, 1996a, p.51).

Industry, which has been largely controlled by the state since the Second World War, employs 30.8 per cent of the labour force and contributes more than half the GDP. Leading industries include machinery, iron and steel, chemicals, textiles and processed food. Poland is an important producer of coal, sulphur and copper. Agriculture employs 25.8 per cent of the labour force (Glowny Urzad Statystyczny, 1996a, p.100). Even under communist rule, most farms were privately run. Agricultural products include rye, potatoes, sugar beet and wheat (Glowny Urzad Statystyczny, 1994).

Poland is a former Soviet bloc country which is in the process of transforming itself into a democratic society. Massive political opposition in the 1980s gave rise to the first non-communist government in 1989 and a transition to a free-market economy. In 1990, an open and free presidential election was held for the first time in Polish history, and 1991 saw the first free parliamentary election since the Second World War. As a result of these democratic changes, Poles now enjoy political and religious freedom. Undoubtedly, some of these changes and the process of privatization have caused hardship and upheavals in the lives of many Polish citizens. Efforts are being made to organize urgently-needed comprehensive social services. A new Social Assistance Act passed in 1990 is intended to provide government aid to the most vulnerable. Social assistance is now governed by the Ministry of Labour and Social Policy (under communism, it was administered by the Ministry of Health and Social Welfare). The organization of child welfare services continues to be the responsibility of the Ministry of Education, as it was previously. However, the Family and Juvenile Court plays a major role in the placement of children in foster care or in residential treatment centres.

History and origins

Poland has a long history of foster care. The first formal foster care programme was organized by the Father Baudoin Home for Children, a foundling hospital that opened in Warsaw in 1736. This institution was the first to try to place children under the care of 'known or recommended' paid foster mothers (Kolankiewicz, 1993, pp.161–2).

In the nineteenth century, when Poland was partitioned between Russia, Prussia and Austria, foster care was a widely applied form of child care in the Prussian sector, while, under Czar Nicholas, abandoned children were placed with paid wetnurses and nannies. Just before the First World War, Kazimierz Jezewski, a distinguished Polish educator, organized 'orphan nests', in which foster families caring for several children worked together on a 'model farm' provided by the state (Czajkowski, 1957; Kepski, 1991).

After Poland gained its independence in 1918, many foster care programmes were established, the best-known being the Lodz programme, founded in 1926 by the municipal authorities (Puternicka, 1930). In this programme, the qualifications of foster families were formulated, as were rules for systematic professional supervision. Foster children were guaranteed free schooling, medical care, medicine and hospitalization, and even summer camps, with costs being covered by the city, and foster parents received remuneration (Majewska, 1948). From 1934, the then Ministry of Social Welfare mounted a Campaign for Foster Families to help expand the idea of fostering throughout the country (Kepski, 1991).

Foster care also played a significant role in the care of war orphans. During both world wars, the lives of thousands of children in Poland were saved when they were placed with foster families. In 1949, there were about 73,000 children in the care of foster families (Majewska, 1948).

However, with the establishment of the communist state in 1945, foster care programmes were no longer encouraged, and they were replaced by large, state-run children's homes. Child care was then placed under the control of the Ministry of Education, which incorporated the newly-formed Department of Child Welfare. For many years thereafter, fostering was not an area of interest to those responsible for child welfare in Poland. However, the Warsaw municipal authorities supported efforts by foster care activists within the state-run Friends of Children Society. This support was manifested through an order promulgated on 9 March 1965 by the Warsaw municipal authorities concerning foster care for children aged 3–7. In 1965, the society began organizing care in foster families through the Adoption and Fostering Centres (Kelm, 1983).

It was not until the 1970s that foster care issues gradually became a focus for attention for the government. Starting in 1971, a number of regulations by the Ministry of Education established general rules governing fostering and financial help to foster families (Regulations by the Council of Ministers, 22 November 1971, concerning financial help for children and youth in foster family care; Order of the Minister of Education, 13 December 1974, concerning general rules for fostering and financial help for children in foster family care). Attempts were made to regulate foster care and the supervision of foster families: schoolteachers served as supervisors. Several forms of foster care were proposed, priority being given to kinship care (Regulations by the Council of Ministers, 26 January 1979). Besides kinship care, there were so-called 'pre-adoptive', 'therapeutic' and 'resocialization' families (Ziemska, 1979).

Since the mid-1970s, the term 'foster family' in Poland has meant the children's next of kin, appointed caregivers or guardians by court order. For years, these relatives received very little help from the state; typically, the subsidy for a child placed in kinship care was only half that for a child placed with non-related caregivers. The subsidy was set at 20 per cent of the average salary for kinship caregivers and at 40 per cent for non-related foster families.

In 1993, new regulations based on the Education Act (1991) provided for equal amounts of 'financial help' to children placed with related and non-related caregivers. At the same time, state supervision of foster families, as well as the organization of supporting services for them, was assured through additional regulations (Education Act, 7 September 1991; Regulations by the Ministry of Education concerning foster family care, 21 October 1993; Regulations by the Ministry of Education concerning establishment of Public Adoption and Fostering Centres, 17 August 1993).

In addition to the kinship foster families, another model of foster care was developed by the Friends of Children Society mentioned above (Kelm, 1983; Ziemska, 1979). 'Family' children's homes – the first came into being in 1958 – function as large foster families, in which one of the foster parents is usually employed to organize the home and provide care. Today, there are 804 children in 117 children's homes of this type (Glowny Urzad Statystyczny, 1996b, p.205).

New regulations and policies in response to recent socio-political changes are much more favourable to foster family care. According to a government policy statement in May 1994, the main task of child welfare is 'the initiation and support of family-like child care' (Ministerstwo Edukacji Narodowej, 1994a, p.24). However, the new policies have resulted in great expectations, so that fostering is now seen as an essential part, or even as 'the future', of child welfare services in Poland. These new rules concerning the development of foster care services (known as 'contract families' – trained persons compensated for providing foster care) are being discussed by the government (Kolankiewicz and Milewska, 1994; Stelmaszuk, 1994a).

Administration and organization

According to the Education Act of 7 September 1991, foster care continues to be under the control of the state. However, the Act delegates responsibility for organizing placement in foster families to a Board of Education (*Kuratorium*) at the provincial level. As in the past, a child can be placed in a foster family either by a court or by an agreement between the child's parents and the Board of Education. Preference is given to caregivers who are related to the child. There is no system for assessment and placement. The child is placed either with a person designated as a foster parent or in residential care. The Board of Education is responsible for providing the foster child with financial support and other help, as well as for the supervision of the foster family. These tasks are carried out, mostly at the provincial level, by the Adoption and Fostering Centres, of which 37 are public and 25 non-public at present (Ministerstwo Edukacji Narodowej, 1994b, p.133).

A number of recently-developed non-governmental organizations (NGOs) that focus on child welfare strongly advocate training and support for foster families (Stelmaszuk, 1995a). However, the government sector controls the distribution of funds and sets eligibility requirements for foster families. It also regulates the agencies within the emerging non-governmental sector. As of 1996, no licensing system for foster caregivers had been established.

Who is placed in foster care?

There are currently 46,101 children and young people in 35,838 foster family homes in Poland. Although foster care is being systematically expanded, most children are placed in various kinds of residential facilities (see Table 17.1).

Table 17.1 Children and young people in out-of-home placements by categories developed by the Central Statistical Office, 1995

Type	Category	No. of placements
Foster care	Foster families*	46,101
(education sector)	'Family' children's homes	804
Residential care	Children's homes	17,874
(education sector)	Children's villages	188
	Emergency care	12,988
Residential care	Residential centres/special educational needs	33,100
Education sector	Residential centres/rehabilitation or behaviour problems	3,356
Justice sector	Juvenile delinquency	2,407
Residential care	Mental disability	3,691
(health/welfare	Physical disability	371
sector)	Psychiatric units	469
	Emergency care**	294
	Not specified	192
Total		121,835

* Includes 1,892 children with special needs
** Shelters for mothers with children.
Source: Glowny Urzad Statstyczny (1996b).

The vast majority of children in foster care are placed with their relatives by the courts: the courts respond to serious problems on the part of the biological parents – predominantly child abuse and neglect resulting from alcoholism (Jaworska-Maj, 1990). According to the Ministry of Justice, 84.7 per cent of the children who were in foster families in 1993 were placed there by the courts (Ministerstwo Sprawiedliwosci, 1996). New data supplied by the Ministry of Education suggest that as many as 98 per cent of children and young people in foster family care were placed there by the courts (Ministerstwo Edukacji Narodowej, 1996). It should be noted that the Ministry of Education statistics include young people who remain in care after reaching the age of majority (18 years) because they are still attending school. These young people may be as old as 26 years whereas the Ministry of Justice keeps records of children only until they reach the age of 18.

As Table 17.2 shows, in 1994, even after the introduction of new regulations the year before, the proportion remained as high as 79.3 per cent, according to the Ministry of Justice figures. (The 1993 regulations resulted in an additional 10,000 foster families in 1994.)

Table 17.2   Placement of children in foster families, 1990–95

	Total	No. placed by court	% placed by court
1990	37,215	31,881	85.7
1991	37,591	32,130	85.5
1992	38,650	32,968	85.3
1993	40,788	34,565	84.7
1994	43,911	34,801	79.3
1995	46,101	36,894	80.0

Source: Ministerstwo Sprawiedliwosci (1996).

A study by Luczak (1994) reports that 46 per cent of biological parents of children in foster care are alcoholics, 34 per cent suffer from alcohol-related disorders, and 37 per cent have committed a crime (these percentages refer to a representative sample of 100 children from the Warsaw area). However, only 4.3 per cent of the children in foster care were classified as having special needs, as Table 17.3 shows.

Table 17.3   Children in foster family care by categories developed by the Central Statistical Office, 1995

Category	No.	%
Special needs	1,982	4.29
Under 2 years of age	641	1.39
Under 2 years of age: special needs	10	0.02
Left care	3,163	6.86
Recently adopted	126	0.27
Total	46,101	

Note: 'Family' children's homes not included.
Source: Glowny Urzad Statstyczny (1996b).

According to Luczak (1994), the majority of children enter foster care between the ages of 3 and 7, and spend at least half their lives until they reach majority in care. For many children, placement with relatives seems to be virtually permanent (Jaworska-Maj, 1990), but more precise data on the whole population of foster children are needed.

Of the 804 children and young people placed in the 'family' children's homes (as of 1995), the majority had great difficulty adapting to life in a large institution. Their placement in the homes is intended to be permanent: they are to be cared for until they are able to live independently (Kelm, 1986; Ziemska, 1979).

Care providers

According to the 1993 regulations, either a couple or a single person with Polish citizenship and living in Poland can be foster parents, on condition that their parental rights have never been terminated. Other requirements are good health and adequate living conditions, an 'appropriate' age difference between the child and foster parents, and agreement to being fostered on the part of the child, if aged over 13. It is also stipulated that those who foster children with special needs should be 'prepared'.

The majority of foster family care providers (35,858 families as of 1995) are the children's grandparents, most often grandmothers, who, in Poland, are usually deeply involved in their grandchildren's upbringing and wellbeing. (Under Polish law, relatives – grandparents, step-parents or siblings – are obliged to support their young relatives if the parents cannot give sufficient care.) Data on the whole population are not available, but research on 256 foster families by Jaworska-Maj (1990) has shown that as many as 91 per cent of foster carers are related to the children, while 79 per cent are grandparents. Almost all are elderly pensioners (68.2 per cent over 60 years old) of rather low socio-economic status. Moreover, over 50 per cent of them have serious health problems, and conflicts with the child's parents are frequent. Non-related foster carers, by contrast, are usually much younger, with better health and higher socio-economic status (Luczak, 1994).

'Family' children's homes are the only form of foster care in which the caregivers are considered service providers. As of December 1995, 135 individuals (usually foster mothers) were employed in 117 homes of this type, the majority of them professionally trained, even though this is no longer a requirement (Glowny Urzad Statystyczny, 1996b, p.205).

Financial support

Foster care is not yet looked upon as a service in Poland. The law clearly states that foster carers are not to be compensated for their efforts: an exception is made for the 'family' children's homes. The allowance received by the foster parents has been defined as 'financial help for the child'. According to the 1993 regulations, this allowance is set at 40 per cent of the average national wage, which is calculated on a quarterly basis. Since, for the second quarter of 1996, the average monthly national wage was 855.35 zlotys (at that time, equivalent to $US320), the monthly allowance given to a foster child amounted to about $US128. Although the allowance has been fixed at 60 per cent of the average national wage for 1995, this rate of payment does not seem to have been achieved.

Only children under 2 years of age (1.3 per cent of foster children) and children with special educational needs (4.3 per cent) are entitled to an allowance of 100 per cent of the average national wage. For children who receive any kind of income or survivor's benefits, the allowance is reduced by half the amount of the income or benefit. An allowance set at 190 per cent of the average salary is earmarked for the accommodation of a new foster child. Those leaving care after reaching majority are entitled to receive a lump sum of 300 per cent of the average salary in order to give them a start in life. Those in foster care who have achieved majority but are still pursuing their education are entitled to foster care benefits (according to the 1993 regulations).

Major problems

The major problems in foster family care in Poland are:

- the quality of care offered in kinship care;
- the dearth of professionals working with existing foster and kinship families;
- the lack of regulations designed to build up the foster care services system.

Recent policies have systematically increased the number of children placed in kinship foster care. The quality of such care is not always satisfactory. Some argue that foster care allowances have been used as a form of public assistance for dysfunctional families, because dysfunctional parents sometimes stay in the same household as the children and their caregivers (Ministerstwo Edukacji Narodowej, 1994b, p.8). There is an urgent need for improved placement policies, such as consultation by child welfare professionals before placement by the court. Professionals should be available at the local level to help both children and their foster parents in existing foster families.

Of the greatest importance is the development of foster care services in which the foster parents are qualified service providers (rather than services recipients). There is a large population of children in institutional settings who have special needs for professional services: such services as can be provided only through fundamental changes in the legal system (Skoczkowski, 1994). Training opportunities for current and prospective foster carers are urgently needed too.

The state/public and non-governmental sectors will need to reach consensus, collaborate with each other, and work out strategies for sharing responsibility and power.

Major trends

The major trends in foster care in Poland are as follows:

- There is an increasing number of children in foster care, since this is the type of placement preferred by the court.
- Reliance is placed mostly upon kinship carers, and they are given priority when children need to be placed.
- Planning focuses on long-term/permanent foster care placement rather than on short-term placement or respite care.
- Children tend to remain in care for longer periods: the state supports children until they have completed their education, sometimes up to the age of 26 if they are still at university.
- Support services for foster carers are being organized through the public (state-funded) adoption and fostering centres.
- Additional service and training opportunities for foster carers are being developed within the non-governmental sector.
- There is an increasing interest in working with biological families.

These 'major trends' should be viewed as a reflection of the great change which has taken place in systems serving children in need, with special reference to foster family care.

Instead of child care measures based on a collective and institutional concept of education, foster family arrangements are based on the principle that bringing up a child within a family is the most important consideration. Unfortunately, the discussions preceding long-anticipated reforms in child care were dominated by the topic of inter-country adoption. The increasing number of Polish children being adopted abroad was the cause of much criticism, even at parliamentary level. These discussions revealed gaps in the existing legislation, as well as errors in the application of the legislation in practice.

Finally, it was decided that the Public Adoption and Fostering Centre in Warsaw would be the organization solely responsible for all adoptions in Poland. The national data bank within the centre is accessible to anyone who wants to seek or provide information. In accordance with the philosophy of the United Nations Convention on the Rights of the Child, inter-country adoption should be regarded as the last recourse for a child who cannot be placed in a family in Poland. It is hoped that the activities of the Public Adoption and Fostering Centre will resolve the very delicate problem of inter-country adoption.

The Socio-Political Committee within the Cabinet began working on a solution to the problem of children still living in institutions in 1994. Changes point most to the foster family care system as an alternative to institutional children's homes for both pedagogical and financial reasons. By the end of 1994, the group of experts working on the problem had devised a scheme involving 'contract foster families'. Under this scheme, professional foster parents (the foster mother or foster father, or both) are employed by children's homes or by public adoption and fostering centres. Foster parents may be employed temporarily or permanently, receiving a regular salary (the average salary in Poland) for as long as they take care of the child. Such foster parents require a certificate, which they can obtain by taking specially organized courses (Kolankiewicz and Milewska, 1994).

The scheme entails the organization of different kinds of foster families according to the child's need: emergency care, assessment care, therapy, rehabilitative care, preparation for moving back to the natural family, or preparation for moving to an adoptive family. The scheme includes a detailed programme for recruiting, training and providing pedagogical support groups for foster parents. When the scheme is realized in its entirety, it will allow children the opportunity to move gradually from institutions to foster families. It is anticipated that the 'contract families' scheme will soon be a permanent part of the child care system in Poland.

In addition to the new professional foster families, there will also be a continuation of the traditional foster family system, where foster parents are related or unrelated to the child. These families will receive 40 per cent of the average monthly national wage, or 100 per cent in the case of a child with special needs. Traditional foster parents will not need to possess any certificate.

Non-public adoption and fostering centres, mainly under the auspices of TPD (The Friends of Children Society, an organization with over thirty years' experience, and active in nearly every province) will continue their work in this field as well. There is also an increasing number of church centres – Catholic Adoption and Fostering Centres – which undertake broad-based work with families in need. They view foster families not as substitute families but as complementary to the natural family, which still has full responsibility for the child. The long-term placement of a child in a foster family is considered a measure of last resort.

In recruiting and preparing future foster parents for their new role, Catholic Adoption and Fostering Centres use non-conventional methods, such as retreats or joint prayers. They stress the moral duty of the Christian family to be open to the needs of others, especially to the needs of children who lack the care of their own parents.

Role of national foster care association

The revival of democratic society in Poland after 1989 favoured the rise of all kinds of citizens' initiatives representing the interests of various social groups. In consequence, a number of organizations, foundations and associations emerged, including associations of foster families. The movement began in major cities such as Warsaw, Cracow and Gdansk in 1993, with the aim of supporting state authorities in their efforts to reform the child care system. The goals were to advise politicians dealing with such matters on the parliamentary level, to respond to consultative documents, and to popularize the idea of foster families, while educating society at large. Associations also aimed to change society's attitudes towards children brought up in institutions or foster families.

As yet, there is no foster care organization at the national level. There are, however, a number of registered foster care organizations and informal groups working independently, mostly at the local level. Some of these organizations were initiated by the authorities or by activists rather than by the foster carers themselves. Others, though never formally registered, were initiated by foster carers and continue to engage in very active work. Several initiatives were undertaken by foster care activists to bring these different organizations together into one national organization: one such initiative occurred before the IFCO conference in Bergen. However, after long discussion, it was decided that a national organization should not be formed officially, but instead, should be allowed to grow out of a natural process facilitated by the foster carers themselves. After so many years of state monopoly, where voluntary organizations and social groups played a very restricted role and were often used or manipulated by the state, people in Poland are very sensitive to any hint of manipulation, and tend to prefer small groups and local activities.

In 1994, the Cracow Association of Adoptive and Foster Families launched a major recruitment drive for foster parents using the local press, TV and radio, but it received rather a small response in Cracow itself. The fact that families with as many as four children, living in small towns and villages around Cracow responded to the appeal makes it evident that information about foster families should also be directed to the lower levels of the state administration, and to local governments, rural communities and parishes in areas where people have better living conditions at present. All possible routes should be utilized.

Based on the experiences of the Cracow Foster Family Association, it may be concluded that the main problem is not how to prepare prospective foster parents, but rather, whether there are sufficient numbers of them to carry on the very difficult task of helping children in need.

Contacts: Association of Foster Families, Public Adoption and Fostering Centre, Nowogrodzka 75, 02-018 Warsaw, Poland *Telephone and Fax*: (+48) 22-62-10-75 (contact person: Krystyna Musial, President *Telephone*: (+48) 22-18-24-11). Foster Parents Support Group of the Warsaw branch of the Friends of Children Society, Szpitalna 5, 00-031 Warsaw, Poland *Telephone*: (+48) 22-26-22-15 (contact person: Grazyna Niedzielska). Family Children's Home Circle of the Friends of Children Society, Os. Rosa 100/2, 61-245 Poznan, Poland *Telephone*: (+48) 61-77-99-82 (contact person: Magdalena Blumczynska, President). Association of Adoptive and Foster Families of the Friends of Children Society, Sw. Marka 20, 31-020 Krakow, Poland *Telephone*: (+48) 12-23-20-20 (contact person: Danuta Wiecha).

Research

Since foster care became a part of the child welfare system, several studies have been conducted, most of them by university researchers. They have, for the most part, been small-scale, descriptive studies, some undertaken for academic theses. They focus on: foster family functioning; foster care providers, their living conditions and motivations for fostering; the social climate, and relationships within the family (Bedkowska, 1979; Jaworska-Maj, 1990; Kelm, 1983; Rozanska and Tynelski, 1981). The majority of researchers, even though they stress the strong emotional bonds between children and their caregivers (Kelm, 1983; Luczak, 1994), have been critical about the quality of kinship care and favour non-related caregivers. They point out that many of those who have left foster care keep in touch with their foster parents more often than with their biological families (Jaworska-Maj, 1990).

In other studies, the focus is on the difficulties experienced by foster children and the causes of these difficulties, contacts with biological parents (Safjan, 1982), performance in school and educational and career plans (Baran, 1985; Kepski, 1991; Rozanska and Tynelski, 1981). A study by Jaworska-Maj (1990) deals with the perception of foster care by those who have been in care, as well as with the foster family's influence on the educational pursuits and professional plans of these people. A comparative study by Baran (1985), which describes the life expectations of children from foster and residential care settings, argues that foster care helps develop more optimistic attitudes than residential care. Another study by Luczak (1994) compares health and development in three representative samples (100 children in each group) from foster care, residential care and natural family settings. The best developmental conditions, outside the natural family environment, were found in non-related foster families.

A number of studies on 'family' children's homes conclude that this form of placement is relatively successful (Kelm, 1976; 1986; Ziemska, 1979).

Recent studies include a critical examination of historical developments in foster care, as well as action research on the development of non-governmental support services for foster families (Stelmaszuk, 1994a; 1995a). Research funded by the Polish Scientific Research Committee, assessing possibilities for the reunification with their families of 300 children placed in three different kinds of settings (residential care, foster family care, and residential school for children with special needs) has recently been completed (Stelmaszuk, 1996). In addition, the Ministry of Education has completed a survey on the entire population of foster families in Poland (Ministerstwo Edukacji Narodowej, 1996).

For further information, the following are suggested:

Jaworska-Maj, H. (1990) *Sytuacja zyciowa bylych wychowankow rodzin zastepczych,* Warsaw: Instytut Badan Pedagogicznych.
Stelmaszuk, Z.W. (1995a) 'Foster care in times of socio-economic changes. Expectations and perspectives, in *Foster Children in a Changing World: Documentation of the European IFCO Conference, Berlin 1994,* Münster: Votum Verlag (in English and German).
Stelmaszuk, Z.W. (1995b) 'Fremdunterbringungsprojekte in Polen und die Unterschiede zu westlichen Systemen', in *Du! Ich brauche Eltern. Pflegekinder. Aktuelle Problene. Zukunftsweisende Modelle. Tagungs-dokumentation,* Salzburg: Kids & Tens.
Ziemska, M. (1981) 'Poland: Foster family homes', in Payne, C.J. and White, K.J. (eds) *Caring for Deprived Children: International Case Studies of Residential Settings,* London: Croom Helm.

Bibliography

Baran, B. (1985) 'Wyobrazenia o wlasnej przyszlosci dzieci wychowywanych poza rodzina', in Tyszkowa, M. (ed.) *Rozwoj dziecka w rodzinie i poza rodzina,* Poznan: Uniwersytet Adama Mickiewicza.
Bedkowska, V. (1979) 'Sytuacja emocjonalna dzieci w rodzinach zastepczych', *Problemy Rodziny,* No. 5.
Czajkowski, K. (1957) 'Kazimierz Jezewski', *Dom Dziecka,* No. 2.
Glowny Urzad Statystyczny (1994) *Wskazniki przemian warunkow zycia w okresie przechodzenia do gospodarki rynkowej w latach 1989–1993,* Warsaw.

Glowny Urzad Statystyczny (1996a) *Maly rocznik statystyczny 1996*, Warsaw.

Glowny Urzad Statystyczny (1996b) *Oswiata i wychowanie w roku szkolnym 1995/96*, Warsaw.

Jaworska-Maj, H. (1990) *Sytuacja zyciowa bylych wychowankow rodzin zastepczych*, Warsaw: Instytut Badan Pedagogicznych.

Kelm, A. (ed.) (1976) *Odzyskane domy rodzinne. Z doswiadczen rodzinnych domow dziecka w Polsce Ludowej*, Warsaw: Wydawnictwa Szkilne i Pedagogiczne.

Kelm, A. (1983) *Formy opieki nad dzieckiem w Polsce Ludowej*, Warsaw: Wydawnictwa Szkolne i Pedagogiczne.

Kelm, A. (ed.) (1986) *Materialy z ogolnopolskiej konferencji naukowo-pedagogicznej poswieconej doswiadczeniom rodzinnych domow dziecka*, Warsaw: Ministerstwo Oswiaty i Wychowania.

Kepski, C. (1991) *Dziecko sieroce i opieka nad nim w Polsce w okresie miedzywojennym*, Lublin: Uniwersytet Marii Curie-Sklodowskiej.

Kolankiewicz, M. (1993) 'Dzieje Domu Ks. Baudoina', *Kwartalnik Pedagogiczny*, Vol. 38, No. 1.

Kolankiewicz, M. and Milewska, E. (1994) 'Kontraktowe rodziny zastepcze – nowa forma opieki nad dziecmi', unpublished.

Luczak, E. (1994) 'Srodowisko wychowawcze rodzin zastepczych', *Opieka. Terapia. Wychowanie*, No. 17.

Majewska A. (ed.) (1948) *Rodziny zastepcze Lodzi*, Lodz: Polski Instytut Sluzby Spolecznej.

Ministerstwo Edukacji Narodowej (1994a) 'Glowne kierunki doskonalenia systemu edukacji w Polsce. Materialy na debate sejmowa', unpublished.

Ministerstwo Edukacji Narodowej (1994b) 'Funkcjonowanie placowek opieki calkowitej nad dziecmi i mlodzieza. Materialy na posiedzenie Sejmowej Komisji Edukacji, Nauki i Postepu Technicznego', unpublished.

Ministerstwo Edukacji Narodowej (1996) 'Informacja dotyczaca przegladu rodzin zastepczych dokonanego w 1995r', unpublished.

Ministerstwo Sprawiedliwosci (1996) *Informacja statystyczna o dzialalnosci wymiaru sprawiedliwosci w 1995r*, Warsaw.

Puternicka, J. (1930) 'Umieszczanie dzieci w rodzinach. Dzialalnosc Wydzialu Opieki Spolecznej Magistratu m. Lodzi', *Opieka nad dzieckiem*, No. 1.

Rozanska, E. and Tynelski, A. (1981) *Rodzina zastepcza jako forma opieki nad dzieckiem*, Kielce: Wyasza Szkola Pedagogiczna.

Rozporzadzenie Ministerstwa Edukacji Narodowej z dnia 17 sierpnia 1993r. w sprawie osrodkow adopcyjno-opiekunczych (Dz. U. Nr 84, poz. 394).

Rozporzadzenie Rady Ministrow z dnia 21 pazdziernika 1993r. w sprawie rodzin zastepczych (Dz. U. Nr 103, poz. 470, z pozn. zm.).

Safjan, M. (1982) *Instytucja rodzin zastepczych. Problemy prawno-organizacyjne*, Warsaw: Wydawnictwo Prawnicze.

Skoczkowski, J. (1994) 'Opinia prawna dotyczaca koniecznych zmian w prawie w celu urzeczywistnienia koncepcji odplatnych kontraktowych rodzin zastepczych', unpublished.

Stelmaszuk, Z.W. (1994a) 'Fostering in Poland', *European Journal of Social Work*, Vol. 1, No. 2.

Stelmaszuk, Z.W. (1994b) 'Family preservation and reunification: A current need in family policies in Eastern Europe', in *Evolution of the Role of Children in Family Life: Participation and Negotiations. Conference Proceedings.* Madrid: Ministerio de Asuntos Sociales and Council of Europe.

Stelmaszuk, Z.W. (1995a) 'Foster care in times of socio-economic changes: Expectations and perspectives, in *Foster Children in a Changing World: Documentation of the European IFCO Conference, Berlin 1994*, Münster: Votum Verlag (in English and German).

Stelmaszuk, Z.W. (1995b) 'Fremdunterbringungsprojekte in Polen und die Unterschiede zu westlichen Systemen', in *Du! Ich brauche Eltern. Pflegekinder. Aktuelle Probleme. Zukunftsweisende Modelle. Tagungsdokumentation*, Salzburg: Kids & Tens.

Stelmaszuk, Z.W. (1996) 'Reintegracja rodziny jako cel i efekt opieki zastepczej nad dzieckiem. Raport z badan wykonanych na zlecenie Komitetu Badan Naukowych', unpublished.

Ustawa z dnia 7 wrzesnia 1991r. o systemie oswiaty (Dz. U. Nr 95, poz. 425 z pozn. zm.).

Ziemska, M. (1981) 'Poland: Foster family homes', in Payne, C.J. and White, K.J. (eds) *Caring for Deprived Children: International Case Studies of Residential Settings*. London: Croom Helm.

18 United Kingdom

Clive Sellick and June Thoburn

Jurisdiction

The United Kingdom, with a population of around 58 million, comprises England, Northern Ireland, Scotland and Wales. Around 20 per cent of the population is aged under 16. Around 6 per cent are from minority ethnic groups, the main groupings being those of South Asian and of African Caribbean ethnic origin. About a third of the ethnic minority population is under the age of 16, compared to around a fifth of the white British population (*Social Trends*, 1995). There is wide variation in the distribution of people from minority ethnic groups across the UK, the majority living in urban areas in England and Wales.

Health services and education from ages 5 to 16 are free, as is higher education for those who secure places. The Department of Health (DoH) and the Northern Ireland Office, Scottish Office and Welsh Office are responsible overall for welfare policy, but the provision of welfare services for those in need of assistance due to age, disability or family problems is delegated to the local authority social services departments in England and Wales, to social work departments in Scotland, and to health and social work trusts in Northern Ireland. In Scotland, probation work with offenders of all ages is the responsibility of the social work departments. In the rest of the UK, some work with child and adolescent offenders is undertaken by the social services departments or trusts, but the probation service undertakes most of the work with adolescents. The age of criminal responsibility is 10.

Although the UK is a comparatively wealthy country, income and wealth are distributed unequally, and the gap between rich and poor is growing. Over 10 per cent of the population available for work are unemployed, and increasing unemployment among young people has led to a higher proportion of 16–18-year-olds remaining in education after the end of

237

compulsory education. There is an income maintenance system which provides an official 'safety net', and in theory, should prevent families slipping into absolute poverty. However, growing numbers are living at or below this basic minimum level (including 1 in 3 children, according to 1994 figures). Young people under the age of 18 who cannot live at home for whatever reason, or who are unemployed and whose parents are too poor to support them, are particularly likely to fall through this safety net, since they are not normally eligible for Income Support in their own right. Black people are more likely than the white British population to be badly housed, to be unemployed and to have a low income (*Social Trends*, 1995).

An important study by Bebbington and Miles (1989) has shown that children in one-parent families, or those whose parents live on state benefits, are badly housed, have more than three children, or are of minority ethnic origin have a 1 in 10 chance of needing to be looked after by the official child care system, compared to a 1 in 1,000 chance if none of these applies.

History and origins

It was not until the 1948 Children Act that services for destitute, maltreated or delinquent children were taken out of the Poor Law, judicial and education systems and put together under the control of local authority children's committees, which adopted a child and family welfare philosophy. Before that date, some large children's charities, which were mainly associated with the Churches, had pioneered a child welfare approach in their children's homes. Under the Poor Law regimes, children were sometimes sent from the workhouses to live with families, but most of them were exploited as free labour. The large charitable institutions developed more child-centred 'boarding out' schemes, and their example was followed by some of the state agencies. However, those who joined the new children's departments in 1948 found much bad practice and exploitation of children in foster care. After 1948, the social work profession took on the major responsibility for the development of the foster care service, which has become increasingly important as the placement of choice for the majority of children who cannot live with their parents. Parker (1990) gives a useful, concise history of child care services.

Legislation and regulation of child care services, including foster care and adoption, is slightly different in the four provinces which make up the UK, but there are more similarities than differences. In England and Wales (and Northern Ireland, with slight differences) the Children Act (1989) and its accompanying regulations and guidance (DoH, 1991a) provide the framework and legislative mandate for all child welfare and family support services. This includes work with children who have disabilities and require additional social support, children whose parents are in dispute following separation or divorce, and children in need of protection or whose families are under such stress that additional support services are necessary to ensure a 'reasonable standard of health or development' for the child. Local authority social workers are also required to provide services to help young people who may be at risk of involvement in criminal activity, but the criminal justice system is regulated by separate legislation, and Youth Courts are separate from the Family Proceedings Courts. In Scotland, Children's Panels make decisions and review the cases of all children where there are serious welfare concerns, including those who have committed offences. A Children Act for Scotland became law in 1995.

Wherever possible, the law requires that intervention, including the provision of accommodation in foster or children's homes, or placement prior to the making of an Adoption Order, should be under the voluntary family support provisions of the Children Act (1989). The court may only make a Care or Supervision Order if 'it considers that doing so would be better for the child than making no order at all'. Even when such an order is granted, parents and older children must be consulted before any important decision is made, and due consideration must be given to their wishes and feelings.

If a child is looked after by foster carers under voluntary provisions (usually referred to as being 'accommodated'), the parents retain their parental responsibility, and the foster family, local authority and parents make an agreement about which aspects of parenting each will be responsible for. Even when a child is subject to a Care Order, the natural parents retain some parental responsibility, which they exercise at the discretion of the local authority and after discussion with the foster carers. There is a presumption that all children in foster care will have regular contact with their birth relatives. If there are difficulties arranging this, the court may make a Contact Order, either to define contact, or if there is strong evidence that it will be harmful to the child, to curtail it. It can be seen that the ability to work in partnership with social workers and birth relatives is an essential attribute for foster carers in the UK.

Administration and organization

Each local authority social services department is responsible for the provision of foster care services within its geographical area. Family placement teams are usually formed to discharge both the fostering and adoption responsibilities of the social services department. They are staffed by specialist social workers, who are responsible for the recruitment, assessment, training and support of foster carers and adopters. The regulations (DoH, 1991a) do not require the establishment of such a distinct service, but acknowledge the value of this, especially with respect to foster carers themselves. A panel of social work, medical and legal staff, usually chaired by a social work manager, approves and reviews foster carers.

Local authorities are the principal agencies which provide and deliver mainstream foster care services. However, some specialist services are purchased from the voluntary sector. Long-established voluntary organizations such as Barnardos have developed specialist fostering schemes for older children or those with disabilities (see for example, Barnardos, 1981 and Westacott, 1988). However, in the main, the older and often religiously founded voluntary agencies, such as the Catholic Children's Society and some of the more recent secular societies such as the Independent Adoption Society or Parents for Children, have concentrated on permanent substitute family placement – usually adoption, but including some permanent foster placements.

In recent years, a number of independent fostering agencies have been established, some in the private sector, others as registered voluntary agencies. These agencies are permitted to recruit and prepare foster carers, but they can only be approved in relation to a particular child by that child's local authority (NFCA, 1995). Although relatively few children are placed in the voluntary foster care sector, its importance is illustrated by the publication of a recent study of the smaller, independent fostering agencies conducted by the Department of Health (DoH, 1995).

There are no overall licensing arrangements specifically governing the establishment of fostering agencies, either public or voluntary, for example with regard to social work staffing levels, numbers of foster carers, methods and levels of payment, and training or support of foster carers. However, the 1991 regulations guide the assessment and approval of foster carers, reviews and termination of approval, the making and reviewing of placements, the number of children placed in each foster household, the supervision and ending of placements, and foster carers' records. General regulations applying to all children in care include promoting the welfare of fostered children, and contact with their parents and other relatives, as well as their health care and education (DoH, 1991a; NFCA, 1991). The Social Services Inspectorate of the Department of Health has established standards for a series of inspections of local authority fostering agencies (DoH, 1994/5).

Who is placed in foster care?

The population of children and young people cared for by local authorities has steadily decreased over recent years. Between 1981 and 1991, the number of children in care fell from 92,270 to 59,834, or by 35 per cent (DoH, 1994, p.36). At the same time, the proportion of children in foster rather than residential care has grown. For example, 65 per cent of all children looked after by local authorities between April 1992 and March 1993 were fostered. The figure rises to almost 90 per cent for children aged under 10 years (DoH, 1994).

Most children spend very short periods in the care of local authorities. About 50 per cent who are aged between 1 and 9 years, the vast majority of whom are in foster care, spend less than 14 days in care (DoH, 1994. p.37). As Rowe and her colleagues remarked in their extensive study of the beginning and ending of placements over two years in six local authorities: 'the day to day, bread and butter work of fostering is still the placement of younger children needing care for a brief period during a family crisis or to give relief to hard pressed parents' (Rowe et al., 1989, p.79). Short-term respite fostering schemes for families with a disabled member or for those under stress and at risk of long-term family breakdown have been extensively described and evaluated (see, for example, Aldgate et al., 1989; Bradley and Aldgate, 1994).

Fostering programmes for those who are looked after for longer periods, including older children, have developed over the past decade. These include teenage foster schemes (Hazel, 1990; Lowe, 1990), foster care for young people charged with offences (Fry, 1994) and schemes to prepare young people, through fostering, for leaving care (Fry and Hazelhurst, 1994; Hill et al., 1993).

Care providers

Although the proportion of children fostered in the UK has risen, the number of foster carers has remained static over many years, and is currently estimated to be 27,000 in England and Wales. The majority of these foster directly for local authorities.

Home studies of potential foster carers are undertaken by social workers, who assess their likely suitability and competence. Applicants are usually assessed individually, and health and police checks are carried out. Most agencies incorporate a training component during this process or soon after approval, and this usually takes place in a group setting, alongside other foster carers. Many agencies use or adopt the National Foster Care Association's training package, *Choosing to Foster: The Challenge to Care* (NFCA, 1994a). This covers a wide range of topics, including listening to children, working in partnership with parents and workers, and the acquisition of other fostering skills. Assessments are stringent and wide-ranging, and include consideration of the applicant's health, personality, religion, employment, leisure and experience of caring for other children. (See Triseliotis et al., 1995, for an extensive discussion of assessment, training and support of foster carers.)

The characteristics of foster families were described in an extensive study of 2,694 foster households in England (Bebbington and Miles, 1990). Typically, foster families comprise two parents, where the father works full-time outside the home. The mother, who is usually aged between 31 and 55, does not have a paid, full-time job. Typical foster carers also have older children of their own, and live in homes with three or more bedrooms.

Financial support

The commonest method of payment to foster carers is an allowance, which is calculated to cover the costs of keeping a child, including clothing, food, heating and recreational activities. This sum is not taxable, does not require foster carers to make National Insurance contributions, and it does not affect eligibility for state benefits such as Income Support. This allowance is sometimes enhanced to take account of an individual child's needs. Some fostering agencies have composited these extra costs and introduced a banding system, often operated on the discretionary judgements of its staff. Such schemes have a built-in financial disincentive – when a child's expensive behaviour lessens, so does the amount of payment. Taxable fees for service have been a feature of specialist fostering schemes for teenagers and children with special needs for some years. Some local authorities, and all independent fostering agencies, have extended these to their mainstream foster carers.

There is no national standard financial award for foster carers. Allowances and fees vary widely, sometimes within the same agency, depending on a variety of factors, including the child's age and perceived difficulties, and the scarcity or availability of foster families. Each year, the NFCA recommends a minimum level of allowances related to the government's Family Expenditure Survey and Equivalence Income Scales, which measure the average costs of caring for a child living in his or her own home. This takes no account of the additional difficulties and costs of fostering a child, yet the majority of local authorities in England still pay foster carers less than the NFCA's minimum recommended allowances.

Major problems

In recent years, and particularly over the last decade, foster carers have experienced a significant increase in what is expected of them. For example, the Children Act regulations (DoH, 1991a) expect carers to participate in review meetings, to document their work with children and families, and to provide skilled assistance to an increasing number of children and young people with emotional and behavioural problems, learning difficulties and disabilities.

Most local authorities have ongoing difficulties in: recruiting and retaining an adequate number and range of foster carers, especially in view of the increase in allegations of abuse against foster carers; the skilled task of facilitating family contact (Waterhouse, 1992); lack of support (Sellick, 1992), and the effects upon foster families' own children (Part, 1993). Bebbington and Miles (1990) found that as a result, hundreds of families each year were giving up fostering altogether, or were turning instead to the independent agencies. These agencies are better able to keep foster carers by placing 'emphasis on factors linked to foster family retention such as substantial group support, respite care and high fostering payments' (Bebbington and Miles, 1990, p.302).

At a time when local authorities are struggling with supply difficulties in respect of the recruitment and retention of foster carers, they are also having to face increased demands for foster placements associated with the steady rise in the birth rate and in social problems linked to HIV infection and drug abuse.

Major trends

Since 1948, there has been a strong emphasis in the UK on foster family care as a temporary service to help families over periods of stress, or to perform a specific task for a young person in need of help and accommodation. In the 1970s, however, a series of research studies, most notably that by Rowe and Lambert (1973), demonstrated that in the UK, as in the USA, children were remaining for long periods in unplanned care. While there, they often lost touch with their birth families, and some were exposed to multiple moves and an uncoordinated system which neglected important aspects of their parenting needs – in particular, their need for a sense of permanence and a sense of personal and cultural identity (see Thoburn, 1994, for a fuller discussion). The research also showed that for some children, the foster family became, quite appropriately, the child's 'permanent' family (Rowe et al., 1984). However, some children who had put down firm roots with their foster families were removed, either by their parents or by the local authorities, against the children's wishes. A change in the law was made in 1975 to give additional legal rights to these children and their foster parents, and also to make it easier for parental contact to be terminated and for children to be placed for adoption without parental consent. As a result, in the 1970s and 1980s, foster carers more often found themselves either encouraged to become the child's permanent carer (sometimes being pushed to apply for an Adoption Order against their better judgement), or helping the child sever links with his or her natural family in order to move to an adoptive family. The emphasis on working with natural families and the development of skills to do so correspondingly diminished.

Over time, the provision of family support services has meant that those who need to be in foster care have more severe problems, and in particular, more of them will have been maltreated by their parents or other carers, or been emotionally harmed by exposure to parental conflict. The Children Act (1989) has brought back more balance and clarity to the foster carer's role. The majority work on a short-term basis to support families and return their children to them, to help young people negotiate the transition to adult life, and occasionally, to help children to move to adoptive or 'permanent' foster families. An important minority provide long-term parenting for children who cannot return home, and often become the children's 'psychological parents' at the same time as helping them to stay in touch with their relatives. These children will often have serious emotional or behavioural difficulties, or may need especially skilled care because of a severe disability.

Role of national foster care associations

The National Foster Care Association

This was established in 1974 and operates across the United Kingdom. It brings together all parties with foster care interests. Its membership includes corporate bodies such as local authorities, voluntary organizations and members of over a hundred local foster care groups, as well as almost 10,000 individual and family members, most of whom are foster carers.

The NFCA produces major training programmes, a wide range of publications, a telephone advice line, advice and mediation, and insurance cover. It regularly engages in specific foster care projects across the country. Its director and her management team and staff are mainly London-based, with some staff posted in Scotland, Wales and the Midlands and North East of England. Its policy direction is set by an elected board which has a number of committees. It actively seeks to involve foster carers in its work to promote the best interests of children and families needing foster care. In addition to membership subscriptions, the NFCA is funded by central government, by local authority service contracts and by the income from sales of publicity materials, training courses, grants and donations.

British Agencies for Adoption and Fostering

This started life as a co-ordinating body for the voluntary adoption societies.

It added fostering to its title and remit in the early 1980s, when these agencies moved from an almost exclusive concern with the placement of babies for adoption to placing children already in care with permanent substitute foster or adoptive families. Many of these agencies also recruit, train and support 'bridge' foster families, who prepare children for the move to a substitute family. Its journal, *Adoption and Fostering*, and its research, practice and training publications are important sources of information on all aspects of child welfare. Its legal and medical groups collate information and provide support for these other professions, which have an important role to play in the provision of family placement services.

Contacts: NFCA, Leonard House, 5–7 Marshalsea Road, London SE1 1EP United Kingdom *Telephone*: (+44) 171-828-6266. BAAF, 200 Union Street, London SE1 0LY, United Kingdom *Telephone*: (+44) 171-593-2000.

Research

There is a long tradition of foster care research in the UK, much of it commissioned by the Department of Health and summarized in two publications: *Social Work Decisions in Child Care* (DoH, 1985) and *Patterns and Outcomes in Child Placement* (DoH, 1991b). Earlier research tended to combine the different fostering tasks, but more recent studies – for example, Rowe et al. (1984), on long–term foster care; Thoburn (1990) and Fratter et al. (1991) on permanent substitute family placement, and Hill et al. (1993) on specialist, task-centred fostering – have provided descriptive accounts of practice and evaluations of outcome for different sorts of children. An important research overview is provided by Rowe et al. (1989), who studied over 10,000 placements, the majority of which were in foster care. Berridge and Cleaver (1987) concluded that about 1 in 10 of placements intended to last up to eight weeks broke down prematurely, but a further proportion lasted too long. Altogether, 1 in 5 short-term placements failed to achieve their aims. Several studies have looked at long-term or 'permanent' placements. Here, outcome is related to the characteristics of the children, with those who are older at placement and those who are emotionally or behaviourally disturbed as a result of earlier deprivation or maltreatment being more likely to experience breakdown. Placement breakdown rates for otherwise similar children placed permanently in foster or adoptive homes are similar, and most studies show that continued contact with birth relatives is a protective factor, even when the placement is intended to be permanent.

Studies on the characteristics of successful foster carers are inconclusive and contradictory, except that the presence of a foster parent's younger child near in age to the foster child has been associated with placement breakdown by several researchers. Other studies have evaluated outcome by considering the wellbeing or educational progress of the child, and have compared the outcome for foster children with similar populations of children (Colton, 1989; Heath et al., 1994; Gibbons et al., 1995). Findings about the likelihood of long-term placement 'repairing' early harm are disappointing, but all studies point to the sorts of families and the sorts of practice which appear to make a difference to outcome. More recent studies in the UK consider the impact which the Children Act (1989) is having on outcomes for children in need or for those who have been abused, including the outcomes of any placements in foster care.

Bibliography

Aldgate, J., Pratt, K. and Duggan, M. (1989) 'Using care away from home to prevent family breakdown', *Adoption and Fostering*, Vol. 10, No. 2, pp.44–5.

Barnardos (1981) *A Professional Fostering Scheme*, London: Barnardos.

Bebbington, A. and Miles, J. (1989) 'The background of children who enter local authority care', *British Journal of Social Work*, Vol. 19, No. 5, pp.349–68.

Bebbington, A. and Miles, J. (1990) 'The supply of foster families for children in care', *British Journal of Social Work*, Vol. 20, pp.283–307.

Berridge, D. and Cleaver, H. (1987) *Foster Home Breakdown*, Oxford: Blackwell.

Bradley, M. and Aldgate, J. (1994) 'Short-term family based care for children in need', *Adoption and Fostering*, Vol. 18, No. 4, pp.24–9.

Colton, M. (1989) *Dimensions of Substitute Care*, Aldershot: Avebury.

Department of Health (DoH) (1985) *Social Work Decisions in Child Care*, London: HMSO.

DoH (1991a) *The Children Act 1989: Guidance and Regulations, Vol. 3: Family Placements*, London: HMSO.

DoH (1991b) *Patterns and Outcomes in Child Placement*, London: HMSO.

DoH (1994) *Children Act Report, 1993*, London: HMSO.

DoH (1994/5) *Inspection of Local Authority Fostering Services*, London: Social Services Inspectorate.

DoH (1995) *A Study of the Independent Fostering Agencies*, London: Social Services Inspectorate.

DoH and Welsh Office (1994) *Children Act Report 1993*, London: HMSO.

Fratter, J., Rowe, J., Sapsford, D. and Thoburn, J. (1991) *Permanent Family Placement: A Decade of Experience*, London: BAAF.

Fry, E. (1994) *On Remand*, London: NFCA

Fry, E. and Hazelhurst, M. (1994) *Supported Lodgings*, London: NFCA/First Key.

Gibbons, J., Gallagher, B., Bell, C. and Gordon, D. (1995) *Development after Physical Abuse in Early Childhood*, London: HMSO.

Hazel, N. (1990) *Fostering Teenagers*, London: NFCA.

Heath, A.F., Colton, M.J. and Aldgate, J. (1994) 'Failure to escape: A longitudinal study of foster children's educational attainment', *British Journal of Social Work*, Vol. 24, No. 3, pp.241–60.

Hill, M., Nutter, R., Giltinan, D., Hudson, J. and Galaway, B. (1993) 'A comparative study of specialist fostering in the UK and North America', *Adoption and Fostering*, Vol. 17, No. 2, pp.17–26.

Lowe, K. (1990) *Teenagers in Foster Care*, London: NFCA.

NFCA (1991) *Foster Care Placement: Regulations and Guidance*, London: NFCA.

NFCA (1994a) *Choosing to Foster: The Challenge to Care*, London: NFCA.

NFCA (1994b) *Foster Care Finance*, London: NFCA

NFCA (1995) 'Appraisal of foster carers: Voluntary organisations', *Foster Care*, 80, January, p.4.

Parker, R. (1990) *Away from Home: A History of Child Care*, London: Barnardos.

Part, D. (1993) 'Fostering as seen by the carers' children', *Adoption and Fostering*, Vol. 17, No. 1, pp.26–31.

Rowe, J. and Lambert, L. (1973) *Children Who Wait*, London: BAAF.

Rowe, J., Hundleby, M. and Garnett, L. (1989) *Child Care Now: A Survey of Placement Patterns*, London: BAAF.

Rowe, J., Cain, H., Hundleby, M. and Keane, A. (1984) *Long Term Foster Care*, London: Batsford.

Sellick, C. (1992) *Supporting Short-term Foster Carers*, Aldershot: Avebury.

Social Trends (1995) Vol. 25, Ch. 1, London: HMSO.

Thoburn, J. (1990) *Success and Failure in Permanent Family Placement*, Aldershot: Avebury.

Thoburn, J. (1994) *Child Placement: Principles and Practice*, Aldershot: Arena.

Triseliotis, J., Sellick, C. and Short, R. (1995) *Foster Care Theory and Practice*, London: Batsford.

Waterhouse, S. (1992) 'How foster carers view contact', *Adoption and Fostering*, Vol. 16, No. 2, pp.42–7.

Westacott, J. (1988) *Bridge to Calmer Waters?*, London: Barnardos.

19 United States of America

Eileen Mayers Pasztor and Kathy Barbell

Jurisdiction

Size, demography and child wellbeing

The USA is made up of 48 contiguous states and the capital, Washington, DC. It is bordered on the east by the Atlantic Ocean, the north by Canada, the west by the Pacific Ocean, and the south by Mexico. Two other states, Alaska and Hawaii, are located north-west of Canada and in the Pacific Ocean, respectively. This covers approximately 10 million square kilometres, with a combined population of 264 million, of which less than 22 per cent are children under the age of 15. Residents include: 0.07 per cent American Indians and Eskimos, 3.3 per cent Asians and Pacific Islanders, 10 per cent Hispanics, 12 per cent African-Americans and 74 per cent non-Hispanic Caucasians (*Encyclopedia Britannica*, 1996, p.741).

Between 1985 and 1992, the wellbeing of children improved, as measured by decreases in the number of high school drop-outs, infant mortality and child deaths. Wellbeing deteriorated as measured by significant increases in arrests of teenagers for violent crimes; violent deaths of young people; single-parent families with children who typically have fewer economic resources, and overall child poverty (Annie E. Casey Foundation, 1995, pp.10–15). Ironically, in a country as wealthy as the USA, the child poverty rate is 20 per cent – higher than many other developed countries – and jumps to 35 per cent for Hispanic children, and over 45 per cent for African-American children (National Commission on Family Foster Care, 1991, p.23). This is generally attributed to inadequate amounts of government assistance for poor families with children. As the economic condition of families has deteriorated along with the lack of essential social supports, there has been a corresponding increase in child abuse and neglect. In 1994, the USA reported almost 3 million cases of abuse and neglect, a 68 per cent increase over the previous ten years. Figure 19.1 provides a breakdown of the numbers of children suffering various degrees of abuse, while Figure 19.2 shows the increase in the number of children in out-of-home care over the past ten years (Curtis et al., 1996, pp.4–5). According to David Liederman, executive director of the Child Welfare League of America (CWLA): 'Too often children get the worst

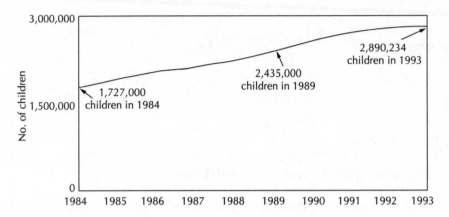

Source: Curtis et al. (1996).

Figure 19.1   Children reported as abused and neglected, 1984–93

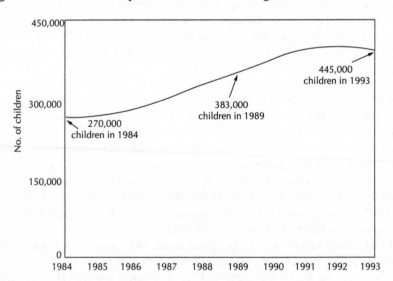

Source: Curtis et al. (1996).

Figure 19.2   Children in out-of-home care, 1984–93

of both worlds . . . neither the privilege accorded to adults nor the care and protection that should be their birthright' (Curtis et al., 1996, p.135).

The challenge of data collection

Current, comprehensive data regarding the status of the USA's youngest and most vulnerable citizens are difficult to obtain. Information collected by federal agencies may be out of date by the time it becomes public, and although several independent national organizations collect important child welfare data, an accurate picture is lacking because every state jurisdiction uses its own definitions of abuse and neglect, foster care, standards of proof, data collection methods and analyses, and time periods (Curtis et al., 1996, p.xiii). It will be a great challenge to adopt standardized definitions and procedures, and to develop the political and public will to make policy changes based on accurate and timely data.

History and origins

Although the traditional term 'foster family care' is used throughout this book, it should be noted that in 1991, the National Commission on Family Foster Care, convened by the Child Welfare League of America in collaboration with the National Foster Parent Association, proposed a new definition of foster care, replacing the term 'foster family care' with 'family foster care' to emphasize that the service occurs in *a family*, and to place the *family* first. As a result, we will use the term 'family foster care' throughout this chapter.

Early foster care

Family foster care has gone through three major phases in its 140-plus year history. Before formal agency-sponsored care, children without parents or extended family lived in orphanages, institutions, and asylums. Early foster care was called 'placing out', and its 'father' is considered to be Charles Loring Brace, the founder of the Children's Aid Society in New York City. Brace saw the family as 'God's reformatory', and began the 'orphan train movement', in which as many as 150,000 destitute and homeless children from eastern cities were placed with families in the midwestern states. Foster parents were to provide education, religious training and job preparation until the young people in their care turned 16 and could be expected to live on their own. Children arriving by orphan trains were put up on auction blocks for selection: hence the term 'up for adoption' is still used in some areas today. Since birth parents were not evident, they were considered to be easily substituted with foster parents. The term 'substitute care' continues to be used today, even though current practice wisdom recognizes that there is no replacement for the family of origin.

Home studies in those early days were really *house* studies, because space and adequate well-water were criteria for matching children with families. In general, perceptions of children's needs focused on their dependency and former neglect, with the expectation that love and training would suffice for their care. It should be noted that children in foster care were mostly Caucasian, as children of colour without parents were generally raised by extended family in what today is called 'kinship care'.

The widespread de-institutionalization of children into family foster care is attributed to the impact of the first White House Conference on Children in 1909, which declared the right of every child to grow up in a family; the creation of the US Children's Bureau in 1912, and the founding in 1920 of the Child Welfare League of America, which began developing standards to influence national policies and practices. In 1961, an amendment to the Social Security Act (1935) provided the first federal reimbursement to states for foster care expenditures.

The 1970s and 1980s

Critical events in the 1970s included:

- the creation of the National Foster Parent Association through the support of the US Children's Bureau and the Child Welfare League of America (CWLA);
- the first national foster parent training programme, Parenting Plus (Stone, 1975), which emphasized that foster parents need skills beyond parenting;
- the passage of federal legislation, the Child Abuse Prevention and Treatment Act (1974), requiring states to promulgate laws mandating professionals such as teachers and physicians to report suspected cases of abuse and neglect;
- the passage of the Indian Child Welfare Act (1978) to keep children within their extended families and tribes;
- studies that documented the harmful 'drift' of children in foster care and the emotional and social need for children to have family continuity and permanency;
- the growth of the foster care population to half a million children.

By the late 1970s, there was a national call to restructure the allocation of federal foster care aid to the states, mandate regular case reviews and provide adequate support for foster parents to care for a new population of children deemed to have 'special needs' because they were older, perhaps members of a sibling group needing placement together, and/or because they had more obvious behavioural and emotional problems.

Hope for foster care reform came with the passage of the federal Adoption Assistance and Child Welfare Act (1980), providing financial incentives for agencies to prevent the unnecessary separation of children from parents, expedite family reunification, and increase adoption opportunities for children with special needs. By 1983, the foster care population had dropped to 225,000, with achievements in working with parents of children in care, respecting the cultural and ethnic identities of children and, in 1985, federal funding for programmes to prepare young people in care for independent living. Treatment foster care (also known as therapeutic or specialized foster care) became recognized as an important service option for children and young people with serious emotional and behavioural disorders but who could be served by an 'integrated constellation of services with key interventions and supports provided by treatment foster parents who are trained, supervised and supported by qualified staff' (Foster Family-based Treatment Association, 1995, p.6).

The 1980s also saw the national development and implementation of standardized models for the recruitment, assessment, selection, training and retention of foster parents and adoptive parents. US foster care providers and educators also began making connections internationally. The Sixth International Foster Care Organization Conference was held in the state of Michigan in 1989, and American and Dutch colleagues began a collaboration to transfer foster parent training technology that today includes Belgium, Sweden and Finland (Van Pagée et al., 1991).

Administration and organization

Family foster care is a service that a state human or social service agency is mandated to offer in the discharge of its child welfare responsibilities. States develop policies, allocate resources and administer services through local offices. In all jurisdictions, there may be voluntary agencies which provide family foster care services on a contractual basis under state or local regulations. There is considerable diversity among the voluntary providers – for example:

- residential treatment centres that work with over 200 children on their campuses and may also have a family foster care programme;
- a single family may own and operate its own 'agency' catering for fewer than six children;
- an agency may provide multiple services, including family

counselling, treatment foster care, residential/group care and adoption;

- a family foster care agency may operate in dozens of communities within a state, or in a dozen states across the country.

Some voluntary family foster care providers are religiously affiliated, while others focus on serving specific ethnic and cultural populations. Most voluntary agencies are non-profitmaking.

Family foster care agencies can be financed by federal, state and county public funding, and agencies may also receive funds from endowments, private donations, foundations and corporations. Whether public or voluntary, state- or county-administered, agencies are responsible for meeting local and state licensing standards and certain federal guidelines. The CWLA's *Standards of Excellence for Family Foster Care Services* (CWLA, 1995) are useful in planning, organizing and administering services, establishing licensing requirements, and helping explain the need for certain programme expenditures. There are national accrediting organizations with specific programme and practice standards for family foster care and treatment foster care. Agencies that meet these standards are recognized as meeting the highest professional standards of organizational strength and quality of service, which often helps with fund development and reducing legal liability.

Who is placed in foster care?

As Figure 19.2 indicates, by 1993, approximately 445,000 children were in residential/group care, family foster care, treatment foster care or kinship care (Curtis et al., 1996, p.49). These children typically have moderate to severe emotional and behavioural problems, alcohol- and drug-related difficulties, tragic effects of exposure to HIV/AIDS, and/or physically handicapping conditions. Growing numbers of very young children who have been physically and sexually abused are entering care, the number of adolescents continues to increase, and the foster care population is more multi-cultural than ever before. Drugs and alcohol are estimated to affect 75 per cent of the children in care. It is projected that by the year 2000, up to 125,000 US children may lose their parents to HIV/AIDS, resulting in the development of practice guidelines to help parents and agencies plan for the long-term care of these children (Merkel-Holguin, 1996). Adolescent pregnancy and parenting also affects the foster care population, as parents who are too young have babies at risk, and many children coming into care have parents who themselves experienced abuse and neglect (CWLA, 1994a).

The foster care population includes children and young people discharged from care but returning at a rate of up to 30 per cent in some jurisdictions. Children and young people previously placed in mental health and juvenile correction facilities are being diverted to family foster care to cut costs. Meanwhile, multiple placements, placements away from their communities and previous school districts, and lack of continuity in educational services exacerbate learning difficulties. Vocational services are essential, but a longitudinal study reports that only 49 per cent of young people discharged from foster care were employed, compared to a national employment rate of 65 per cent for their cohorts (Westat, 1991).

Children of colour continue to be disproportionately represented, which is attributed to the declining wellbeing of the USA's families of colour (Stehno, 1990; Tatara, 1993) and rapidly-changing racial/ethnic patterns. Between 1980 and 1990, the Caucasian population decreased nationally by 3 per cent, whereas the African-American population grew by 13 per cent, the Native American/Alaskan Native population by 42 per cent, the Hispanic population by 53 per cent, and the Asian and Pacific Islander population by 97 per cent (US Bureau of the Census, 1992). Between 1982 and 1990, the number of Hispanic children in care increased 172 per cent, and African-American children represent over 40 per cent of the foster care population. Children of colour are noted for receiving less adequate services than their counterparts, especially related to service planning, family contacts, and counselling services.

Parents of children in care have many special and extraordinary needs that mirror those of their children. They need skilled casework services and community resources that include: economic assistance and job training, drug counselling, housing, health care and child care, and the message that they can and should have a valuable role in the lives of their children. Reunification and after care services, and participation in open adoption opportunities, are also essential.

Care providers

The foster parent population is estimated at between 100,000 and 130,000 families, with a steady decrease in the past decade. A shortage of 65,000 foster families is projected over the next few years (James Bell Associates, 1993). These declines are attributed to both social and economic factors and programmatic issues. The need for paid employment, housing costs and the lack of child day care affect recruitment. Retention studies emphasize that foster parents might continue service longer if there were more congruence between their responsibilities and supports, more respite care, more consultation and collaboration from skilled staff, and comprehensive, competency-based pre-service and in-service training (Pasztor and Wynne, 1995).

Appropriate numbers of qualified casework staff are also needed. With an annual turnover of 30–70 per cent in some agencies, it can be impossible to maintain frequent and consistent contact with parents and children and to collaborate effectively with foster parents. Most child welfare workers who provide direct services have little or no formal social work education, and even fewer have graduate degrees in social work or related fields. Low salaries not commensurate with the risks and responsibilities of child welfare work are also of national concern. It is revealing that treatment foster care programmes have fewer of these problems; this may be attributed to such factors as the provision of salaries for treatment foster parents, 24-hour staff availability and support, planned respite care, intensive training, and status within the agency and the community. Given the constraints, however, there are still thousands of dedicated and committed foster carers and caseworkers who provide remarkable services, despite a prevailing lack of resources.

Financial support

During the early years of family foster care, most foster carers were farm families, and the children and young people placed with them could be a source of labour. Today, there remains a public notion that fostering is a lucrative endeavour. Historically, however, foster parents have been reimbursed at very low rates. While treatment foster parents may typically be paid a salary or an enhanced cost of care rate for the intensive work they do, most foster parents find that they must use their own money to pay for additional clothing, school events, holidays, gifts, child care and home repairs when children are destructive. In 1993, the average monthly foster care reimbursement rate ranged from $US319 for children under age 2 to $US393 for teenagers (American Public Welfare Association, 1994). Demographically, foster parents – especially those who are single, older or minority – have incomes lower than many other American families, and the personal expense of fostering cannot be minimized as a disincentive to both recruitment and retention (Pasztor and Wynne, 1995, p.47). The CWLA *Standards of Excellence for Family Foster Care Services* recommend reimbursement rates which cover the full cost of care and are commensurate with the foster parents' level of competence (CWLA, 1995, p.102). The Foster Family-based Treatment Association (FFTA) *Program Standards for Treatment Foster Care* also recommend full coverage for fostering costs, and compensation for 'special skills, functions and responsibilities' (FFTA, 1995, p.17).

Major problems

By 1990, deteriorating social and economic conditions – including the devastating impact of crack/cocaine, HIV/AIDS and poverty – had resulted in rapid growth in the numbers of children in foster care. This group included children whose medical, social, emotional and behavioural problems moved them from the category of 'special' to 'extraordinary' needs. This escalation, combined with a substantial decrease in the foster parent population with the willingness, ability, and resources to foster, prompted national concern that family foster care was no longer a viable service option, and perhaps widespread institutional care should be considered.

The National Commission on Family Foster Care (NCFFC) was thus convened in 1990 to address this debate, and after a year of work, produced *A Blueprint for Fostering Infants, Children, and Youths in the 1990s* (NCFFC, 1991), which provided a new definition of family foster care and the rationale for it. It detailed specific foster parent and social worker responsibilities, child welfare agency responsibilities, and public policies and legislation to make family foster care a viable service option. The work of the NCFFC provided a foundation for the development of new national standards for family foster care, national attention to kinship care, a conceptual framework for national training programmes for foster parents and adoptive parents, and new collaborations among national organizations and associations concerned with family foster care.

Despite many achievements, family foster care today still suffers from a lack of congruence between child welfare values, state policies and federal legislation. Despite the devastating impact on children of poverty, homelessness, chemical dependency, violence and other tragedies, there remains a lack of public will and political authority to systematically develop and implement prevention strategies, or to transfer the wealth of programme and practice knowledge about family foster care and treatment foster care developed over the past twenty-five years into service delivery on a local level. Because family foster care is designed to react when families and other systems cannot keep parents and children together, it is especially affected by social, economic and political trends. Both the problems and trends can lead to worse conditions, or conversely, perhaps produce reforms that make families and communities much safer places for children.

Major trends

Kinship care

In 1990, about 1.4 million children were living with relatives. Approximately a quarter of the 445,000 children in foster care are living with kin, and in some large city jurisdictions, that proportion climbs to 50 per cent. Growth is attributed to the increasing number of children needing foster care, the declining pool of foster parents, and the commitment by kin to take care of their young family members – prompting a recognition of kinship care as an essential child welfare service option. The consideration of kin as the first placement option for children has historical roots in traditional family practices that pre-date formal foster care, and indeed, the federal Indian Child Welfare Act (1978) stipulates that the first placement preference should be with a member of the child's extended family or tribe.

Kinship care has several significant and emotionally charged benefits and concerns. The benefits include: caring for children within their own families; minimizing trauma associated with family separation and placement with unknown individuals; preserving cultural identity, and a documented reduction in placement disruptions (compared to children placed with foster parents). The concerns include: less protection from abusive parents; increased lengths of stay in foster care, and less casework support to the kinship family (compared to children placed with foster parents).

Not surprisingly, most controversy involves family values and financial costs. States prefer relatives to receive federal welfare assistance (Aid to Families with Dependent Children) to support the children, but judicial rulings provide relatives with the same financial support that foster parents can receive, if the kin can meet foster care standards. This support can be greater by more than $US100 per month per child. In addition, some states have waived foster care standards for kin. The argument is: why should foster parents, unrelated to the children in their care, receive more financial support than relatives? But at the same time, why should relatives receive more financial support than parents for the care of a child? In response, a number of jurisdictions are developing special programmes so that well-functioning kinship families have the necessary financial support for the care of children, but the administrative costs for monitoring and casework intervention are reduced. A special issue of *Child Welfare* devoted to kinship care policies, programmes, practice and research was published in autumn 1996, and a national conference on kinship care was held in 1997.

Collaboration in the development and support of foster parents and adoptive parents

Inspired by a request for more training from foster parents in the state of Illinois, that state's public child welfare agencies and numerous voluntary ones formed a collaboration with the CWLA, more than a dozen other state and voluntary child welfare agencies, schools of social work and community colleges and foundations, to pool resources to develop PRIDE (Parent

Resources for Information, Development and Education). As Figure 19.3 shows, PRIDE is a 14-step, comprehensive, competency-based approach to developing and supporting foster parents and adoptive parents (Pasztor and Wynne, 1995, p.35).

PRIDE places foster parent and adoptive parent knowledge and skills into five categories:

1 protecting and nurturing children;
2 meeting developmental needs and addressing developmental delays;
3 supporting relationships between children and their families;
4 connecting children to safe, nurturing, lifetime relationships;
5 working as a member of a professional team. (CWLA and Illinois Department of Children and Family Services, 1996).

Work tools include videos, a desk reference, training guides and resource workbooks that cover recruitment, assessment, pre-service and in-service training, and much more. The strength of the programme is its comprehensive, competency-based focus, the credibility of a national development team, and the strategy of using a collaborative model to create new programmes when financial resources may be in short supply. There is a wealth of knowledge that can be shared domestically and internationally.

Family-centred services

While keeping children with their families and reunifying children and families continue to be the primary goals, there is a broader recognition that families come in a variety of forms: two-parent, single-parent, blended, extended, foster, adoptive, and so on. Services must be guided by culturally competent strengths/needs assessments, and interventions must engage the whole family – however defined – in order to be effective. Those children who cannot grow up with their parents must be connected to other safe and nurturing relationships which are intended to last a lifetime. In either case, there is a clear shift towards serving children by supporting their families and their communities.

The shift to families and communities as the locus of child welfare services parallels shifts that are occurring in other fields, such as mental health and developmental disabilities. It encourages a more participatory and horizontal approach in service delivery, focuses on promoting self-sufficiency as well as caregiving, is centred in the home and community, values and embraces diversity and is non-hierarchical in its approach to information-sharing and problem-solving. At its core, family-centred practice recognizes the actual and potential strengths of family relationships, and builds on those strengths to achieve optimal outcomes for children and families.

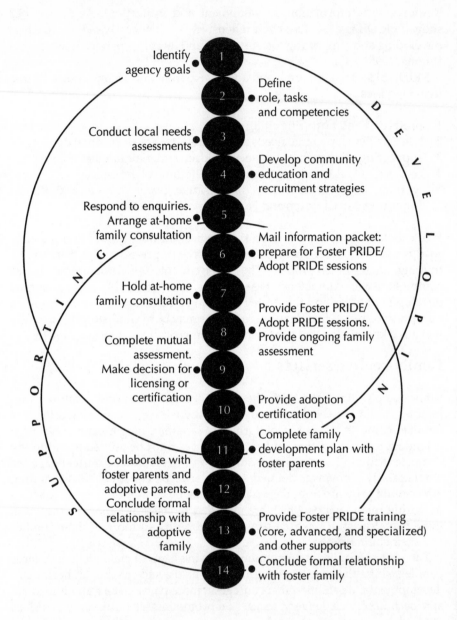

Source: Pasztor and Wynne (1995).

Figure 19.3   The Foster PRIDE/Adopt PRIDE process to develop and support resource families

A particularly significant development in support of this approach is the Family Preservation and Family Support Program, the first major federal legislation addressing children in more than fifteen years. It translates current family-centred theory and practice into public policy, and requires states to engage in a comprehensive planning process for the development of a meaningful and responsive family support and family preservation strategy. Five themes are critical:

1 the importance of family to children;
2 children's lifelong connections to their families;
3 the uniqueness of families;
4 the shifting availability of family members;
5 the need to broadly define family or family-like support.

Family foster care has a significant role in family-centred work. There are successful endeavours to identify, develop and support foster parents from the communities in which children and families at risk are located. Foster parents are being trained to develop the competencies and resources to support relationships between children and their families. Residential/group care agencies have also developed programmes to keep children and families more connected. Adoption services also include more opportunities for a range of continuing connections, recognizing that the termination of parental rights does not have to include the termination of relationships.

Managed care

An approach long used by the health care industry, the principles of managed care are now being applied extensively to behavioural (mental) health services, and are increasingly being used in the delivery of residential/group care, family foster care and other child welfare services. This approach is considered attractive because of its incentives to reduce costs, improve access to care, improve the quality of care and increase the focus on prevention rather than crisis-driven treatments (McCullough, 1996, p.4). Public child welfare agencies are now looking at such strategies as risk-based contracting with voluntary providers, and outcomes that focus on reduced lengths of stay in care and recidivism. If managed correctly, managed care may indeed improve services and decrease costs; conversely, it risks harming the populations intended to be served, because of inadequate funding, poor planning and unrealistic expectations regarding outcomes.

Agency executive directors and commissioners – from both the private and public sectors – are meeting locally, state-wide and nationally to address such issues as system design, pricing, best practices and procedural protocols, utilization management and monitoring, shared risks and rewards for qualified providers, information access and data collection, and meaningful and measurable outcomes, including client and provider satisfaction. A book on managed care and child welfare has been published, recently (Emenhiser et al., 1995), and the CWLA has created a national Managed Care Institute to conduct research and to provide consultation and training for child welfare agencies – especially those delivering residential and family foster care services. How organizations can prepare for, survive and even prosper in this new arena so that children and families are well served is an issue of enormous national attention.

Welfare reform

Child welfare has become enmeshed in the national debate over welfare reform. Proposed legislation to reduce welfare benefits also threatens to remove important and essential entitlement protections for vulnerable children, with the risk of propelling thousands of children into greater poverty. Considering a relationship between poverty and child maltreatment, these major legislative changes are projected to increase the number of children needing foster care – at costs per child that are, ironically, far greater than individual family welfare payments. Child welfare professionals and advocates have mobilized locally and nationally to stop, or at least minimize, the impact of welfare reform on fragile children and families. Their message is clear: do no harm to children.

Role of national foster care association

The US National Foster Parent Association was established in 1972 as a non-profit, volunteer organization with membership open to anyone interested in and committed to improving foster care. Its main objectives are in the areas of communication, collaboration, networking and information-sharing, programme and legislative advocacy, foster parent retention and recruitment, and education.

Organized and operated by its foster parent volunteers, the NFPA provides an array of services and supports, which include: a national publication, *The Advocate* (the only major national newsletter devoted solely to family foster care), an annual national conference – in its 26th year – typically attended by over 1,000 participants, and committees focusing on membership, minorities issues, finance, public relations, adoptions, awards, education, legal issues, legislation and nominations. The NFPA is governed by an executive committee, and is also supported by ten regional vice-presidents and professional advisers.

Contact: Charles Black, Director, NFPA Information and Service Office, 9 Dartmoor Drive, Crystal Lake, Illinois 60014, USA *Telephone*: (+1) 815-455-2527.

Research

Foster care research over the past several decades has made numerous contributions resulting in: federal permanency planning legislation; models for foster parent retention and recruitment; best practices in supporting the relationships between children in care and their parents to facilitate reunification; recognition of the unique needs of young people in transition to independent living; better understanding of the impact of foster care on child growth and development, and most recently, the strengths and needs of kinship care. Despite these contributions, research continues to receive minimal financial support, with a large gap between research findings and their application to policy and practice development.

Faced with managed care, welfare reform and other forces, a timely collaboration has been initiated with a longitudinal study to assess the outcomes of family foster care, treatment foster care and residential care, and to identify which services are more effective for which populations of children. Entitled The Odyssey Project, over twenty CWLA member agencies nationwide are pooling financial resources, data collection and staff to achieve the goals of the project – the first of its kind in the USA.

Publications and other resources

The CWLA is the world's largest publisher of child welfare books, monographs and training resources – including publications for professionals, parents and children. The publications catalogue can be obtained by contacting: CWLA, c/o CSSC, PO Box 7816, Raritan, New Jersey 08818-7816, USA *Telephone*: (+1) 800-407-6273 or (+1) 908-225-1900 *Fax*: (+1) 908-417-0482.

Resources related to young people in care, independent living services and residential care can be obtained by contacting: National Resource Center for Youth Services, 202 West 8th Street, Tulsa, Oklahoma 74119-1419, USA *Telephone*: (+1) 918-585-2986 *Fax*: (+1) 918-592-1841.

Bibliography

American Public Welfare Association (1994) 'Foster care rates', *W-Memo*, Vol. 6, No. 2, pp.23–4.

Annie E. Casey Foundation (1995) *Kids Count*, Baltimore, MD: Annie E. Casey Foundation.

Barbell, K. (1995) *Foster Care Today* (briefing paper for CWLA National Advisory Committee on Foster Care), Washington, DC: Child Welfare League of America.

Barth, R. (1990) 'On their own: The experiences of youth after foster care', *Child and Adolescent Social Work*, Vol. 7, No. 5, pp.419–40.

Centers for Disease Control and Prevention (1993) *HIV/AIDS Surveillance Report: Third quarter edition*, Atlanta, GA: CDCP.

Close, M. (1983) 'Child welfare and people of color: Denial of equal access', *Social Work Research and Abstracts*, Vol. 19, No. 4, pp.13–20.

Cohen, F. and Nehring, W. (1994) 'Foster care of HIV-positive children in the United States', *Public Health Reports*, Vol. 109, No. 1, pp.60–7.

Cook, R. and Ansell, D. (1986) *Study of Independent Living Services for Youth in Substitute Care*, Rockville, MD: Westat.

Curtis, P. and McCullough, C. (1993) 'Impact of alcohol and other drugs on the child welfare system', *Child Welfare*, Vol. 72, No. 6, pp.533–42.

Curtis, P., Boyd, J., Liepold, M. and Petit, M. (1996) *Child Abuse and Neglect: A Look at the States – The CWLA Stat Book*, Washington, DC: CWLA.

CWLA (1994a) *Welfare Reform and the Minor Mothers' Residency Requirement*, Washington, DC: CWLA.

CWLA (1994b) *Kinship Care: A Natural Bridge*, Washington, DC: CWLA.

CWLA (1995) *Standards of Excellence for Family Foster Care Services*, Washington, DC: CWLA.

CWLA and Illinois Department of Children and Family Services (1996) *Model for Developing and Supporting Resource Families: A Practice Handbook*, Washington, DC: CWLA.

DeWoody, M., Ceja, K. and Sylvester, M. (1993) *Independent Living Services for Youths in Out-of-home Care*, Washington, DC: CWLA.

Dubowitz, H. (1990). *The Physical and Mental Health and Educational Status of Children Placed with Relatives – Final Report*, Baltimore, MD: Department of Pediatrics, School of Medicine, University of Maryland.

Emenhiser, D., Barker, R. and DeWoody, M. (1995) *Managed Care: Surviving and Thriving During Your Agency's Transition*, New York: CWLA.

Fahlberg, V. (1991) *A Child's Journey Through Placement*, Indianapolis, IN: Perspectives Press.

Fein, E., Kluger, M. and Maluccio, A. (1990) *No More Partings: An Examination of Long-term Foster Family Care*, Washington, DC: CWLA.

Festinger, T. (1983) *No One Ever Asked Us*, New York: Columbia University Press.

Fitzharris, T. (1984) *The Foster Children of California*, Sacramento, CA: Children's Services Foundation.

Foster Family-based Treatment Association (1995) *Program Standards for Treatment Foster Care*. New York: FFTA.

Gershenson, C. (1990) 'Preparing for the future backwards: Characteristics of the ecology for children and youth in long-term out-of-home care', paper presented at The Casey Family Program Symposium on Children and Youth In Long-Term Out-of-Home Care, Seattle, WA.

Ingalls, R., Hatch, R. and Meservey, F. (1984) *Characteristics of Children in Out-of-home Care*, Albany, NY: New York State Council on Children and Families.

James Bell Associates (1993) *The National Survey of Current and Former Foster Parents Executive Summary*, Washington, DC: US Department of Health and Human Services, Administration for Children, Youth and Families.

Jones, M. and Moses, B. (1984) *West Virginia's Former Foster Children: Their Experience and Their Lives as Young Adults*, New York: CWLA.

Lieberman, A., Hornby, H. and Russell, M. (1988) 'Analyzing the educational backgrounds and work experiences of child welfare personnel: A national study', *Social Work*, Vol. 33, No. 6, pp. 485–9.

McCullough, C. (1996) 'Managed Care and Child Welfare: A Child Welfare League of America Perspective' (unpublished paper), Washington, DC: CWLA.

Merkel-Holguin, L. (1996) *Children Who Lose Their Parents to AIDS – Agency Guidelines for Kinship Care and Adoptive Placement*, Washington, DC: CWLA.

Michaels, D. and Levine, C. (1992) 'Estimates of the number of motherless children and youth orphaned by AIDS in the United States', *Journal of the American Medical Association*, Vol. 268, pp.3,456–61.

National Commission on Family Foster Care (1991) *A Blueprint for Fostering Infants, Children and Youths in the 1990s*, Washington, DC: CWLA.

North American Commission on Chemical Dependency and Child Welfare (1992) *Children at the Front: A Different View of the War on Alcohol and Drugs*, Washington, DC: CWLA.

Ooms, T. (1990) *The Crisis in Foster Care: New Directions for the 1990s*, Washington, DC: Family Impact Seminars.

Pasztor, E.M. and Wynne, S. (1995) *Foster Parent Retention and Recruitment: State of the Art in Practice and Policy*, Washington, DC: CWLA.

Pasztor, E., Polowy, M., Leighton, M. and Conte, R. (1992) *The Ultimate Challenge: Foster Parenting in the 1990's*, Washington, DC: CWLA.

Schor, E., Aptekar, R. and Scannell, T. (1987) *The Health Care of Children in Out-of-home Care*, Washington, DC: CWLA.

Shyne, A. and Schroeder, A. (1978) *National Study of Social Services to Children and Their Families* (DHEW publication No. 78-30150), Washington, DC: Department of Health and Human Services, US Children's Bureau.

Siu, S. and Hogan, P. (1989) 'Public child welfare: The need for clinical social work', *Social Work*, Vol. 34, No. 5, pp.423–30.

Stehno, S. (1990) 'The elusive continuum of child welfare services: Implications for minority children and youth', *Child Welfare*, Vol. 69, No. 6, pp.551–62.

Stone, H. (1975) *Parenting Plus*, New York: CWLA.

Tatara, T. (1993) *Characteristics of Children in Substitute and Adoptive Care: A Statistical Summary of the VCIS National Child Welfare Data Base*, Washington, DC: American Public Welfare Association.

Timberlake, E., Pasztor, E.M., Sheagran, J., Clarren, J. and Lammert, M. (1987) 'Adolescent emancipation from foster care', in *Child and Adolescent Social Work*, Vol. 4, Nos. 3 and 4, pp.116–29.

US Bureau of the Census (1992) *Statistical Abstract of the United States, 1992* (112th Edn), Washington, DC: US Government Printing Office.

US Bureau of the Census (1993) *Poverty in the United States: 1992. Current Population Report*, Series P60–185, Washington, DC: US Government Printing Office.

US Department of Health and Human Services, National Center on Child Abuse and Neglect (1994) *Child Maltreatment 1992: Reports from the States to the National Center on Child Abuse and Neglect*, Washington, DC: US Government Printing Office.

US Department of Health and Human Services, Centers for Disease Control and Prevention, National Center for Health Statistics (1993), 'Advance report of final natality statistics, 1991', *Monthly Vital Statistics Report*, Vol. 42, No. 3.

US General Accounting Office (1991) *Foster Care: Children's Experiences Linked to Various Factors: Better Data Needed*, report to the US Senate, Committee on Finance,

GAO/HRD-91-64, Washington, DC: US Government Printing Office.

US House of Representatives, Committee on Ways and Means (1994) *1994 Green Book, Overview of entitlement programs*, Washington, DC: US Government Printing Office.

US House of Representatives, Select Committee on Children, Youth and Families (1989) *No Place to Call Home: Discarded Children in America*, Washington, DC: US Government Printing Office.

Van Pagée, R., Van Miltenburg, W. and Pasztor, E.M. (1991) 'The international transfer of foster parent selection and preparation technology: The example of the Netherlands and the United States', in McFadden, J. (ed.) *Child Welfare Around the World*, Washington, DC: CWLA, pp. 113–21.

Wald, M., Carlsmith, J. and Liederman, P. (1985) *Protecting Abused/neglected Children: A Comparison of Home and Foster Placement*, Palo Alto, CA: Stanford Center for the Study of Youth Development.

Westat (1991) *A National Evaluation of Title IV-E Foster Care Independent Living Programs for Youth, Phase 2, Final Report*, Rockville, MD: Westat.

Wulczyn, F. and Goerge, R. (1990) *Public Policy and the Dynamics of Foster Care: A Multi-state Study of Placement Histories. New York, Illinois, and Michigan*, Chicago, IL: Chapin Hall.

20 Venezuela

Elsa Levy and Iliana Kizer

Jurisdiction

The republic of Venezuela is situated in northern South America, bounded to the north by the Caribbean Sea, to the north-east by the Atlantic Ocean, to the south-east by Guyana, to the south by Brazil, and to the west by Colombia. Venezuela encompasses an area of 915,567 square kilometres. Its capital city is Caracas, and the official language is Spanish. Venezuela has a population of about 14.5 million people, distributed by age as shown in Table 20.1. The life expectancy at birth is 70 years, and the infant mortality rate is 2.4 per cent (as of 1991). The average annual income is $US2,730. The population comprises a heterogeneous mixture of various ethnic strains: Indian, white European and black African.

Table 20.1   Age distribution

Age range	%
0–19	48.1
20–39	31.5
40–64	16.7
65+	3.7

History and origins

The concept of foster family care, as understood in the USA, for example, does not exist in Venezuela. However, legal adoption has existed since 1867,

267

when it was first legislated in the Civil Code. There have since been various reforms to this law, the latest in 1983. The law embraces the modern concept of adoption, stating that adoption is an institution basically established in the interests of the child.

At one time, the Venezuelan government did support foster care as such, paying foster families to look after indigent, abandoned, violated or endangered minors, but this system was soon abandoned. It was found that foster care did not fulfil the purpose intended, which was to provide substitute homes for abandoned children in which they would receive affection as well as nourishment, education, and so on. Instead, paid foster care had been subverted as a means of obtaining income under the pretence of maintaining a family group. Children placed in this kind of foster care encountered situations similar to those which had given rise to state intervention in the first place.

However, a system of 'family placement' does exist in Venezuela. The state places the child in a foster home with a view to adoption. During the three-month trial period, and during the period when the various requirements for formal adoption are being met, the foster parents receive no financial support whatsoever from the state.

Administration and organization

This section will concentrate on the history and practice of state institutional care for children in irregular situations, since, as stated above, true foster family care is not practised in Venezuela.

The Venezuelan Children's Council was created in 1936, and was later renamed the National Institute for Minors (INAM), under the Ministry of the Family. The INAM currently cares for children from irregular situations (abandonment, violation, danger) through its children's homes and work-shops. Three separate programmes have been organized through the INAM to provide care for children from 0 to 17 years of age in irregular situations. There are 144 prevention centres, 74 centres for the care of abandoned or endangered children and 61 centres for therapy for behaviourally disordered children.

The INAM exercises guardianship over children who have been declared to be in a state of abandonment by the courts. Once such a declaration is issued, the INAM Adoption Department presents to the court a list of three married couples (or single, married, widowed or divorced individuals) whom it has evaluated and approved. From this list of people who wish to adopt a child, the family most appropriate for the particular child is selected. The family chosen then receives an institutionalized child under the 'family placement with a view to adoption' scheme.

Later, the prospective adoptive parents must present a formal Adoption

Request to the Family and Children's Court, accompanied by all the requisite documents. A Certificate of Approval from the INAM Presidency must be attached to the request. After the judicial review phase and the meeting of all legal requirements, the request will be processed. The judge will then notify a representative from the government ministry, who then has ten working days to review the request and make any pertinent observations.

Adoption of a child cannot be decreed until the child has remained in the home of the foster family for an uninterrupted trial period of at least three months. If the adoption is inter-country, permission must be requested from the judge for the child to travel to the place of residence of the prospective adoptive parents: a proposal to emigrate must be made. A Venezuelan passport with the name of the child and his or her biological parents will then be issued.

The requirements for inter-country adoption specified by the INAM Adoption Department are:

- a biographical letter addressed to the president of the INAM;
- a copy of the passport;
- approval by the receiving country for the adoption of a foreign child;
- birth certificates of the prospective adoptive parents, notarized by the Venezuelan Consulate;
- a copy of the adoption law of the receiving country, translated into Spanish;
- a marriage certificate, notarized by the Venezuelan Consulate;
- job certification, indicating position, salary and years of service;
- three personal reference letters (one from a Church official and two from reputable persons);
- a photograph of the proposed home and neighbourhood;
- two recent colour identity photographs of each prospective adoptive parent;
- a medical certificate stating that the couple is unable to procreate;
- a psychological evaluation;
- a social report prepared by a recognized social service agency in the receiving country.

All documents must be translated into Spanish and notarized, and photocopies must be sent by post. In the event that the request is accepted, instructions will be given for the delivery of the original documents. Inter-country adoption is covered by Article 21, Paragraph B of the United Nations Convention on the Rights of the Child and is considered as an alternative when the child has not been placed in Venezuela.

The INAM does not intervene in cases of private adoption. In these cases, the holders of *patria potestas* (the legal guardians of the child, usually the biological parents) must appear before a Family and Children's Court to sign an Act of Consent, expressing their willingness for their child to be adopted, and thereby renouncing all their parental rights.

The holders of the *patria potestas* must state in the Act of Consent that they have received no type of payment or remuneration, and that they have not been pressurized in any way to take this decision – that the agreement is pure and simple, unconditional and irreversible. The adoptive parents then request that they be granted guardianship and custody by the appropriate Family and Children's Court judge. Article 12 of the Adoption Law states: 'For the adoption of minors, the consent of those who hold the *patria potestas* is required. When the biological parents are themselves minors, such consent must be given on their behalf by their legal representative or through authorization by the Children's Court.'

Who is placed in foster care?

Table 20.2 shows the number of children declared abandoned by the government from 1987 to 1990 inclusive, and the number of children placed with a view to adoption by the INAM over the same period.

Table 20.2   Children declared abandoned and placed for adoption, 1987–90

	No. of children abandoned	No. of children placed for adoption
1987	93	104
1988	102	143
1989	110	97
1990	113	111

A reduction of financial resources in real terms and an increase in the population of children in irregular situations over the last few years has resulted in a decrease in the number of children served through the INAM.

In Venezuela, 4,062 children were cared for in state institutions in 1992, with 2,464 (60.7 per cent) housed in centres for boys, 1,385 (34.1 per cent) in centres for girls, and 213 (5.2 per cent) in mixed centres. The institutionalized population increased by 10.8 per cent between 1989 and 1992. As of 1 January 1993, the INAM had 50 children placed in final adoption and 81 in family placement with a view to adoption.

Compensatory assistance programmes exist in Venezuela. These charitable programmes, which benefit the children of the poor, among others, are non-contributory and provide direct subsidies towards such items as food, milk, student travel and meals in school and public lunchrooms. Generic medicines are free.

Financial support

In Venezuela, endangered or abandoned children are placed in a state children's home or in a private children's home. The child remains there until the Children's Court judge decrees a 'state of abandonment', when the child is transferred to another long-term home or is returned to his or her family environment. As previously noted, in the event that a child is placed with a view to adoption, the state provides no type of financial support to the foster family.

The cost of maintaining a child in a private Children's Home is between $US1,500 and $US2,900 annually. The term 'child custodianship' is used. These homes are maintained through contributions received from private companies and individuals. Such donations are not taxed by the government.

Children's homes, public as well as private, are subject to inspection by the INAM Adoption Service. Follow-up studies of children adopted through family placement are theoretically conducted by the institutional centre, the home itself, or by other social services, but unfortunately, they are not carried out frequently or systematically.

Major problems

The greatest difficulties encountered in the maintenance of children's homes include:

- The distribution and concentration of the centres does not correspond to the distribution of needs and the local population.
- Few centres can provide complete care encompassing all fields of child development.
- Problems with the homes' fabric include operational areas in a poor state of repair (lunchrooms, kitchens, playgrounds), with little remodelling or improvement.
- The number of children housed is too small or too large in certain centres.
- Difficulties arise in assigning staff. There is a lack of training and selection.
- With respect to education, a high proportion of institutionalized

children have not completed primary school, although they are old enough to have done so. It is difficult to engage these children in formal education.

- Follow-up studies of children are infrequent and non-systematic.
- There is a lack of individual and specialized care during institutionalization.

The average period of residence in a state centre varies between one day and six years or more. In the case of institutionalized children between the ages of 0 and 7 years, the average stay is from six to twelve months.

Visiting periods for the biological family vary according to the institution and the judgment of the Children's Court.

Major trends

In Venezuela, a high percentage of children remain throughout their lives with the family which took the child 'with a view to adoption', even though, according to the Child Guardianship Law, the child is only supposed to remain in family placement for a test period of three months before adoption is decreed.

Few children are returned to the homes by their prospective adoptive parents. In the case of FUNDANA (Foundation of Friends of the Abandoned Child), a private organization founded to care for abandoned children in its private children's home, Los Chiquiticos, 48 children were given family placements with a view to adoption in 1994, and only four were later returned to be placed again with another prospective adoptive parent.

Role of national foster care association

A national foster care association does not exist in Venezuela, but there is a registry of adoptive families, maintained by the INAM Adoption Department.

Contact: INAM Adoption Department, Torre Oeste, Parque Central, 46th Floor, Caracas, Venezuela *Telephone*: (+58) 2-507-8430.

Research

Articles on foster care and adoption appear from time to time in Venezuelan magazines and journals published by the CECODAP and the FUNDAICI, but no major research studies have been carried out.

21 Zimbabwe

Rodreck Mupedziswa and Leontina Kanyowa

Jurisdiction

Zimbabwe is a developing country situated in Southern Africa. It is bordered to the south by South Africa, to the east by Mozambique, to the north and north-east by Zambia, and to the west by Botswana, the Caprivi Strip and Namibia. It has a total land area of approximately 390,000 square kilometres (Auret, 1990). This land-locked country has a population of 10.4 million, approximately half of whom are children aged 15 years or less.

The distribution of the country's population by age is shown in Table 21.1. The 1992 national census (Central Statistical Office, 1992) shows that of the population of 10,401,767, 5,075,549 are male, and 5,326,218 are female. The population growth rate between 1982 and 1992 was 3.13, and the average household comprises about 4.8 persons. Population density is 26.62 persons per square kilometre. Thus fertility for the country as a whole is rather high (UNICEF, 1994).

Table 21.1   Age distribution

Age range	%
0–4	17
5–14	31
15–64	49
65+	3

Source: CSO (1987).

Historically, the first people to settle in Zimbabwe were the Shona tribes, who displaced the Bushmen (Koisan people) between the eighth and tenth centuries. The first white people to penetrate the land were the Portuguese traders, missionaries and soldiers, who arrived as early as the 1500s. A few more white people arrived in the 1850s and 1860s, before the major influx, which occurred with the Pioneer Column in 1890. These people were initially interested in precious minerals, but later decided to settle when they realized the agricultural potential of the country (Auret, 1990).

Attempts by the indigenous black population to resist white penetration were quickly crushed (1893–96), and until 1923, the country was administered by the British South African Company. In 1923, the country became a self-governing colony, with foreign affairs issues being handled by the British Foreign Office in London. Between 1923 and 1979, several settler regimes ruled Zimbabwe, the most notable being the Rhodesian Front regime, which acceded to state power in 1962.

The Rhodesian Front advocated separate development among the races, and it proceeded to introduce a dual economy which made life unbearable for the indigenous black population. The disgruntlement felt by the black population culminated in a protracted armed struggle, which ended with the coming into power of a majority-rule government in April 1980, following the signing of the Lancaster House Agreement, in which the UK conceded to demands for majority black rule.

Zimbabwe has had a fairly robust economy. In particular, it has considerable agricultural potential, in addition to a relatively sophisticated mining, industrial and manufacturing base. The country is fairly wealthy compared to its neighbours, and even the entire African continent. However, great inequalities exist in terms of the distribution of wealth and income. This dates back to the colonial era, and means that many of the people remain poor. Because of the dual nature of the economy, poverty and deprivation – with the attendant problems of unemployment and underemployment, hunger, inadequate shelter and homelessness, disease, illiteracy and ignorance – remain predominant features of the country's way of life.

The Central Statistical Office (CSO, 1987) estimates that, as of 1987, 73 per cent of the population of Zimbabwe was rural-based. Communal areas exhibit a rather higher population density than other areas. The languages spoken as the mother tongue in various parts of Zimbabwe are: Shona (74 per cent), Ndebele (18 per cent), English (4 per cent) and other languages, for example Nyanja (4 per cent) (CSO, 1987). However, English is widely spoken, particularly in urban areas, as it is used for all official business.

The government of Zimbabwe has a responsibility to provide the usual social services to its people: health care, education, housing, social welfare, and so on. However, the government appreciates that since resources are always in short supply, there is no way it can meet the demands for these services on its own. Consequently, it has encouraged the private sector (including Church organizations, private non-profit agencies, industrial firms and mines) to take an active part in the provision of social services. In addition, self-help and local initiatives have also been encouraged. Government services are generally financed from public funds, while non-governmental agencies depend largely on grants both from established donor agencies and from the general public (Mupedziswa, 1995).

With respect to social welfare provision in particular, the magnitude of the social problems in the country makes it necessary for both public and private institutions to organize welfare services for people in need. Groups benefit from various forms of social provision, including public assistance, social insurance and workman's compensation. Public assistance is financed from public taxation, and is non-contributory and means-tested. Those who may benefit from public assistance include the disabled and the handicapped, the aged, the unemployed, the destitute, the sick, and also children and young people. Both government and non-governmental organizations (private and non-profit agencies) play a role in providing services to these target groups. Minors, including orphans and other types of children in need of care, also benefit for a variety of welfare provisions, as will be discussed later.

History and origins

During the colonial period in Zimbabwe, social welfare services were based on racial segregation, and this was reflected even in the way foster care cases were handled. White and coloured people were catered for in separate offices to those serving black people. White and coloured people were served either directly by the government through segregated offices in the Department of Social Welfare, or through a non-profit agency called the Child Protection Society. This organization worked closely with the Department of Social Welfare, which had the ultimate responsibility in law to dispose of cases. The Child Protection Society maintained a pool of potential foster parents, whom they vetted. This organization ceased to operate on the basis of its original mandate after independence was attained in 1980, since racial segregation was abolished. Now it focuses on the protection of abandoned children and also operates a day care centre for single mothers.

Among the black population, the situation was rather different. To begin with, there was no registered private organization to facilitate family foster care. Cases had to be handled by offices dealing with foster care in the Department of Social Welfare. These offices were grossly under-utilized because, traditionally, foster care occurred informally, since it was held that there was no need for court action to place children with suitable foster parents.

As a result of the racial segregation in the years before 1980, mixed-race foster care was also very rare. When it did happen, it mainly involved white couples seeking to foster black children, but not vice versa. This trend has continued to the present day. With respect to same-race, formal foster family care, generally more white than black people have shown interest in fostering children, and again, this trend has continued. Since the percentage of white people in the country is very small (about 4 per cent or less), statistical records show the names of more black people than white on the foster care register, but this is misleading, as more white people than black, proportionally, are involved in formal fostering. Among the black population, foster care continues to occur informally, largely involving the children of relatives.

Zimbabwe has committed itself to guaranteeing the protection of the rights of the child. The Zimbabwean legislation reflects the rights of children as enshrined in the United States Convention on the Rights of the Child and the African Charter on the Rights of the Child (UNICEF, 1994). The legislative basis for family foster care is essentially the Children's Protection and Adoption Act (Chapter 33) of 1972. The Act provides for: the establishment of Juvenile Courts; the protection, welfare and supervision of children and juveniles; the establishment, recognition and registration of certain institutions and institutes for the reception and custody of children and juveniles; the contribution of certain persons towards the maintenance of children and juveniles; the adoption of minors; other matters connected with the welfare of children, juveniles and minors, and other matters incidental to and connected with the foregoing.

The Act also addresses foster care issues, with particular emphasis on such aspects as: jurisdiction and procedure in relation to Foster Orders; power to make Foster Orders; restrictions on making Foster Orders; terms and conditions of Foster Orders; effects of Foster Orders; rescission of Foster Orders; minors already subject to an order; consent to foster care given by a parent of a child (where appropriate); matters about which the court has to be satisfied; registers of applicants for fostering, and registers of foster children.

Not much has changed with respect to the Act over the years, despite the fact that it was promulgated before independence in 1980. While many of the provisions have been seen as being stringent enough, there has been dissatisfaction over some provisions which many consider relics of the colonial past. For example, in various sections, the Act makes reference to certain instances where minors can be taken to South Africa – an arrangement which has long been overtaken by events. Critics argue that such aspects show that the Act needs to be reviewed.

Administration and organization

Today, the delivery of foster family care for children and young people is administered only by the Department of Social Welfare, which falls under the Ministry of Public Service, Labour and Social Welfare. As noted earlier, the administration of foster family care is governed by Chapter 33 of the Children's Protection and Adoption Act. Although the Department of Social Welfare is the only agency that administers foster family care in Zimbabwe, non-governmental organizations, both religious and non-religious, assist the department in identifying potential foster parents, who are then screened by the Department of Social Welfare.

As mentioned above, traditional foster care still exists among black Zimbabweans. In this instance, foster care takes place informally within the family, and there is generally no need to go to the Department of Social Welfare or the courts to formalize the placement of the child. However, if prospective foster parents who are also relatives so wish, they may formalize the placement of the child through the Department of Social Welfare. In such cases, the screening is less stringent compared to the screening involving prospective parents who are not related to the child.

The procedures followed in cases of formalized family foster care placements are:

1 Interest in fostering a child is expressed, and the prospective parent's name is placed on a register.
2 The prospective foster parent is screened by a social worker in the Department of Social Welfare.
3 The social worker makes visits to the home of the prospective foster parent to assess the suitability of the home environment for foster care.
4 A court session is convened, and the magistrate is helped to arrive at a decision by a probation officer's report.
5 A court order for foster care may then be issued by the magistrate.
6 The case is reviewed after three years, with the two options being either to terminate the relationship or to allow it to continue, with the consent of all parties.

Who is placed in foster care?

Foster family care in Zimbabwe is intended for minors termed 'children in need of care' who are aged between 0 and 18 years. Children attain majority at the age of 18. In Zimbabwe, children deemed in need of care fall into the following categories:

- destitute children;
- orphaned children;
- abandoned children;

- children whose legal guardians cannot be traced;
- children whose legal parents or guardians are unfit to exercise control over them;
- children who are habitual truants;
- children who find themselves in the company of vicious or immoral persons;
- children living in circumstances calculated to cause or contribute to their seduction, corruption or prostitution;
- children who cannot be controlled by their parents or guardians;
- child beggars;
- children engaged in street trading;
- children found in possession of drugs;
- children used to 'avenge angry spirits';*
- street children;
- any children who find themselves in circumstances detrimental to child development and upbringing.

There are far more children in need of care than there are foster parents. As a result, most, if not all institutions are over-enrolled. This state of affairs could be attributed to the fact that black Zimbabweans, who constitute the vast majority of the population, are generally reluctant to take a strange child into their family due to some of the traditional beliefs that exist. Another contributing factor is the low level of public awareness about foster family care. If information were made more readily available to the public, more people would probably be willing to foster children.

While this is the case among black Zimbabweans, the situation is different among the minority population of white Zambabweans. Finding foster parents for white children in need of care is generally not a problem, although a waiting list does exist, and this is lodged with the Department of Social Welfare. As previously noted, white Zimbabweans have formally fostered black children over the years, but formal foster care of white children is not common among black Zimbabweans.

---

* According to local custom, if a person is murdered, an avenging spirit of the deceased will trouble not only the murderer but also members of the murderer's entire extended family, some of whom may die in inexplicable circumstances. It is therefore necessary to appease the avenging spirit, and this is done by giving away a young daughter as a wife to some relative of the deceased. Many girls, some as young as 6 or 8 years old, have been abused in this way. The law vetoes such practices and prosecutes the culprits: the children are declared as 'children in need of care' since they cannot easily be sent back home.

Care providers

There are a number of different types of foster family care providers in Zimbabwe. They include:

- people who foster children in the context of the extended family network (relatives);
- paid families or individuals;
- unpaid families or individuals;
- people who wish to adopt the child.

According to the records kept by the Head Office of the Department of Social Welfare, the current count for registered foster parents in Zimbabwe by province is as follows: Harare, 179; Bulawayo, 241; Gwanda, 21; Masvingo, 93; Gweru, 90; Mutare, 85; Chinhoyi, 15, and Marondera, 7. Thus, there are currently 755 families legally fostering children in Zimbabwe. These numbers fluctuate of course, as some people are removed from the register while others are added. Unfortunately, figures for informal foster arrangements, though thought to be higher than the formal arrangements, are not readily available, as no registers are kept.

Screening of prospective foster parents is carried out by the Department of Social Welfare, and this is done with the best interests of the child in mind. Some of the requirements prospective foster family caregivers should meet are:

- they must be citizens of Zimbabwe;
- they must be aged 25 years or over;
- they should be active – that is, they should be able to work and earn an income;
- they should have no criminal record.

The motivation behind the prospective foster parent's desire to foster a child is also considered. It would appear that the motives are generally positive, although some more sinister ones have been known. The most common reasons for wishing to foster include religious grounds and a desire by childless couples to have a child. The Department of Social Welfare does not place a foster child with single foster parents of the opposite sex, for obvious reasons.

Financial support

Foster care providers who indicate that they need financial assistance receive a grant of $Z150 (approximately $US18) per month from the Department of

Social Welfare. In addition, the Department of Social Welfare issues requisitions which enable foster children to obtain free medical attention from state-owned medical institutions. The Department of Social Welfare also covers the cost of tuition and school fees for foster children attending school. If the child is in the care of a foster parent who is also a relative, the Department of Social Welfare pays $Z75 (approximately $US9) per month. No financial assistance is given to foster parents for the care of foster children after an adoption has been effected, or after the child attains the legal age of majority.

Major problems

There are numerous problems associated with foster family care in Zimbabwe. To begin with, there is the problem of the sheer number of children who could benefit from this service, which far outnumbers the pool of potential foster parents. The number of children in need of care is increasing daily, partly as a consequence of the scourge of AIDS, which has orphaned many. Conservative estimates put the number of children orphaned by AIDS at approximately 60,000 currently, and a projected 600,000 by the year 2000 (Department of Social Welfare, 1993). This shortage of potential foster parents is compounded by lack of public awareness. Also, as previously noted, the local culture is a factor. Members of the black community in Zimbabwe are often reluctant to take strangers into their homes for extended periods. Admittedly, foster care implies a temporary arrangement, but many do not view it that way: hence, there is a general reluctance to accept the idea of foster care.

Coupled with this is the fact that some people do not appreciate the difference between foster care and adoption. Therefore, when they enter into a foster care relationship, they are reluctant to let go of the child at the end of the stipulated period. When they hear about cases elsewhere in which foster children have been taken away from a foster parent, they become reluctant to enter into such an arrangement themselves.

In terms of length of stay in a foster family home, the law stipulates that the Foster Order must be reviewed after three years, at which time the arrangement can either be renewed or terminated. Cases where Foster Orders have had to be revoked after a mismatch or mishap are apparently on the increase. Many such cases are due to abuse of the child or a change in the circumstances of the foster parent, and in these circumstances, children may stay in care for less than three years.

Low levels of grants are a perennial problem in Zimbabwe where social services provision in general is concerned. This is particularly true in the case of non-contributory services, and the area of foster care is no exception. As noted, foster parents receive only $Z150 per month, which is not enough for the upkeep of a child. In some cases, the foster parents themselves also depend upon that meagre amount. This can create problems related to poverty, such as malnutrition, which may adversely affect the welfare of the child in foster care.

There is virtually nothing available to foster parents in Zimbabwe that can be viewed as resembling training. Foster parents receive some counselling, but even this is often inadequate, largely because of the shortages of time and staff in the Department of Social Welfare. There is a critical lack of adequate supervision by Social Welfare officers, again largely due to the limited resources at their disposal. Monthly visits are supposed to occur, but these, more often than not, remain on paper only. The three-year review is supposed to be based on a comprehensive and adequately prepared report, partly founded on a number of home visits, but in many instances this does not happen because of the limitations alluded to earlier.

There seems to be a general lack of involvement on the part of the biological parents of children in foster care, even when these parents are living. Although the law does not bar them from having contact with their children (unless the court specifically makes such a stipulation), many biological parents prefer not to get in touch with their children. This obviously creates problems with respect to re-integration, since one or both parties may experience long-term feelings of alienation. Some problems in foster placements are a consequence of the delinquent tendencies of some of the children themselves. For instance, petty thieving may occur in some cases. In other cases, difficulties such as bed wetting may create friction between the child and the foster parent. Some potential foster parents have insisted on knowing the child's HIV status before they agree to take the child in. Such a stance, though understandable from the perspective of the foster parent, may create untold stress for the child.

The question of the motive for fostering a child can be a source of numerous problems too. In some cases, foster parents do abuse foster children. There have been a few instances reported of foster parents who lock up their foster children while they go about their daily errands, because they cannot afford a childminder. Some parents use foster children as a source of cheap labour, while others treat them as virtual slaves. Sometimes, foster parents are motivated not by compassion or the wish to help, but by greed. They see the child as a source of income, since if they take the child in, they can claim a grant from the government.

Yet another problem concerns what is to happen to the child once he or she reaches the age of 18. Frequently, there is no employment waiting for the child, and neither is there a home. These children often have to be placed in children's homes until a solution is found, and none may be available for a lengthy period.

Major trends

Slowly, more and more people, particularly among the black population, are beginning to appreciate the role of formal foster care – the need to bring 'children in need of care' into foster family care. Hence, more black people are beginning to respond favourably to calls to foster a child.

What is also emerging is a situation where, sadly, more and more people are beginning to view foster children as a source of financial gain. This is being exacerbated by the economic hardships brought about by the Economic Reform Programme, with its concomitant austerity measures. It is also partly due to the poverty largely brought about by the intermittent episodes of drought experienced in the country.

There are increasing numbers of cases of abuse in which the children are treated as cheap labour. Some parents use the children to earn money in the informal sector: for example, by selling items, or even by begging or stealing on the streets. Some even encourage the children to engage in prostitution to raise money. The fact that children in foster care normally qualify for free medical care vouchers and free education is an added advantage for such foster parents, as it essentially means that they are getting free labour, 'all expenses paid'.

The children are increasingly becoming more 'sophisticated' in terms of their world view, so some bring more complex problems to the foster relationship. For instance, as noted above, some engage in delinquent behaviour, perhaps because they have lived as street children before they were brought into the foster family home. Such children may have been in contact with 'hard core' peers, who may have influenced their thinking in a negative way. In Zimbabwe, the policy has been to round up street children and then place them in children's homes, whence some could easily end up in foster care. It is such children, with behaviour 'too mature' for their age, who are an increasing cause for concern among potential foster parents. Because of their background, such children may steal or may abuse the natural children of the foster family, sexually or otherwise: worse still, the natural children may be badly influenced by this 'stranger' in their home.

Role of national foster care association

There is no national foster care association in Zimbabwe, although such an association would certainly be desirable. Perhaps, if the Child Protection

Society had remained operational on the basis of its original mandate, it could have formed the nucleus for such an association. As it is, there is only the Child Welfare Forum, an organization set up in September 1990 to promote co-ordination among organizations involved in child welfare and to minimize duplication.

Unfortunately, foster parents are not directly involved with this Forum (Powell et al., 1994). There are two reasons for this. First, the Forum does not focus specifically on foster care issues. Second, it consists simply of a monthly meeting involving various organizations working in the field of child welfare, chaired by the government's Department of Social Welfare, and, thus, it has no contact person or address.

The Zimbabwe National Council for the Welfare of Children (ZNCWC) is the umbrella body for all organizations involved in child welfare in the country. This council does not focus specifically on foster care issues: as an umbrella body, its mandate includes monitoring the activities of all the various agencies working in the area of child welfare, as well as other things.

Contact: ZNCWC, c/o National Association of Non-governmental Organizations, 16–18 Samora Machel Avenue, Box CY 250, Causeway, Harare, Zimbabwe *Telephone*: (+263) 4-791251/2/3 *Fax*: (+263) 4-794973.

Research

There has been very limited research into foster family care in Zimbabwe. The following essentially summarizes such research:

Powell, G.M., Morreira, S., Rudd, C. and Ngonyama, R.P. (1994), 'Child Welfare Policy and Practice in Zimbabwe', Department of Paediatrics and Child Health, University of Zimbabwe and Department of Social Welfare, mimeo.
Department of Social Welfare (1994) 'Orphans and Children in Need: A Situation Analysis of Masvingo and Mwenezi Districts', research report.

Bibliography

Auret, D. (1990) *A Decade of Development: Zimbabwe 1980–1991*, Gweru: Mambo Press.
CSO (1987) *Inter-Censual Demographic Survey (ICDS)*, Harare: Central Statistical Office.
CSO (1992) *Census 1992, Zimbabwe Preliminary Report*, Harare: Central Statistical Office.
Department of Social Welfare (1993) *Strengthening the Community Response to Orphans*, report from the National Conference, 17–19 November, Mutare.
Department of Social Welfare (1995) 'Orphans and Children in Need: A Situation Analysis of Masvingo and Mwenezi District', research report.

Fuglesang, A. and Chandler, D. (eds) (1992) *Children's Rights Through Community Care – A Collection of Resource Materials for Staff Training*, Harare: Norwegian Save the Children Fund.

Ministry of Labour, Manpower, Planning and Social Welfare (1991/92) *Not Making Worse: Recognizing and Enhancing Strengths of Displaced Children and Their Families*, summary Report of Chimanimani Workshop, 1–6 December, 1991, and follow-up Symposium, 29 April 1992.

Mupedziswa, R. (1995), 'Social welfare services in Zimbabwe', in Hall and Mupedziswa, R. (eds) *Social Policy and Administration in Zimbabwe*, Harare: JSDA.

Powell, G.M., Morreira, S., Rudd, C. and Ngonyama, R.P. (1994) 'Child Welfare Policy and Practice in Zimbabwe', Department of Paediatrics and Child Health, University of Zimbabwe and Department of Social Welfare, mimeo.

UNICEF (1994) *Children and Women in Zimbabwe: A Situation Analysis Update*, Harare: UNICEF, June.

22 Overview and conclusions

Matthew Colton and Margaret Williams

The issues raised in the preceding chapters will be familiar to many readers. All over the world, in different regimes and cultures, foster care providers are struggling with essentially the same difficulties. Therefore, it will be worthwhile in this chapter to revisit and summarize these difficulties in order to see how others are coping and what conclusions they may have reached.

The first difficulty, as often seems to be the case, revolves around the question of definitions. What is foster family care? What is its purpose? For whom is it intended? What kinds of services are provided under its umbrella? Different countries have answered these questions in different ways. In Ireland, for example, new regulations have given 'formal recognition to placement with relatives, as distinct from foster care, which is seen as placement with non-relatives' (page 136). Hence, part of the definition of foster care here is that the carer should not be related to the child. Conversely, since the mid-1970s in Poland, 'the term "foster family" has meant the children's next of kin, appointed caregivers or guardians by court order' (page 223). Under Polish law, relatives are under an obligation to support their young relatives if the parents cannot give sufficient care. There are also cultures, such as that in Hong Kong, where the majority of people engage in regular ancestor worship, and the acceptance of an unrelated child into one's home is alien to the concept of continued ancestral lines. Similarly, black Zimbabweans are generally reluctant to take a strange child into their families, on the basis of traditional beliefs.

Informal care by relatives seems to be an integral part of the cultural framework of a majority of countries, and even in those countries where kinship links are weaker, relatives are increasingly being seen as an under-utilized resource: a possible addition to the diminishing pool of foster carers, and a way of maintaining the child's links with the biological family. Naturally, all sorts of questions arise when relatives assume the role of foster carers. Should they be paid less than unrelated carers? Indeed, if it is assumed that they have a moral obligation to the child which is not shared by unrelated carers, should they be paid at all? Should they be obliged to meet the same selection criteria as unrelated carers, or should screening and selection standards be relaxed on their behalf? Should they be supervised, and if so, to what extent? Should the same level of supportive service be provided for them in terms of counselling, respite or access to state facilities? Will a long-term placement – essentially a form of adoption – still count as 'foster care' with respect to access to services? What happens if a placement with a relative breaks down?

We will come back to these questions: and indeed, they lose some relevance if part of the definition of 'foster care' is placement with a non-relative. Meanwhile, there is still the matter of other criteria which may help us to think about what the term 'foster care' entails. One criterion from the Netherlands is that the child is placed with the foster family through the mediation of a recognized authority. This criterion excludes all informal arrangements between parents and relatives or friends, and restricts the notion of 'foster care' to placement of a child with another family (related or not) by means of a regulated system. Hence, carers who have not gone through formal channels will not be eligible for services provided to those carers who have been formally approved. There is a dual advantage here, in that scarce resources are husbanded, and a formal system offers some protection to a child whose relatives are more interested in economic benefits or cheap labour than in nurturing the child. On the other hand, formal systems in some countries either do not exist at all or are impossibly cumbersome or slow. For example, in Argentina, potential carers who wish to foster babies are often lost because the required legal process takes so long that the child may be over 12 months old before the process is completed. In Zimbabwe, where children have traditionally been fostered informally, people do not believe that there is any need for an official system to place children with suitable foster parents, and the offices of the Social Welfare Department have been grossly under-utilized .

Yet another criterion, also from the Netherlands, is that 'foster care' should mean a temporary placement: 'The placement of a child in a foster family is thus quite different from settling a child permanently with substitute parents who take on the full responsibility for raising the child and officially have parental control over the child. In this latter case, the parents are adoptive parents, not foster parents' (page 199). Of course, having 'official' parental status and control is not the same thing as acting unofficially in a parental role towards a child who has stayed in the foster home for years. Nevertheless, in the majority of countries, cases abound where a child has arrived, formally or informally, for a temporary period, and has remained to adulthood or beyond. One question here is whether these pseudo-adoptive parents should still be viewed as 'foster carers'. Another more basic question is whether this 'permanent foster care', for want of a better phrase, should be viewed as a good thing. These, again, are questions that we shall return to.

In the mean time, there is a fourth criterion which may be of interest in deciding how 'foster care' should be defined. In Finland, ' "foster care" means arranging the care, upbringing or other round-the-clock tending of a person outside his or her own home in a private home' (page 58). The operative words here are 'round-the-clock', which would seem to deny the possibility that a child who is cared for outside the home for part of the day may also be 'being fostered'. Conversely, in Italy, foster family care 'can be used for part of the day or week, when parents cannot guarantee that they will always be able to be with their children' (page 167). Future plans in Torino, Italy, include giving priority to the development of daytime foster and residential care for a number of excellent reasons which will be addressed in more detail later in this chapter. However, the idea that 'foster care' may be provided for a child who is still resident in his or her own home runs counter to the generally accepted notion that 'foster care' means ' "the relocation or transfer of children from biological or natal homes to other homes where they are raised and cared for by foster parents" ' (Chapter 3, page 34).

A fifth and final criterion centres around the notion of a private home. There is a clear distinction between an institution which houses hundreds of children and a foster carer's home which houses one or two. However, the distinction becomes less clear when we consider 'cluster' models, such as those in Israel, where up to 20 foster families living in a single neighbourhood take up to 12 children each. The criterion for defining a 'private home' is possibly not the number of foster children housed, but whether the 'staff' consists of a number of people working shifts, as would be the case in a residential home, or a single couple, invariably present, who assume a parental role. Even if we can distinguish between a residential and a foster home, it is as well to remember that there are children who inhabit both worlds, living in a residential home during the week, and moving to a foster home for holidays and weekends.

In sum, then, we have five criteria to juggle in deciding what should be meant by 'foster care':

1 It may or may not include care by relatives.
2 It may or may not include only those placements which are mediated by a recognized authority.
3 It may or may not include only temporary placements (whatever is meant by 'temporary').
4 It may or may not mean round-the-clock care.
5 It may or may not involve a 'private home' in the accepted Western sense.

Probably, few would deny that some of the possible combinations of these criteria would not constitute 'foster care'. For example, a child staying for a few days with an aunt is not being fostered, and neither is a child in day care – unless, perhaps, the day care placement has been arranged for the specific purpose of resolving the child's behavioural difficulties or providing support to the parent. We have perhaps arrived at the idea that foster care can only be defined in terms of what it is intended to accomplish.

In early Ireland, fostering was used for political rather than welfare purposes, as a means of forging links or defusing conflict between the family placing and the family receiving the child. More commonly, however, the intention behind foster care has been to provide substitute homes for children in difficult circumstances, where they will receive not only the basic necessities of life, but also training and affection. The purpose has been to care for abandoned, abused and neglected children, so that they will have similar opportunities to more fortunate children: to redress the balance, so to speak. In Indonesia, the purpose is possibly to contribute to an increase in the overall standard of education. In Western countries, in recent years, the purpose has been to look after the best interests of the child.

In all these traditional purposes, whether they stem from concern for the child or concern for the status of the government, the role of the biological parents appears to have been ignored. They may be involved before the child is fostered or adopted, but afterwards, they are either not involved at all, or their involvement is viewed as problematic. In Argentina, there is still a widely-held assumption that successful fostering or adoption necessitates the breaking of biological ties. However, in other places, the focus of foster care has shifted from the child to the natural family, not in denial that the best interests of the child still need to be served, but on the assumption that the child can usually best be served through serving the natural family. This is an assumption which has sometimes led to problems, but it does mean, nevertheless, that the traditional purpose of foster care – to provide substitute homes for children in difficult circumstances – has been replaced with another purpose: to make the original home fit for the child to live in. Of course, it is not always possible to return the child home, but even in these cases, the emphasis tends to be on providing two families for the child: the foster or adoptive family, and the family of origin. Hence, the foster parents are no longer 'substitute' parents, but are expected to complement the child's own parents. Indeed, the term 'carer' has been coined specifically to avoid the implication that the child's biological parents have been replaced by foster parents.

Thus it might appear that traditional definitions of foster care have been based on traditional ideas of what foster care is for. If we accept that in many countries, the purposes have shifted, it seems only sensible to accept that the definitions should change as well. Before proceeding further, it might be as well to clarify these new purposes – if only to provide those who disagree with our definitions with a sound basis for refuting the changed definitions of foster care which will inevitably follow upon an altered statement of purpose.

The first purpose is what it always was: to care for abandoned, abused and neglected children. If the child has a parent or parents, we might suggest that a second, intermediate purpose – a way of accomplishing the first – should be to reunite the child with these parents, in a physical sense if possible, or failing that, in the psychological sense of trying to establish in the parents and the child a feeling of mutual belonging to the family of origin. If the child is still residing with the parents, then obviously, the purpose is to prevent removal. Some readers will undoubtedly think that there is nothing new in this: one of the primary purposes of foster care is already to promote reunification with the natural family, on the grounds that children need a sense of personal and cultural identity.

Some of the readers who think it is not new may also think it is disastrous. Many professionals in Hungary argue against reuniting children with their natural parents, and most children grow to adulthood in their foster homes once they have been placed there. A recent study in Finland showed that 'children placed in foster care considered cohabiting as the main factor in the development of a child–parent relationship. Consequently, foster children felt that it was easier, on a psychological level at least, to regard substitute parents rather than biological parents as their real parents' (page 62). In Germany, the psychoanalytic approach to foster care assumes that 'a child who has lived in a foster family for a relatively long period (about two years) develops ties to his or her foster parents through which social parenthood is established' (page 96). Proponents of this approach believe that such newly-emerging ties to substitute parents 'should be protected by the state through legislation' (page 96). Similarly, in Australia, some feel that the outcome of the shift from child-centred to family-centred service has been to 'undermine the security of long-term placements for both child and foster parent, as magistrates were forced to review the option of returning the child to the natural parent, even when the child has been in the placement for a number of years' (page 18).

There is no doubt that relationships between foster carers and natural parents, even – or perhaps especially – when the foster carers are kin, are often problematic. There is also no doubt that physical reunification runs a high risk of failure and is often unsuccessful. Nevertheless, it might be argued that failures with respect to the natural family reflect a traditional mind set, as opposed to an inherent obstacle. In Italy, 'current legislation provides a commitment to successful reunification in principle, but neither the regions nor the local authorities have provided adequate resources to implement reunification in reality' (page 169). Reunification is seen merely as a goal, rather than as a new stage in the child's care career which requires support: it is managed in a 'fragmentary and intuitive way', and it is therefore not surprising that the failure rate is high. In Germany, by way of contrast, social workers have increasingly started to make the foster family and the natural family acquainted before placing the child into care, in an effort to combat the antipathy which so often arises between the families and has a negative impact upon the child. Efforts of this kind may possibly inhibit the development of 'social parenthood', in the sense that children's ties to their foster carers will no longer require a break with their natural families.

Perhaps successful reunification depends upon the spirit in which it is attempted, bolstered of course, by legislation, resources and systems of service provision which reflect that spirit. However, spirit is not the same thing as revolutionary fervour. There are fashions in child welfare, as there are in everything else, and it is a mistake to assume that the current fashion, no matter how enlightened, is as good for every child as the previous one was bad. Some biological families ought never to be reunited. Some children need substitute families rather than complementary families, and the social worker should have the opportunity – and, of course, the training – to pick these children out from all the rest.

Hence, we might hedge the purpose we suggested with the provision that one of the goals of foster care (or one of the stages in the foster care process, to give credit to the Italian experience) is to reunite the natural family, *where appropriate*, and also, naturally, to prevent the child's removal, *where appropriate*. Given this purpose, we might revisit the five criteria we identified as useful in deciding what is meant by 'foster care'.

Relatives, whether or not they get on with the natural parents (and often they do not), succeed in maintaining family ties because they *are* family. It seems sensible, therefore, to include care by relatives in the definition of foster care.

With respect to including only those placements which are mediated by a recognized authority, it is only those kinds of placements which can yield the necessary data. Informal placements, unregistered, uncounted and, of course, never evaluated, may be wonderful in many ways and lacking in other ways, but we shall never know. The term 'foster care', in its common usage, will doubtless continue to include informal placements, as it always has, but professionals working in the field are only concerned with placements established through some system. For our purposes, therefore, 'foster care' means *formal* foster care.

The third suggested criterion was that 'foster care' should include only temporary placements. The only possible reason for distinguishing between 'temporary' and 'permanent' placements is that services and rates of pay to carers would be different: perhaps less so on both counts as initial adjustment difficulties were smoothed, hopes of reunification with the family of origin receded, and the carer began to assume more closely the role of parent, including financial responsibility. There is the obvious difficulty of deciding at what point 'temporary' becomes 'permanent' and there is also the consideration that, failing reunification, permanency is desired. Although the amount and type of services will inevitably alter as the placement is prolonged, foster carers should not be penalized for having succeeded in providing a child with a home. In addition, most studies show that continued contact with birth relatives is a protective factor, even when the placement is intended to be permanent, and foster carers may continue to need support in dealing with this. Thus 'foster care' might best be defined as including placements of *any* length, short of actual adoption.

In the Philippines, families are not permitted to adopt the child they foster, presumably to prevent 'child shopping': an event which 'supposedly occurs when prospective adoptive parents apply to become foster parents and accept children into foster care, until they find a child they want to adopt' (page 216). In Zimbabwe, as in India and Hungary, people do not appreciate the difference between foster care and adoption, and are reluctant to foster when they realize that they may have to relinquish the child. In Venezuela, children are placed in a 'foster home' solely with a view to adoption. In many countries, it is emphasized that foster care is not a route to adoption, and there are good reasons for this, since the desired motivations, attitudes and skills may differ markedly between adoptive and foster parents. Although it may seem unconscionable that children should lose a good adoptive home merely because they have been fostered in it, the definition of 'foster care' derived in this chapter will *not* include fostering with a view to adoption.

To return to our criteria, the fourth criterion concerned round-the-clock care, as opposed to care for part of the day or week, or care for a short or long predetermined period, when parents have to leave home, for example to go into hospital. The real distinction here is the child's official place of residence – with the foster carer or in the natural parents' home – and the question being addressed is whether care given while the child is still at home should be defined as 'foster care'. If one of the purposes of foster care is to prevent the child's removal from the natural home, then the answer must be that such care *does* count as 'foster care', and foster carers in this sense should receive the appropriate reimbursement, training and support.

The fifth and final criterion revolves around the concept of a 'private home'. We have already noted that a 'private home' might be defined not in terms of the nature of the dwelling or the number of children housed, but in terms of whether the 'staff' consists of a number of people working shifts or a single couple who assume a parental role. Thus 'foster care', as distinguished from residential or other types of care, means care by a couple (or individual) provided *in their home*.

In sum then, we have defined 'foster care' as:

care provided in the carers' home, on a temporary or permanent basis, through the mediation of a recognized authority, by specific carers, who may be relatives or not, to a child (differently defined in different countries) who may or may not be officially resident with them.

This is a somewhat cumbersome definition, which could certainly be improved, but it will suffice as a basis to continue the discussion.

Once we have decided what foster care is, the next interrelated questions are:

- What is it for?
- Whom does it serve?
- What services does it provide?
- How does it provide them?
- What constraints exist on service provision?

To some degree, we have already dealt with the question of what it is for, but there still remain a large number of intermediate purposes, obviously linked to the nature of the children being served. In the Philippines, about 75 per cent of the children fostered are aged 6 years or less. In Argentina, carers prefer to foster healthy babies. In India, there is a greater demand for newborn children – and for boys, in a patriarchal society. In the majority of countries, in fact, healthy, newborn children are the foster carer's choice.

However, in Canada, 'Fostering has changed from a voluntary service that provided temporary care for most children to a system of taking in older children with multiple individual and family problems' (page 46). In Ireland, 'There is strong anecdotal evidence of increasingly challenging behaviour among the children placed, and of a growing risk of disruption in placements' (page 142) and 'There is growing recognition of the implications of providing for a population of children who may have experienced abuse' (page 142). In Australia, 'children who require out-of-home placement are now more likely to be older, more behaviourally disturbed and/or emotionally damaged' (page 17). In Zimbabwe, the number of children orphaned by AIDS is approximately 60,000 currently, and is projected to be 600,000 by the year 2000. In Argentina, physically or mentally handicapped children are not fostered to any significant extent.

In countries all over the world, those most in need of foster care are older, less healthy or more troubled children; and there can be no doubt that the skills and services required to cope with them are different in kind from the skills and services required for healthy babies. Many countries have already established separate programmes for such children. In Australia, foster parents prepared to take adolescents (aged 12–17) are administered in a separately funded programme. In Australia, there is also a shared family care programme targeted to meet the needs of children with developmental delay and intellectual disability: 'It incorporates the funding of disability resource worker positions, targeted recruitment of carers, additional support to carers, high payments to agencies for placements made under the programme, and in some instances, higher reimbursement to foster parents caring for children with disabilities. The caseload ratio is 1:6, compared to 1:12 in programmatic foster care' (page 13). Similarly, in Germany, 'under the title "special care", there is a nationwide organization which employs pedagogically qualified foster parents. The organization provides these foster parents with counselling, supervision and further education if they take in a child who is developmentally disabled' (page 90).

It seems that we are moving perforce away from a system in which well-meaning and largely untrained people volunteered to take in 'children in difficult circumstances', towards a set of systems in which highly-trained professional carers, supported by other highly-trained professionals, try to deal with children whose 'difficult circumstances' have led to the children themselves becoming disturbed. The move is slow, fragmented and strenuously resisted by many people in many places, for a large variety of reasons. It might be useful to examine these reasons in order to understand the constraints being put upon change.

First, foster carers in the Philippines 'see themselves as providing a service of "love": a religious or charitable act undertaken for love of children or as one's share in nation-building. Foster care administrators tend to take advantage of the fact that low pay reinforces the idea of a charitable act so that no cognitive dissonance is felt by those who wish to foster a child from charitable motives' (page 218). The belief that love and money cannot mix is widely held, not just by administrators who wish to save money, but by foster carers themselves, and most importantly, by the children receiving the service. No doubt, it will require a sweeping change in public attitudes before children can bring themselves to believe that a person who is paid at a professional rate for looking after them is also capable of loving them deeply – and sweeping changes are invariably slow.

Not only have traditional foster carers been expected to act out of love, but they have also been expected to stay at home full-time. In Australia, as elsewhere, 'Changes in community work patterns have meant that the assumption that women will be at home full-time, on which the volunteer system of foster care was based, no longer applies in the majority of families. This has caused difficulties . . . in the recruitment of adequate numbers of carers' (page 17).

In almost every country, one of the major difficulties cited was the difficulty of recruiting foster carers. It might be argued that this is because we are continuing to look for charitably-disposed, full-time homemakers, who only now exist in decreasing numbers. However: 'foster care in Israel is being transformed into a profession, and may well be on its way to becoming a realistic career option. Such a process is immensely important, since its success should ensure a constant and consistent supply of carers, ready and able to meet market demands' (page 159). In other countries too, the trend towards the professionalization of foster care is proceeding slowly, although many foster carers still tend to be treated as service recipients rather than service providers: a type of treatment which, unfortunately, is often commensurate with volunteer status.

A number of issues arise with respect to the professionalization of carers. Selection processes, pay scales, benefit packages, competency standards, respite, support, and training, supervision and registration procedures immediately come to mind – complicated by the fact that carers will be variously employed by public and private agencies, and will be caring for children who are experiencing various levels of difficulty. There is also the matter of fairness to foster parents already caring for children on a voluntary basis and being paid, in the majority of countries, at abysmal rates. In Australia, 'there is some evidence that "professional" levels of payments are being introduced in an *ad hoc* fashion through the development of specialized foster care services for hard-to-place children which have higher carer payments, and also through retention of a residential care placement level of funding for children and young people transferred into home-based care' (page 18). In Canada, 'The development of specialist foster care in the private sector initially created conflict between public and private foster care providers, because specialist foster care providers received more training and support, and generally, better pay. In addition, conflict was created between residential and treatment foster care agencies because funds were diverted from residentially-based centres to treatment foster care. In Alberta, the tension has been resolved to a certain extent through the sharing of professional development opportunities between public and private agency providers. The government has maintained control over setting foster care standards, but has also worked with specialist foster care agency associations to standardize the two systems' (page 44).

So far then, we have identified the following constraints on the move towards the professionalization of foster carers:

- the perceived divorce between love and money;
- the reluctance of professionals in the field to look upon carers as partners;
- the fragmented development of specialized services; resentment over the unequal treatment of volunteer and professional parents;
- matters concerning selection, training, supervision, respite, support,

registration, competency standards and, of course, pay and benefits;
- conflict between public and private foster care providers;
- conflict between residential centres and specialist agencies because of the diversion of funds from the former to the latter.

Conflict between residential centres and foster care agencies has a long and nasty history. The usual question is whether residential or foster care is 'better', and the answer to that is that neither is 'better', but both have their uses. For example, not all children can tolerate the intimacy of contact with a foster carer, and they do better in residential care. Some children need to be prepared for foster care. Some children, because of mental or physical handicaps or severe behavioural or emotional disturbance, are not suited to even specialist foster care programmes. Some children need a place to go when a placement breaks down and no emergency home is available. Some parents in some cultures feel that an institution is less shameful than a foster home. In Canada, 'the introduction of foster care did not replace institutional care, but broadened the continuum of out-of-home services for children' (page 43). This possibly optimistic statement represents the ideal: a system based not on turf-and-territory jealousies, but on deciding which of the many available options will best meet the needs of a particular child at a particular time.

If we accept that the trend is towards professional specialist carers, we must nevertheless remember that there will still be healthy babies needing to be fostered, and there will still be charitable people who want to help a child but have careers of their own. Specialist carers will necessarily work in the short term towards the amelioration of specific difficulties, and afterwards, a child who cannot go home may move to a more traditional foster placement. Moreover, there will still be relatives who are unwilling to obtain a certificate in order to take in a needy child. Hence, more traditional forms of foster care must run in parallel with newer forms: and here again there should be no question of which is 'better', but only of which is better for *this particular child*.

So we have defined what foster care is, and we have looked briefly at what it is for, whom it serves, and how it is likely to develop. Before closing, it is also worthy of note that many countries have developed innovative methods of service provision. For example, in Poland, 'professional foster parents . . . are employed by children's homes or by public adoption and fostering centres . . . The scheme entails the organization of different kinds of foster families according to the child's need: emergency care, assessment care, therapy, rehabilitative care, preparation for moving back to the natural family, or preparation for moving to an adoptive family. The scheme includes a detailed programme for recruiting, training and providing pedagogical support groups for foster parents' and 'there will also be a continuation of the traditional foster family system' (page 230). In Australia, the need to recognize and accommodate the demands of contemporary lifestyles within a volunteer-based foster care programme has led to the development of innovative ways of supporting foster parents through, for example, accessing community-based child care, after-school care, holiday programmes and respite services (see Chapter 2). In Italy, Torino has arranged a foster project for 1995 with the aim of giving priority to the development of daytime foster and residential care which would have the consent of the parents (see Chapter 15). In Finland, work methods of welfare services have been adapted towards strengthening child rearing by natural parents. Maternity and child health clinics have expanded, family training has been diversified, and co-operation with families has intensified. In the day care service, various forms of co-operation to encourage and support parental participation have been developed. Home help services have also been developed to support child rearing by parents (see Chapter 5).

There has only been space in this chapter for the briefest of overviews, but we would like to say, in conclusion, that editing this book has been a fascinating experience. A greater degree of international sharing of problems, innovations and experiences must surely contribute in considerable measure to caring for the children of us all.

Index

Note: Page numbers in bold denote entries of particular significance